# The Best of
# SEWING and EMBROIDERY

# The Best of
# SEWING and
# EMBROIDERY

*Consultant Editor*
**Susan Janes**

HAMLYN

*To our American readers:* throughout this book,
the American term, when it differs from the
British, is given in parentheses following the
British word. The u.s. Standard/Imperial
equivalent measurement is given in
parentheses after the metric figure.

*Additional material by Carol Peyton*

Published 1985 by
Hamlyn Publishing,
Astronaut House, Hounslow Road,
Feltham, Middlesex

ISBN 0 600 30551 1

Printed in Spain

# CONTENTS

# PREFACE

Making things yourself gives a unique sense of accomplishment and satisfaction and, happily, often saves you money. This book brings you lots of good sewing and needlework ideas, along with step-by-step instructions which help you to achieve success. We have chosen many attractive projects, among them simple-to-make designs which will enable beginners to produce professional-looking results. The more experienced needleworker has not been forgotten. She will find a wide range of makes which will show her expertise off to advantage.

The projects, all designed and selected by talented experts, offer you the opportunity to make pretty and practical things for yourself, your family and your home. As you make these items, you will acquire useful new skills and practise familiar ones. For instance, in the sewing section, we introduce you to leathercraft and millinery work, and also tell you how to handle special fabrics. You will find many timeless and chic designs for apparel, soft toys (stuffed toys) and household textiles. The embroidery section features many projects in the popular technique of counted cross-stitch, as well as needlepoint and openwork designs. Most of the embroidery techniques are multi-purpose and can be used to beautify clothing as well as bed and table linen.

The comprehensive course section at the end of each part is clearly arranged and easy to follow, so that you can conveniently check up on the things you need to know. We hope that this book will help you to really enjoy sewing and embroidery.

# SEWING

This section features lots of well-designed clothing for adults and children, fashion accessories and items for the home. All the projects are smart and have classic appeal. The detailed instructions will help you to enjoy making them. We have deliberately avoided selecting complicated garments like coats or jackets which require tailoring expertise. Our aim was to create a book which offers everyone a chance to practise sewing pleasurably. Both you and your family will appreciate the pretty and practical makes which are ideal to give as gifts. The clear and concise Sewing Course will serve as a handy reference for future endeavours.

**2**

## Travelling Companions

Attractive and practical vanity and make-up bags are hard-to-find necessities. To solve the problem, here are two different styles, both ideal for travel. The green vanity bag has two convenient and spacious compartments for your toiletries. It is also suitable for use as a man's shaving holdall.

We have equipped the small beige organizer on the right with make-up, but you might wish to outfit it as a sewing repair kit. Side flaps hold the contents securely in place and it folds up compactly for packing. Both bags are easy to sew and make useful gifts.

Instructions for making these bags are on pages 18 and 19.

3

## Waistcoats with Back Interest

Heads will turn when you wear one of these unique waistcoats (vests). Teamed with a matching blouse and coordinating skirt, the waistcoat will be the focal point of your outfit. Unusual and witty, each of these machine-appliquéd designs is as much fun to make as it is to wear.

Apart from the sewing involved in making the appliquéd motifs, there is very little dressmaking to do. The garment itself is simple and uncomplicated. There are few seams to stitch and all the edges are bound with bias binding. The

front view is simple and uncluttered. It is cut from the background fabric and sports patch pockets at hip level.

We have included instructions for the Mother Goose and Tropical Paradise designs, but you may wish to create an original masterpiece. Bits of fabric from the sewing basket can spark your imagination. The possibilities are endless. For instance, you may wish to create a geometric or abstract design instead of a recognizable picture.

Instructions for the Mother Goose and Tropical Paradise waistcoats are on pages 21 and 21.

4

## Smart Fashion Accessories: Simple to Craft

The projects on these pages provide brief introductory excursions into the areas of millinery and leathercraft.
Hats are coming back into fashion now, and this makes sense, too, protecting your head against sun and wind. This casual cloche is made from a double layer of fabric, has a panelled crown and ample brim. Best of all, it folds up compactly for travelling. We show you three versions of the same pattern: a plain (solid-coloured) fabric hat with ribbon-trimmed brim, a sporty denim version for jeans enthusiasts and another made from coordinating floral prints. Why not sew several?

Making this chic, envelope-style clutch is a wonderful way to get acquainted with leathercraft. It is an easy first project which produces gratifying results.

The spacious cowhide bag is made by threading leather strips through pre-punched holes. As a bonus, the instructions tell you how to make a matching wallet.

Instructions for sunhats, bag and wallet are on pages 21, 22 and 23.

5

# 6

## A Skirt For All Seasons . . . With Matching Shawl

The distinction between summer and winter fashions has been lessening in recent years. An attractive skirt is welcome at any time of the year and, if you choose your fabric well, it can span the seasons beautifully. This flowing skirt with matching shawl is just such a design. Make it out of soft, lightweight woollen fabric (or brushed cotton as a budget-conscious alternative) and wear it all the year round. Choose brightly printed material.

The fullness of this ultra-feminine skirt is controlled by gentle released tucks encircling the hips. Its main pattern piece is a simple rectangle of fabric.

The versatile bias-bound shawl can be worn as a chill-chaser on a summer evening, or you can use it to top your winter coat. If you are more adventurous, drape it round your hips. It's actually a diagonally folded square of fabric.

Instructions for the skirt and shawl are on pages 23 and 24.

# 7

## Easy Glamour: Long Tiered Skirt

This long, billowy skirt is ideal for casual wear or lounging. It is frilly and romantic, but you'll also appreciate its practicality in warm weather because it is comfortable and lightweight to wear. There is elastic in the waistband, so you can just slip it on. The skirt consists of five gathered lengths of coordinated, printed fabrics in toning colours. To make the skirt more festive, just stitch a matching satin or velvet ribbon between each layer. You can, of course, stop at any length by making a shorter three- or four-tiered version.

Instructions for the long tiered skirt are on page 25.

# Vanity Bag

**Finished Size:** 24 x 16 cm
(9½ x 6¼ in)

**Materials:** 0.4 m (½ yd) of
120 cm (48 in)-wide
canvas, rubberized or
plasticized fabric. One
10 × 50 cm (4 × 20 in) strip
of leather or suede for
carrying strap and trim.
Two 22 cm (9 in) zips
(zippers). Matching sewing
thread. Craft knife. Leather
glue.

**Cutting out:** Cut out the
bag front/back piece twice
across the width of the
fabric; do the same for the
inner pocket. Add 8mm
(⅜ in) seam allowance all
round. Using the craft knife
on the protected surface,
cut out the following pieces
from leather: one carrying
strap without seam
allowance, two trims with
1 cm (⅜ in) seam allowance
on short sides only and
centre zip slits as shown;
two tabs without seam
allowance.

**Sewing:** The vanity bag is
made up of two individual
bags which are seamed
together along the top edge
in the middle. Each bag
contains a multi-sectioned
interior pocket. Sew each
bag separately first.
*Inside pocket:* to make a
tuck in each pocket section,
match each **x** to an **o** and
stitch along vertical line.
Turn under and clean-
finish all pocket seam
allowances. With wrong
sides together, baste the
inside pocket on to the
back of the bag as shown
on diagram, matching
vertical lines to form the
pocket sections. Stitch
inside pocket on to the
back of the bag along
vertical seams, then along
the bottom of the pocket.
*Bag assembly:* with right
sides together, stitch the
narrow tuck along the base
of the bag. As shown on
diagram, stitch leather trim
to the narrow extension on
the upper edge of the bag
back part of the bag front/
back piece, matching

length **e–f**, and with the
wrong side of the leather to
the right side of the fabric.
Insert zip beneath slit in the
leather trim strip and stitch
in place all round, close to
the inner edge. Now stitch
the remaining long free
edge of leather trim to the
seam allowance of the front
part of the bag front/back
piece, matching length **e–f**,
and with the wrong side of
the leather to the right side
of the fabric. (A tube will
be formed. Do not catch the
fabric in the seam.) The
bag seam allowance is now
sandwiched between the
leather trim and the zip
tape. Sew it down to the
bag interior. Open zip
(IMPORTANT: this permits
completed bag to be turned
right side out). Stitch side
seams (match **e–g** to **h–e**)
with right sides together;
clean-finish edges. Now
stitch the short seams on
the base of the bag from
corner to corner over the
tuck, matching **g** to **g** and
**h** to **h**. Clean-finish edges.
Before stitching the short

seams across the bag top,
clip the seam allowance on
the front part of the bag
diagonally into the corners.
Stitch seams, clean-finish
edges. Turn bag right side
out. Make the second bag
in the same way.
*Finishing:* Stitch the
completed bags together
along the upper fold line of
the back part of bag,
seaming very close to the
edge. Now glue the
rectangular leather tabs
over the ends of the
carrying strap, just above
the semi-circular strap
ends, as shown in diagram.
Topstitch all round the
carrying strap, using the
width of the machine foot
as a stitch guide. Sew tab
and carrying strap ends
securely on to either side of
the bag at the point
marked **i** in the diagram.

**How to enlarge pattern:**
The pattern for the vanity
bag is shown in reduced
size. Using the
measurements given (in
centimetres or inches)

enlarge the pattern pieces
to full size. The dotted lines
are guidelines. It may be
helpful to use graph paper.
The broken lines on the
bag front/back piece
indicate folds. Seam
allowances are not included
on the pattern diagram;
they are indicated in the
cutting-out instructions.

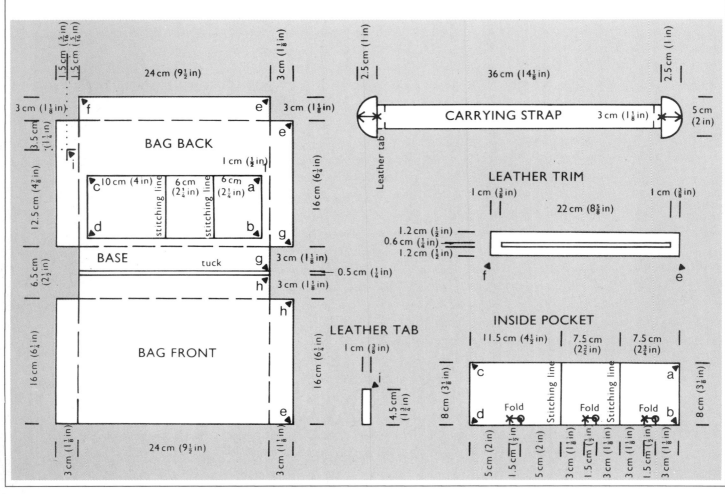

# 2

## Make-up Organizer

**Finished size:** 23 x 46 cm (approx. 9 x 18 in), unfolded

**Materials:** 0.5 m (⅝ yd) of 150 cm (60 in)-wide canvas. 0.1 m (⅛ yd) of 150 cm (58–60 in)-wide supple imitation leather. Scraps of clear plastic for the two upper pockets (available as shower curtaining). 0.25 m (10 in) of 2 cm (¾ in)-wide elastic. Two 1.5 cm (⅝ in)-diameter press-studs (snap-fasteners) and tool for insertion. Two 3.5 cm (1¼ in)-diameter metal rings (for fastening). Matching sewing thread.

**Cutting out:** Cut out all pieces without seam allowances, except for the bottom pocket front which has a 2 cm (¾ in) allowance along top edge.
*Cut out the following pieces from imitation leather:* one fastening strap (twice the finished width plus 5 mm (¼ in) seam allowance all round), four pocket tabs without seam allowance, 2.5 cm (1 in)-wide binding strips for organizer edges as shown (cut across width of 'leather'). For elastic ends cut four rectangular tabs, each 2 cm (¾ in) × 1 cm (⅜ in). Cut two 12 cm (4¼ in) strips of elastic.

**Sewing:** Bind the top edge of each clear plastic pocket with imitation leather. Position the 'leather' strip along pocket edge, with right side of strip to plastic. Stitch a 5 mm (¼ in) lengthwise seam. Roll binding over pocket edge and to other side. Finger-press binding flat, aligning lower edges. Stitch through all thicknesses, close to lower edge of binding. Be careful to catch all layers in seam. (HINT: masking tape helps to hold binding in place for stitching.) Place short plastic pocket on top of tall plastic pocket, aligning bottom edges. Bind them as one, stitching through all layers. Position the completed plastic pocket unit on the main section as shown on diagram and stitch the seam through all layers, close to lower edge of bottom binding. Attach elastic strips as shown,

stitching 'leather' tabs over the raw ends. Stitch lines across elastic where indicated, forming divisions. Bind curved edges of side flaps and baste the straight raw edges to the main section. Turn under and sew a double hem on top edge of bottom pocket front. Place two 'leather' pocket tabs wrong sides together and stitch close to the curved edges. Repeat with the other pair. Bind the flap of the bottom pocket flap/back piece, catching tabs in seam, as shown. Position bottom pocket flap/back piece on bottom of main section (right sides together). Sandwich the bottom pocket front on top (wrong sides together). Baste all round the main section, close to edges. Apply binding all round the main section, stitching through all layers and overlapping it 5 mm (¼ in) at the join. Fold under seam allowance on fastening strap and stitch round all edges using machine foot as guide. Fold the short straight edge of

the strap over rings; sew down. Stitch across strap at point **h** to attach it to the main section below plastic pockets (point **h**).
*To finish:* with insertion tool, punch a press-stud into each pocket tab and sockets into the pocket front piece at corresponding points (**x**).

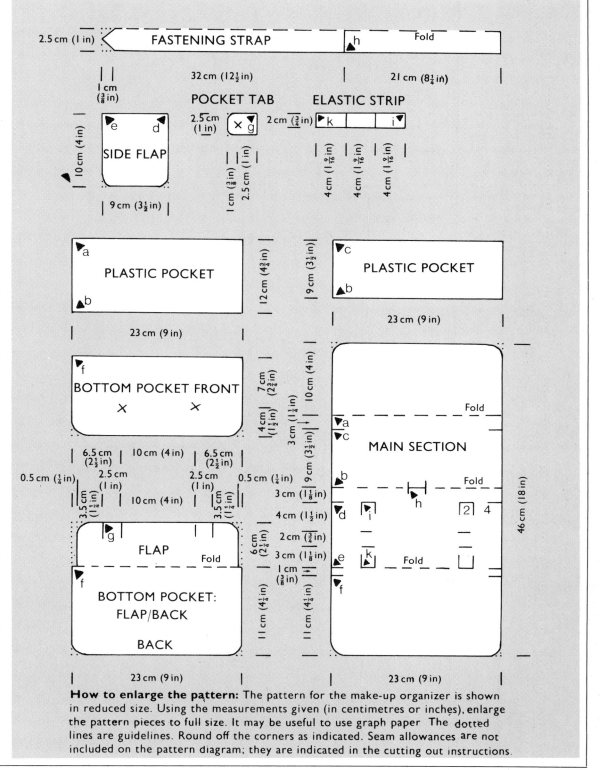

**How to enlarge the pattern:** The pattern for the make-up organizer is shown in reduced size. Using the measurements given (in centimetres or inches), enlarge the pattern pieces to full size. It may be useful to use graph paper The dotted lines are guidelines. Round off the corners as indicated. Seam allowances are not included on the pattern diagram; they are indicated in the cutting out instructions.

# 3

## Mother Goose Waistcoat (Vest)

**Size:** One size fits 10–14 (8–12 U.S.)

**Materials:** 1.4 m (1⅝ yd) of 120 cm (48 in)-wide navy blue/white floral printed quilted cotton fabric (half for waistcoat front, half for back). One large white/blue and smaller yellow/white and white/red printed cotton remnants. Scrap of strawberry-coloured satin. 0.5 m (½ yd) white lace trim. Two white buttons. One pin-on fabric flower. Small amount of synthetic wadding (batting). One sequin. Waterproof marking pen (optional). 5 m (5½ yd) of 24 mm (1 in)-wide pink bias binding. Matching sewing thread.

**How to enlarge pattern:**
Each box of the grid measures 5 cm (2 in) square. To enlarge the pattern, draw grid to scale on paper. Copy each design line into exactly the same position in the corresponding box of the full-size grid. Remember to make separate pattern pieces for waistcoat front, front patch pocket, waistcoat back and for each part of the appliqué motif (large and small goose bodies, apron, apron facing (lower half of apron, to broken line), large and small beaks, large and small legs, hat). (NOTE: lower half of apron has an oddly-shaped cut-out. When apron is stitched on to goose body, this space will create the illlusion of a wing.) Seam allowances are specified in cutting-out instructions.

**Cutting out:** From navy blue/white quilted fabric cut out one waistcoat back, two fronts (right and left sides) and two pockets, adding a 2 cm (¾ in) seam allowance to shoulders, side seams (to asterisk only) and pocket edges (except top). Remaining edges are without seam allowance. Cut out appliqué pieces as follows: cut large and small goose bodies from white/blue fabric with 5 mm (¼ in) seam allowance all round. Cut apron and apron facing

from white/red fabric with 5 mm (¼ in) seam allowance all round. Cut small beak and legs from yellow/white fabric without seam allowance. Cut out large beak twice from yellow/white fabric, with 5 mm (¼ in) seam allowance. Cut hat from strawberry satin without seam allowance.

**Sewing:** *Back appliqué:* turn under seam allowances of large and small goose bodies and baste into position on waistcoat back. Stitch on to back of waistcoat, machining close to edges. Machine-stitch legs, small beak and hat on to waistcoat back, using a closely spaced narrow zigzag stitch (satin stitch) all round edges. Pin lace trim to bottom half of apron, on right side of fabric and with bottom edge of lace facing inwards. Stitch the semicircular apron facing to bottom half of apron, with right sides together and catching lace trim in the seam. Turn right side out. Turn under and baste down remaining apron seam allowances; then baste apron in place on goose body. Poke a small amount of wadding under the upper half of the apron to create a 'tummy'. Stitch upper half of apron to waistcoat back, stitching across waistline of apron. Stitch two concentric rings within hat, as shown. With

### PATTERN FOR WAISTCOAT FRONT AND POCKET

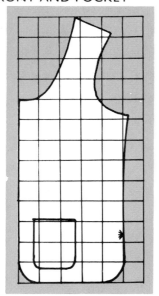

TROPICAL PARADISE WAISTCOAT

MOTHER GOOSE WAISTCOAT

right sides facing, sew large beak together, leaving an opening for turning. Turn, sew opening shut, stitch all round beak close to edge. Fold beak in half, sew beak to goose face along folded edge. Sew flower to hat. Sew on button eyes. Machine-embroider wing-line on to small goose with narrow zigzag stitch; sew on sequin for eye. Using small backstitches, outline the wing and tail section of the large goose. If you wish, draw sunglasses and bootlaces on the large goose using a waterproof marking pen.
*Finishing the waistcoat:* Stitch shoulder seams and side seams (to asterisk only). Apply bias binding to raw edges of waistcoat and to pocket tops, mitring it at front neckline corner and at side notches. (To apply binding: open out one folded edge. Pin binding to edge of fabric with right sides together. Stitch along binding foldline. Fold binding up and over the raw edge of the fabric, so that the other folded edge of the binding meets the stitching line on the wrong side of the fabric. Pin binding in place, slipstitch it to seamline. Turn under and finish the pocket seam allowances. Baste pockets in place on each side of the waistcoat front, as shown on diagram. Attach each pocket to the waistcoat front, stitching close to the edges. If you wish, add a folded and stitched length of bias binding to each side of the neckline edge, for a 'tie' closure.

## Tropical Paradise Waistcoat

**Size:** One size fits 10–14 (8–12 u.s.)

**Materials:** 1.4 m (1⅝ yd) of 120 cm (48 in)-wide white/blue floral printed quilted cotton fabric (half for waistcoat front, half for back). One large blue and one sandy-beige cotton fabric remnant. Small brown, green and yellow scraps of printed cotton. Approx. three dozen silver sequins. Small piece of yellow fishnet. 4 m (4⅜ yd) of 24 mm (1 in)-wide blue bias binding. 1 m (1⅛ yd) of 24 mm (1 in)-wide beige bias binding. Matching sewing thread.

**How to enlarge the pattern:** Enlarge pattern to scale as for Mother Goose Waistcoat. Remember to make separate pattern pieces for waistcoat front, front patch pocket, waistcoat back and for each part of appliqué motif (sky, island, palm leaves, tree trunk, fence pole, moon). Seam allowances are specified in cutting-out instructions.

**Cutting out:** From white/blue quilted fabric cut out one waistcoat back, two fronts (right and left sides) and two pockets, adding a 2 cm (¾ in) seam allowance to shoulders, side seams (to asterisk only) and pocket edges (except top).

Remaining edges are without seam allowance. Cut out appliqué pieces as follows: cut out blue cotton sky with seam allowance on shoulder and side seam only. Cut island from sandy-beige fabric with seam allowance on side seam only. Cut out the following pieces without seam allowance: palm leaves (from green patterned fabric), tree trunk and four fence poles (from brown patterned fabric) and the crescent moon (from yellow fabric).

**Sewing:** *Back appliqué:* position 'sky' on waistcoat back, matching outer edges; baste in place. Machine-stitch along lower edge using a closely spaced narrow zigzag stitch. Position 'island' as shown, baste, then zigzag-stitch it on to back along the irregular upper edges. Position and stitch tree trunk, fence poles, palm leaves and moon to back (in that order) in the same manner. Sew the fishnet over the fence poles and tree trunk by hand. Sew the sequin 'stars' into the sky by hand, spacing them evenly apart. Machine-embroider the waves using wide, closely spaced zigzag stitches.
*Finishing the waistcoat:* finish waistcoat as for Mother Goose waistcoat, but apply beige seam binding to bottom edge of back, blue binding to all other edges and pocket tops.

## 4 Summer Sunhats

**Size:** To fit an average-sized head (circumference 58 cm [22¾ in])

**Materials:** 0.5 m (⅝ yd) of 115 cm (45 in)-wide fabric.
*Style 1:* plain (solid-coloured) cotton.
*Style 2:* lightweight denim.
*Style 3:* printed cotton.
*For Style 1:* four 1 m (1⅛ yd) lengths of 1 cm (⅜ in)-wide ribbon, in contrasting colours.
*For all hats:* matching sewing thread.

**Cutting out:** Copy pattern pieces as directed, then add a 5 mm (¼ in) seam allowance to all seams. Cut out the brim twice, placing centre front on fold of fabric and also on the straight grain. (An arc-shaped pattern piece results.) Cut out the crown section ten times.

**Sewing:** The hat is made out of a double thickness of fabric.
*Crown:* stitch together two sets of five crown sections to form a cone shape, always stitching from bottom upwards to peak. Press seams open and

topstitch 3 mm (⅛ in) on either side of each seam. You now have two completed hat crowns. With wrong sides together, pin one crown inside the other, matching seams and raw bottom edges. Stitch crowns together, close to the bottom edges.
*Brim:* With right sides facing, stitch the centre back seam of each brim piece together to form a ring; press seam open. With right sides facing, pin brims together along the outer edges, matching seams. Stitch all round the outer edge, turn to right side; press outer edge. Join brim to crown: with right sides together, stitch one layer of brim fabric to crown, aligning the brim seam with a crown seam. Press seam towards brim. Turn under the seam allowance on the inner edge of brim underside. Slipstitch this edge to the crown, concealing the brim/crown seamline.
*Finishing: Style 1:* stitch ribbons on to brim at equal distances apart.
*Style 2:* topstitch ten evenly spaced concentric rings round brim.
*Style 3:* topstitch round outer edge of brim, using width of machine foot as a guide.

*Continued overleaf*

21

Centre Back Seam

BRIM

Grain

CROWN

Fold

Fold

**Hat pattern:** These partial pattern pieces are full-size. Given above are half the crown section (crown has five sections in all) and a quarter brim (piece is seamed at centre back). To copy each pattern, start with a folded piece of tracing paper. Align paper fold with broken line of pattern. Trace pattern outline. Turn tracing paper over and trace the mirror image of the outline. Open out tracing paper for full crown section and half brim. Seam allowances are not included on pattern pieces; they are specified in the cutting-out instructions.

## 5
### Leather Envelope Clutch and Wallet

**Size:** *Bag:* approx. 20 × 32 cm (8 × 12½ in) *Wallet:* approx. 15 × 21 cm (6 × 8¼ in)

**Materials:** Approx. 100 sq.cm (3½ sq.ft.) of natural cowhide (enough for bag and wallet). 30 × 70 cm (2 × 2½ sq.ft) piece of lining leather (for bag flap). Leather thonging (lacing): Bag: approx. 3 m (3⅜ yd) of 5 mm (³⁄₁₆ in)-wide. Wallet: approx. 2 m (2¼ yd) of 3 mm (⅛ in)-wide. One medium-sized press-stud (snap fastener) and setting (insertion) tool. Revolving punch plier (rotary leather punch). Metal ruler. Stanley knife. Rubber solution (rubber cement). Thonging (lacing) needle (optional).

**Cutting out:** Enlarge pattern pieces and make the side gusset template as directed. Inspect leather for flaws and blemishes; try to avoid these when positioning pattern pieces. Weight the pattern pieces, then outline the shapes on the right (grain) side of the leather. (Bag flap lining only: trace pattern on to *rough* side of leather. Add a 2 cm [¾ in] seam allowance to the angled sides.) Start by cutting along straight lines of pattern pieces. Place the ruler on each marked line. Lean the Stanley knife against the ruler and cut with a firm, even pressure. Now cut out two side gussets using the card template as a guide for accuracy. (Pull knife round template edges.) Next, carefully cut the remaining pattern curves freehand. Work on a steady, protected surface.

**Making up:** Mark the placement line of the bag

flap on the rough side of the main section. Insert the ball half of the press-stud (snap fastener) into the grain side of the flap lining, 2.5 cm (1 in) from the point. Insert the socket half into the front part of the main section, centred 16 cm (6¼ in) from edge on the grain side of the leather. Apply adhesive to the rough side of the bag flap and lining. Wait until tacky. Starting at straight edge, smooth on the lining up to the fold. Bend the fold, then smooth on the rest of the lining. (If necessary, apply extra pressure with a rolling pin.) Trim the protruding lining edges flush with the bag. Now mark the position of the lacing holes on the grain side of the leather. For the bag, space the holes 5 mm (¼ in) from the edge and 1 cm (⅜ in) from centre to centre. For the wallet, space the holes 4 mm (³⁄₁₆ in) from the edge and 8 mm (⁵⁄₁₆ in) from centre to centre. Punch a test hole in a leather scrap to check that the thonging passes through easily. Make holes with the punch. Trim thong ends to a point for easy threading or use a special needle. Lace the pieces together using whipstitch, beginning with bag side gussets. Let a bit of thong extend at the start. Pull firmly as you stitch. If thong runs out, splice it: leave end to hang out; begin new thong in next hole. Thin each thong end by scraping the underside with a Stanley knife. Apply adhesive to scraped ends; join them together. Pound the splice flat.
*Wallet:* this is made in the same way as the bag. Place the pieces on top of each other as shown in photo. The divisions of the credit card compartment are sewn with running stitch.

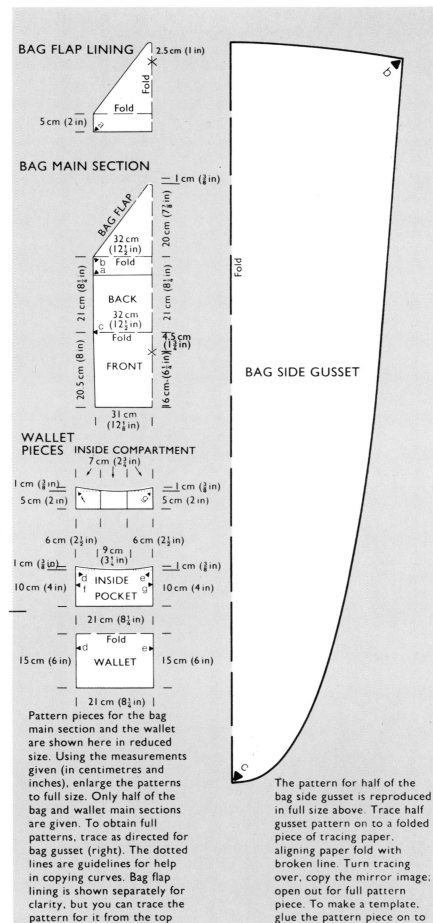

**BAG FLAP LINING** 2.5 cm (1 in)

Fold

Fold

5 cm (2 in)

**BAG MAIN SECTION**

BAG FLAP

1 cm (⅜ in)

20 cm (7⅞ in)

32 cm (12½ in) Fold

b
a

21 cm (8¼ in)

21 cm (8¼ in)

**BACK**

32 cm (12½ in)

c

Fold

4.5 cm (1¾ in)

20.5 cm (8 in)

**FRONT**

16 cm (6¼ in)

31 cm (12⅛ in)

BAG SIDE GUSSET

Fold

b

Fold

c

**WALLET PIECES** INSIDE COMPARTMENT

7 cm (2¾ in)

1 cm (⅜ in)

5 cm (2 in)

1 cm (⅜ in)

5 cm (2 in)

6 cm (2½ in)

6 cm (2½ in)

9 cm (3¼ in)

1 cm (⅜ in)

10 cm (4 in)

d INSIDE

POCKET

e

f

g

1 cm (⅜ in)

10 cm (4 in)

21 cm (8¼ in)

Fold

15 cm (6 in)

d

**WALLET**

e

15 cm (6 in)

21 cm (8¼ in)

Pattern pieces for the bag main section and the wallet are shown here in reduced size. Using the measurements given (in centimetres and inches), enlarge the patterns to full size. Only half of the bag and wallet main sections are given. To obtain full patterns, trace as directed for bag gusset (right). The dotted lines are guidelines for help in copying curves. Bag flap lining is shown separately for clarity, but you can trace the pattern for it from the top portion of the bag main section.

The pattern for half of the bag side gusset is reproduced in full size above. Trace half gusset pattern on to a folded piece of tracing paper, aligning paper fold with broken line. Turn tracing over, copy the mirror image; open out for full pattern piece. To make a template, glue the pattern piece on to card (cardboard); cut it out.

## 6
# Skirt With Matching Shawl

**Size:** 14 (12 u.s.)

**Materials:** 3 m (3⅜ yd) of 140 cm (54 in)-wide printed woollen challis fabric (1.5 m [1¾ yd] for skirt only) *or* 2.4 m (2⅝ yd) of 90 cm (36 in)-wide brushed cotton (for skirt only). 0.1 m (¼ yd) of 90 cm (36 in)-wide, medium-weight, iron-on interfacing. One 18 cm (7 in) zip (zipper). 5.7 m (6¼ yd) of 24 mm (1 in)-wide bias binding (for shawl). Matching sewing thread.

**How to enlarge the pattern:** The pattern for the rectangular skirt front and back piece is shown in reduced size. Using the measurements given (in centimetres or inches), enlarge the pattern piece to full size. Slightly reduced patterns for skirt waistband and a tuck stitching guide are given in grid form. Each box of the grid measures 1 cm (⅜ in) square. To enlarge the pattern pieces, draw grid to scale on paper. Copy each line into exactly the same position in the corresponding box of the full-size grid. Trace the full-size, tuck-pleat stitching guide on to a piece of card (cardboard); cut it out. The guide will help you to stitch the skirt's released tucks accurately.

**Cutting out:** Add a 1 cm (⅜ in) seam allowance and a 4 cm (1½ in) hem to the skirt front/back piece. Cut the piece out twice, placing the long dimension along the 140 cm (54 in) fabric width (for brushed cotton, place the long dimension along length of fabric). Add a 1 cm (⅜ in) seam allowance all round waistband. Cut out the waistband four times on the fold (twice for the waistband and twice for the self-fabric facing). Using the waistband pattern, cut out two pieces of iron-on interfacing. Trim seams, clip diagonally across corners and iron on to wrong side of waistband pieces. For the shawl, cut a 140 cm (54 in) square from

*Continued overleaf*

the remaining woollen fabric.

**Sewing:** *Skirt:* stitch the right side seam; press open. Mark the position of the released tucks on the wrong side of fabric. The skirt has a total of 38 released tucks. Each tuck takes up 3 cm (1⅛ in) of fabric (distance **x-o**). Distance between tucks is 2.5 cm (1 in). Now stitch tucks using the wedge-shaped stitching guide. On the wrong side of the fabric, match **x** to **o**, forming a fold. On a flat surface, align the straight edge of the stitching guide with the fold edge of the tuck. Stitch an 8 cm (3⅛ in) seam along the tapered edge of the guide.

Press each finished tuck to the right. Leave the tuck at the left side seam unstitched. Stitch the left side seam, leaving an 11 cm (4½ in) slit at the top for the zip. Baste this opening shut; press side seam open. Fold the side seam tuck; baste; press towards skirt front; remove basting. Now stitch the right side seam of the waistband and waistband, with right sides together. Press open. Press under the seam allowance on the lower edge of the waistband facing. Apply waistband to skirt top, with right sides of fabric together and right side seams matching. (Waistband seam allowance will extend beyond the folded edge of

the tuck-pleat on skirt front.) Press waistband/ skirt seam upwards. *Insert zip:* the zip is inserted into the tuck-pleat at the left side seam. This tuck is, therefore, longer than the rest. To apply zip, make a horizontal cut into the tuck-pleat which lies flat against the skirt front. This permits the tuck to open out. Insert zip with a lapped application, so that the top of the zip is level with the top of the waistband. *Now apply the waistband facing:* pin facing to top waistband edges with right sides together. Stitch seam; trim. Turn facing to inside. Turn under the side seams of the facing. Slipstitch facing side seams and

bottom edge of facing to skirt. Hem the skirt. If you wish, belt carrier loops can be sewn on to waistband at the right side seam and close to the zip at the left side seam. Fashion these out of fabric strips or thread.

**Shawl:** Open out one folded edge of the seam binding. Pin binding to the raw edges of the fabric square, pivoting at corners and with the right side of binding to wrong side of fabric. Stitch binding to shawl along the binding foldline, pivoting the machine needle at corners. Clip diagonally across shawl corners. Fold binding over so that its full width lies flat on the right side of

the fabric; press. Mitre binding at corners and lap a diagonal seam at the corner where binding ends meet. Baste the free folded edge of the binding to the fabric. Machine-stitch across the lapped corner seam and all round binding, close to folded edge. Fold the fabric square in half diagonally to form the triangular shawl.

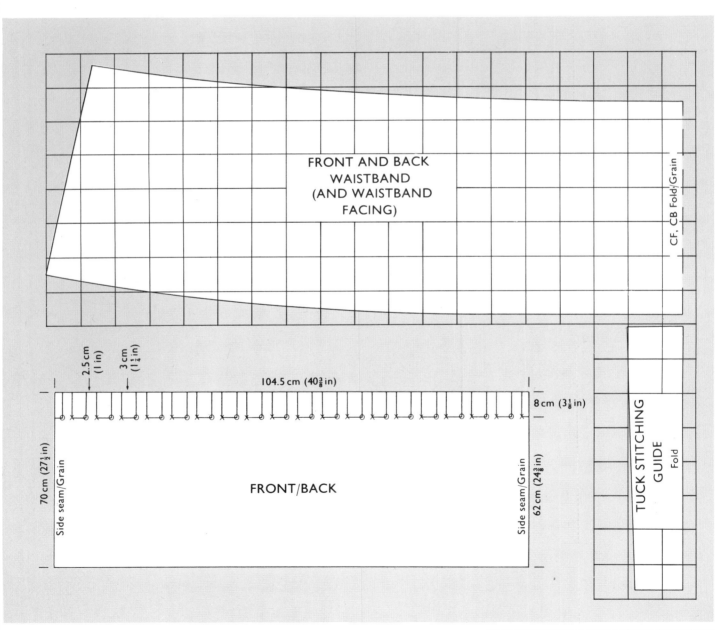

# 7

## Long Tiered Skirt

**Size:** One size fits 12–14 (10–12 u.s.)

**Materials:** Printed cotton or cotton blend fabric in coordinating patterns and similar colours.
*First tier:* 0.6 m ($\frac{3}{4}$ yd) of 90 cm (36 in)-wide.
*Second tier:* 1.1 m ($1\frac{1}{4}$ yd) of 90 cm (36 in)-wide.
*Third tier:* 1.2 m ($1\frac{3}{8}$ yd) of 90 cm (36 in)-wide.
*Fourth and fifth tiers (each):* 1.7 m ($1\frac{7}{8}$ yd) of 90 cm (36 in)-wide.
4 cm ($1\frac{1}{2}$ in)-wide elastic for waistband. Matching sewing thread.

**Enlarging the pattern:** You will need a roll of brown paper, a ruler, set square (right triangle), flexible curve (available at art supply shops) and a pencil. First, draw a 21 cm ($8\frac{1}{4}$ in) vertical centre line on to a piece of paper and extend each end a few centimetres (inches). Copy the dotted guidelines on to the paper at right angles to the centre line. Transfer the short vertical marks on to the paper at the specified distances from the centre line (measure these distances along the dotted guidelines). To copy a pattern curve, lay a flexible curve between the short vertical marks so that it goes upwards from one dotted line level to the next. Run your pencil along the edge of the flexible curve to record the curved line. NOTE: Seam allowances are not included on pattern diagram. They are specified in cutting-out instructions.

**Cutting out:** For some of the tiers fabric must be joined. Follow cutting instructions carefully.
*First tier:* Broken line marks centre of pattern piece to be placed on fold of fabric. Cut out the whole piece twice, adding a 15 mm ($\frac{5}{8}$ in) seam allowance all round each piece. (This is the standard seam allowance for the skirt.) Cut waistband from same fabric: cut two strips, each 8 cm ($3\frac{1}{8}$ in) × 48 cm (19 in) plus seam allowance.
*Second tier:* this tier has a centre seam at front and back. Cut piece out four

times from single fabric, adding seam allowance all round each piece.
*Third tier:* same as second.
*Fourth tier:* skirt front and back each have a centre panel with a curved section on either side. Cut out rectangular centre panel twice on the fold, curved side section four times. Be sure to add seam allowance all round each piece.
*Fifth tier:* same as fourth.

**Sewing:** Stitch the centre seams of the second and third tiers and the seams within the fourth and fifth tiers. Clean-finish seam allowances; press seams open. Now gather the top of the second tier to fit the bottom width of the first tier. (To gather: run two

parallel rows of machine basting 6 and 12 mm ($\frac{1}{4}$ and $\frac{1}{2}$ in) from the edge of the fabric, then carefully draw up the threads from either end.) Gather the other tiers in the same manner. With right sides together, pin gathered top of second tier to ungathered bottom of first tier, distributing gathers evenly. Stitch the tiers together. Trim and clean-finish seam allowances; press upwards. Repeat to join other tiers. Stitch side seams, carefully matching the tiers; clean-finish seam allowances. Turn under a narrow double hem and stitch. With right sides together, join the short ends of the waistband strips to form a ring. Stitch one

long edge of waistband to skirt top, with right sides together and side seams matching. Press under seam allowance on unstitched waistband edge. Fold waistband in half to inside, then stitch close to seamline, leaving a small opening for elastic. Cut elastic to waist measurement plus 2.5 cm (1 in), thread it through the casing, overlapping ends slightly; sew ends together. Slipstitch waistband opening closed.

Pattern pieces for the long tiered skirt are given in reduced size, at right. Enlarge the measurements given (in centimetres or inches) to full size. The dotted lines are guidelines.

1    FIRST TIER
2    SECOND TIER
3    THIRD TIER
4    FOURTH TIER
5    FIFTH TIER

**CF** = CENTRE FRONT
**CB** = CENTRE BACK

Pattern diagram — First tier (1): 2.5 cm (1 in) guidelines; 24 cm ($9\frac{1}{2}$ in); 29 cm ($11\frac{3}{8}$ in); CF and CB Fold; 21 cm ($8\frac{1}{4}$ in).

Second tier (2): 4.5 cm ($1\frac{3}{4}$ in); 47 cm ($18\frac{1}{2}$ in); gather; 52 cm ($20\frac{1}{2}$ in); CF and CB seam; 21 cm ($8\frac{1}{4}$ in).

Third tier (3): 6 cm ($2\frac{1}{4}$ in); 70 cm ($27\frac{1}{2}$ in); gather; 75 cm ($29\frac{1}{2}$ in); CF and CB seam; 21 cm ($8\frac{1}{4}$ in).

Fourth tier (4): 6 cm ($2\frac{1}{4}$ in); 52 cm ($20\frac{1}{2}$ in); 43 cm (17 in); gather; Seam; 57 cm ($22\frac{1}{2}$ in); 43 cm (17 in); CF and CB Fold; 21 cm ($8\frac{1}{4}$ in).

Fifth tier (5): 6 cm ($2\frac{1}{4}$ in); 78 cm ($30\frac{3}{4}$ in); 42 cm ($16\frac{1}{2}$ in); gather; Seam; 83 cm ($32\frac{5}{8}$ in); 42 cm ($16\frac{1}{2}$ in); CF and CB Fold; 21 cm ($8\frac{1}{4}$ in).

# 8

## House Clothes You Look Good In

What you need for an enjoyable morning, a lazy weekend or the odd tranquil evening are comfortable house clothes you feel really good in. They must possess certain qualities: soft fabric which is pleasant to the touch, an easy fit and a trace of elegance. For day-to-day convenience, they must be washable and practical to wear. We have styled the robes on these pages bearing these features in mind.

A well-designed dressing-gown is invaluable on hectic home-based mornings when you haven't had time to dress. Pop it on over your nightie and you're both warm and presentable. In the evenings, slip on a comfortable robe and it will help you to unwind from daily tensions.

For the 'A.M.' style on the left, we selected a soft knitted fabric. The kimono-style cut provides freedom of movement. The sleeves are wide enough to be roomy and graceful without being clumsy. The ties are sewn on to the robe, so they'll never get lost. Hem and sleeves are decorated with borders of printed jersey in matching colours. The ties are also made out of the same fabric. The combination of geometric and flowered prints is very effective. Remember, though, that to mix prints successfully, you must match colours carefully. The scale of the patterns must also be harmonious.

Our 'P.M.' robe, in jewel-like green, is made out of luxurious stretch velour, a knitted-pile fabric. Only the sleeves have been trimmed with bands of colourful knitted cotton. The side seams are provocatively slit. In other respects, it is identical to the 'A.M.' version.

When making the dressing-gowns, it is essential to choose compatible fabrics. Match knitted fabrics with knitted trim.

Instructions for these robes are on page 38.

## Patchwork for the Playroom

Children love to play on the floor, so we've designed these projects with them in mind.

The strip patchwork scatter rug provides a soft, warm and washable play surface. It's made from fabric remnants which you may already have or can purchase cheaply. The coordinating quilted and patchwork cushions on the bench are made from the same fabrics. All contain synthetic wadding (batting).

These patchwork 'play puffs' are as much fun for you to make as they are for children to play with. The multi-coloured balls are made from interlocking five-sided shapes. It's fascinating to see how the puzzle-like pieces fit together. You'll feel like a magician when the finished ball emerges from a pile of scraps.

The balls are thrifty scrap-bag creations and are stuffed with light-as-a-feather synthetic filling. They are perfect for safe indoor play because they don't hurt and won't break anything on impact. Toss them into the washing machine when they get dirty.

Instructions for rug, cushions and balls are on pages 39 and 40.

9

I I

## The Well-Dressed Kitchen: Things to Make for You and Your Home

Cheerful surroundings do much to take the tedium out of housework. We've translated this belief into the projects on these pages.

These colourful, easy-fitting pinafore-style aprons are perfect for kitchen duty, but they're anything but matronly, and you wouldn't be ashamed to receive your guests in them. Cut straight and wide with a gathered tie casing, both are stylish enough to lead a double life, and be worn outside the kitchen too – wear the long version for lounging and the short one as a summer top. And they're easy to sew.

There's more to the humble tea-towel (dish towel) than just wiping up, as you can see from the photo at right. We've designed a full range of household textiles, all made from those familiar linen rectangles. The mother/daughter butcher-style aprons, cushion covers, serviettes (napkins), tablecloth, tea-cosy and even the curtains are all created from one or more towels. What could be more appropriate kitchen decor?

Instructions for aprons and tea-towel makes are on pages 40, 41, 42 and 43.

12

13

## Clever Things to Make for a Cosy Bedroom

For those who like lounging around or reading in bed, this handy bag is ideal. Simply hang it over the bed-frame or tuck its flap under the mattress and you can use it for storing magazines and bedside odds and ends. It is thriftily made from fabric remnants and pieces of card (cardboard).

The rustic machine patchwork cover on the right-hand page is made out of colourful mixed plaids and checks.

You'll appreciate its inventive easy-sew construction. The top side consists of 36 squares, while the back is a single layer of fabric. To pad it, a triple layer of wadding (batting) is slipped into the individual square pockets, as sewing progresses row by row. This quilt measures 0.9 m (35½ in) wide by 1.8 m (71 in) long, including the frill (ruffle), but our instructions tell you how to make it up in any size.

Instructions for the bedside bag and quilt are on pages 43–44.

14

# 15

## Nursery Menagerie: Jungle Mascots for Children to Treasure

Soft toys have been popular since before the days of grandmother's youth. Lots of parents are proud to display the battered soft (stuffed) toys which were cherished childhood playmates. This kind of toy is a perennial favourite and it's easy to see why: a cuddly pet *like this* is the right friend in any situation. An elephant or teddy is always there for a child to confide in. It shares triumphs and secrets. It comforts him when he's sad. Even when the child is angry, a few punches and thumps don't bother these stalwart pals. Whatever its owner's mood, a toy like this will remain a devoted companion for many years.

Soft toys must be tough enough to withstand rough treatment, and nothing can match the quality and durability of the ones you sew yourself, made with good fabric and lots of love.

The domesticated jungle creatures on these pages are enchanting variations on the traditional teddy bear. All are created from man-made fur and synthetic filling, which makes them completely washable (just remove the felt eyes before laundering).

The perky little elephant is furry, warm and huggable. Its floppy ears are lined with flowered fabric, which is also used for the soles of its feet. The long-necked giraffe is ideal for putting young arms round. Its tiny mouth is embroidered. The enormous jaws of the tame crocodile are lined with red cotton fabric. Its teeth are white felt triangles.

When you've finished sewing our miniature zoo, use your own imagination to create other animals for it.

Instructions for these soft toys are on pages 44 and 45.

17

# 18

## Household Extras with the Personal Touch

We all get tired of selecting from the range of identical mass-produced goods available to us. Here are some useful household items that carry the stamp of *individuality*, because they are home-made

in the very best sense of the word. Our designs are already a bit different from what's on the market, and when you make them up in the fabrics of your choice, they are truly unique.

These vivid, streamlined oven gloves make an attractive addition to

any kitchen. They're also useful for barbecues. The thumb is situated in the palm of the hand, which, although it may seem unusual at first, is actually quite practical.

The serviette (napkin) pouch and coordinating serviette combine elegance with

informality. Use them to add a gracious air of hospitality when you're entertaining.

Hang these 'tidies' in a well-used passageway to encourage your family to deposit odds and ends of washing. Each laundry bag has a large back slit for big

items and front patch pockets as catch-alls for small bits of clothing. They are appropriately made out of old linen (the more washings it's had, the better).

Instructions for these projects are on pages 46 and 47.

# 8

## Kimono-style Robes

**Size:** 16–18 (14–16 u.s.)

**Materials:** 2.6 m (2⅞ yd) of 140 cm (54 in)-wide cotton jersey (Style 1) or stretch velour (Style 2). Fabric trim in matching colours:
*Style 1:* 1 m (1⅛ yd) each of 90 cm (36 in) printed cotton knits A and B.
*Style 2:* 0.3 m (⅜ yd) of 140 cm (54 in)-wide printed cotton knit C, 0.4 m (½ yd) of 140 cm (54 in)-wide printed cotton knit D. Small amount of sew-in interfacing (for tieband slits). Matching sewing thread.

**Cutting out:** Enlarge pattern pieces and refer to cutting layout for placement. For each robe: cut out two fronts and one back piece, adding a 4 cm (1½ in) seam allowance for sleeve hems and hem and a 1 cm (⅜ in) seam allowance elsewhere. Cut out one back neck facing and two front facing strips, adding a 1 cm (⅜ in) seam allowance to outer edges.
*Tiebands:* for each robe cut four 10 × 75 cm (4 × 30 in) strips (Style 1: cut tieband from fabric B. Style 2: use fabric D.). Tieband measurements include a 1 cm (½ in) seam allowance.
*Sleeve trim (both styles):* cut out continuous strips of fabric, eliminating the sleeve top seam and adding 1 cm (⅜ in) seam allowance all round.
*Style 1 trim:* cut out hem border strips with side seams and 1 cm (⅜ in) seam allowance all round.

**Sewing:** Use a flat zigzag stitch to prevent seams from pulling. Baste the placement lines for trim on to the pattern pieces. Each robe front has a slit through which a tieband is threaded. To make each slit, baste a small piece of interfacing behind the marked slit on the wrong side of each robe front; work a machine buttonhole. (Alternatively, you can make a bound buttonhole using self-fabric strips.) Stitch sleeve top seams joining the robe fronts to back; clean-finish seam edges; press them open; slipstitch seams to garment. Stitch the interior seams of the trim strips for sleeves and hem (Style 1), pinning long edges together with right sides facing (join strips together as in photo). Press seams open.
*Style 1:* with right sides facing, stitch side seams of the hem trim.
*Both styles:* press under seam allowances on outer edges of trim strips. Baste hem strips into position on the base fabric of robe, then stitch along each interior seam and close to outer edges. Stitch the underarm/ side seams, matching trim strips carefully (IMPORTANT: stitch Style 2 only as far as the slit markings). Finish underarm/side seam edges; press open; slipstitch to garment (including the seam allowances of Style 2 slits).
*Tiebands:* each robe has a pair of tiebands (finished width: 4 cm [1½ in]). To make a tieband, stitch the short ends of two strips together with right sides facing; press seam open. With right sides facing, fold strip in half lengthwise; stitch long edges and one short end. Turn the tieband right side out; press.
*Facings:* stitch facings together at shoulder seams, with right sides together. Clean-finish the outer edges. With right sides together, pin facing to robe, matching shoulder seams and catching in the raw ends of the tiebands (tiebands face inwards). Stitch facing to robe. Turn facing to inside, baste down along edges.
*Finishing:* topstitch along front and back neck edges, 5 mm (¼ in) from edge. Turn up and hem sleeves and robe hem.

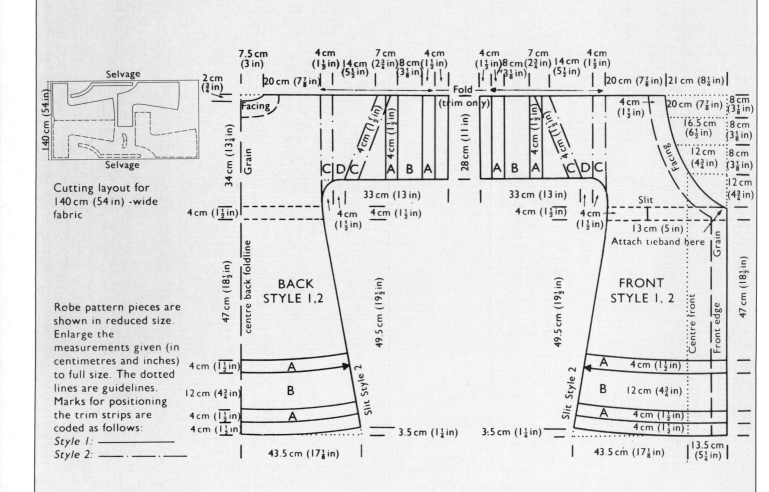

Cutting layout for 140 cm (54 in)-wide fabric

Robe pattern pieces are shown in reduced size. Enlarge the measurements given (in centimetres and inches) to full size. The dotted lines are guidelines. Marks for positioning the trim strips are coded as follows:
Style 1: ——————
Style 2: —— · —— · ——

# 9

## Strip Patchwork Rug and Coordinating Cushions

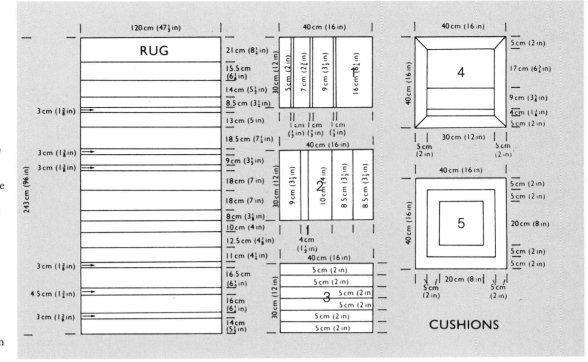

RUG

CUSHIONS

**Sizes:** *Rug:* approx. 120 × 243 cm (47½ × 96 in) NOTE: actual size of rug is slightly smaller. The rug loses a bit of length because of the bulk of the filling. *Cushions 1,2,3:* 30 × 40 cm (12 × 16 in) *Cushions 4,5:* 40 × 40 cm (16 × 16 in)

**Materials:** *For top of rug:* assorted cotton fabrics, plain (solid-coloured) and printed. *For rug backing:* 2.5 m (2¾ yd) of 120 cm (48 in)-wide (or wider) plain cotton furnishing fabric. *For rug binding:* four 8 cm (3¼ in)-wide strips of plain cotton: two strips 1.2 m (1⅜ yd)-long, two strips 2.5 m (2¾ yd)-long. *Filling:* 2.5 m (2¾ yd) of 120 cm (48 in)-wide (or wider) synthetic wadding (batting). *Cushions:* assorted cotton fabrics, plain and printed, as required. *Filling (for all five cushions):* 3.2 m (3½ yd) of 120 cm (48 in)-wide (or wider) synthetic wadding. *For rug and cushions:* matching sewing thread.

## Rug

**Cutting out:** Cut out one layer of wadding and one piece of backing fabric to the measurements given in the pattern diagram. Sort the fabrics for the top of the rug according to pattern and colour, then place them in a pleasing arrangement. Cut out 22 strips in the dimensions indicated on the diagram, adding a 1 cm (⅜ in) seam allowance to the long edges.

**Sewing:** Join the strips, with right sides together, following the sequence shown on the diagram. Press seams open. Sandwich the rug backing, the layer of wadding and the top fabric together, with wrong sides facing. Baste the layers together by hand, using large stitches. (It is best to baste in a

Patterns for the patchwork rug and coordinating cushions are shown in reduced starburst pattern, starting from the rug centre and working out to the edges.) Machine-quilt the rug by stitching *through* the seamlines of all the strips. (To reduce bulk while sewing, roll the quilted portion of the rug up tightly beneath the machine arm.) Press under a 1 cm (⅜ in) seam allowance on the long edges of the binding strips. Bind the short sides of the rug first, to a width of 3 cm (1¼ in): open out one folded edge of binding. With right sides together, pin binding fold 3 cm (1¼ in) from fabric edge. Stitch along binding foldline. Fold binding up and over raw edge of fabric, so remaining folded edge meets the stitching line on rug back. Slipstitch binding to the stitching line. Bind the long sides of the rug in the same way, but with binding ends extending 15 mm (½ in) beyond rug edges. Fold under the binding ends before slipstitching long edge of binding to the rug back.

## Cushions

**Cushion 1** (quilted): For cushion front and back, cut out two 30 × 40 cm (12 × 16 in) pieces of fabric,

size. Enlarge the measurements given (in centimetres or inches) to full size. Cushions 1, adding 1 cm (⅜ in) seam allowance all round. Cut out five layers of wadding without seam allowance. Baste one layer of wadding to the wrong side of one fabric piece. Referring to the diagram, mark the stitching lines for quilting on to the padded piece of fabric (use basting or chalk). Machine-quilt through both layers.

**Cushion 2** (patchwork/ quilted): For cushion back, cut out one 30 × 40 cm (12 × 16 in) piece of plain fabric, adding 1 cm (⅜ in) seam allowance all round. Cut out strips for cushion top, following the pattern measurements and adding 1 cm (⅜ in) seam allowance all round. Cut out five layers of wadding without seam allowance. With right sides facing, stitch the strips together and press seams open. Baste one layer of wadding to the wrong side of the patchwork top. Machine-quilt the cushion top, stitching through seamlines.

**Cushion 3** (quilted): Cut out one 30 × 40 cm (12 × 16 in) piece of plain and another of printed fabric, adding 1 cm (⅜ in) seam allowance all round each. Cut out five layers of wadding without seam

3 and 5 are quilted. The interior lines on their pattern diagrams represent stitching lines.

allowance. Baste one layer of wadding to the wrong side of the printed piece (cushion top). Machine-quilt the cushion top, stitching lines at 5 cm (2 in) intervals as shown on diagram. (A quilter guide-bar sewing machine attachment is helpful, if you have one.)

**Cushion 4** (patchwork): For cushion back, cut out one 40 cm (16 in) square of plain fabric, adding 1 cm (⅜ in) seam allowance all round. Cushion top: for border, cut four 5 × 40 cm (2 × 16 in) strips of plain cotton, adding 1 cm (⅜ in) seam allowance all round. For centre, cut out one 30 cm (12 in) plain fabric square and one 9 × 30 cm (3⅝ × 12 in) fabric strip, adding 1 cm (⅜ in) seam allowance all round both. Cut out five layers of wadding without seam allowance. With right sides together, mitre the corners of the four borders; press open. Press under seam allowance on the long sides of the printed strip. Appliqué the strip on to the centre square, stitching close to the folded edges and positioning it as shown on diagram. Press under the seam allowances of the square. Centre square on top of the border with the

folded edges of the square overlapping the inner edges of the border. Stitch the square on to the border, close to the folded edges of the square.

**Cushion 5** (quilted): For cushion front and back, cut out two 40 cm (16 in) squares of plain fabric, adding 1 cm (⅜ in) seam allowance all round. Cut out five layers of wadding without seam allowance. Baste one layer of wadding to the wrong side of one square. Referring to the diagram, machine-quilt the pattern of concentric squares through both layers. (A quilter guide-bar attachment eliminates the need for marking the pattern on to the fabric).

*Finishing* (all cushions): with right sides together, stitch cushion fronts to backs, leaving most of the fourth side open. Turn each cushion right side out, fill with the wadding layers; slipstitch the opening shut.

# 10

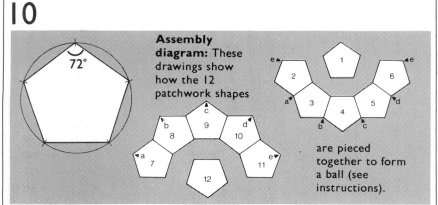

**Assembly diagram:** These drawings show how the 12 patchwork shapes are pieced together to form a ball (see instructions).

## Patchwork Play Puffs

**Sizes:** as desired

**Materials:** For each ball, you need: assorted printed cotton fabric scraps (enough for 12 five-sided shapes). Synthetic filling (stuffing): quantity required varies with size of ball. Matching sewing thread.

**Making the templates:** For each different-sized ball, make a five-sided pattern template out of card (cardboard). To draw the shape, follow either of these simple methods: the first uses a compass and tape measure, the other a protractor and ruler.
*Method 1:* inscribe the pentagon in a circle. With compass, draw a circle of the desired radius. Measure the circumference of the circle with the tape measure; divide by five. Using tape measure and pencil, measure along the circle's circumference and mark each of the five equal divisions with a point. Connect adjacent points with a straight line, as shown in diagram. When using this method, label each template according to radius size.
*Method 2:* use the protractor and ruler to

draw five equal lines of the desired length at an angle of 72° to each other. A pentagon will result. When using this method, label templates according to side length.
*Both methods:* add a 1 cm (⅜ in) seam allowance all round each template; cut out.

**Cutting out:** For each ball, cut out 12 pentagons from assorted fabrics using the template as a guide.

**Sewing:** With right sides together and referring to assembly diagram, stitch together two semicircular groups of pentagons (shapes 2–6 and 7–11). With right sides facing, stitch the ends of each semicircle together to form a ring (join shape 2 to shape 6 and shape 7 to shape 11). Press seams open. With right sides facing, stitch both rings together along their zigzag edges, carefully matching the lettered points (see diagram). Press seams. With right sides facing, stitch on the two remaining pentagons (1 and 12), carefully matching corners to seams and leaving two seams open on one of the shapes. Press. Turn the ball right side out. Fill the ball; sew seams shut by hand.

# 11

## Short and Long Pinafore-style Aprons

**Size:** 12–14 (10–12 U.S.)

## Short Apron

**Materials:** 1.6 m (1¾ yd) of 90 cm (36 in)-wide cotton or cotton blend fabric. 0.2 m (¼ yd) of iron-on interfacing. Matching sewing thread.

**Cutting out:** Enlarge the pattern and cut out the apron body in one piece, following the cutting layout. Add a 4 cm (1½ in) hem allowance, 2 cm (¾ in) to side seams and a 1 cm (⅜ in) seam allowance elsewhere. Following the pattern, draw a separate pattern piece 3 cm (1¼ in) wide for the one-piece neckline facing. Add a 1 cm (⅜ in) seam allowance to all edges and cut out once each from fabric and

interfacing (see cutting layout). Trim 5 mm (¼ in) from inner and outer interfacing edges, then iron it, centred, on to wrong side of facing. Cut out two 5 × 60 cm (2 × 23⅝ in) strips for the casing (finished width: 3 cm [1⅛ in]) and two 5 × 95 cm (2 × 37½ in) strips for the ties (finished width: 2.5 cm [1 in]). These measurements include a 1 cm (⅜ in) seam allowance all round. (See cutting layout for casing and tie placement.)

**Sewing:** Clean-finish the edges of the neckline facing. With right sides together, stitch the facing on to the apron. Clip facing corners diagonally to the stitching line. Turn facing to the inside, baste round the neckline, then topstitch close to edge. Turn hem allowance under twice and stitch. With right sides together, stitch the side seams between the arrows only, leaving armholes,

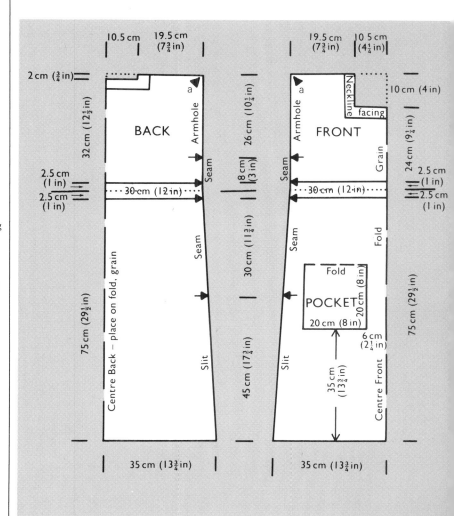

casing ends and bottom slits open. Tie the thread ends securely. Press under seam allowances to the top of the slit and topstitch the width of the sewing machine foot. Repeat for armholes. Press under the seam allowances on the long sides of the casing strips, then press under the short sides. With wrong sides together, stitch the top and bottom edges of the casing strips to the wrong sides of the apron front and back sections, at marked positions. (Each strip ends 1 cm [⅜ in] inside side seams.) With right sides together, fold each tie in half lengthwise; stitch together leaving an opening for turning. Turn tie right side out, sew opening shut and topstitch all round. Thread each tie through a casing using a safety pin.

## Long Apron

**Materials:** 3.3 m (3⅝ yd) of 90 cm (36 in)-wide cotton or cotton blend fabric. 0.2 m (¼ yd) of iron-on interfacing. Matching sewing thread.

**Cutting out:** Enlarge the pattern, making separate front and back pieces. Cut them out following the pattern layout, adding a 4 cm (1½ in) hem allowance, 2 cm (¾ in) to side seams and 1 cm (⅜ in) elsewhere. Following the pattern, draw separate pattern pieces 3 cm (1¼ in)-wide for the front and back neckline facings. Add a 1 cm (⅜ in) seam allowance to all edges and cut out front and back facings once each from fabric and interfacing (see cutting layout). Trim 5 mm (¼ in) from all edges of front and back interfacing, then iron each piece, centred, on to wrong side of the

corresponding facing piece. Cut out the patch pocket twice on the fold, with 1 cm (⅜ in) seam allowance all round. Cut out two 7 × 60 cm (2¾ × 23⅝ in) strips for the casing (finished width: 5 cm [2 in]). Cut out four strips for the ties, two strips 11 × 150 cm (4¼ × 59 in) and two strips 11 × 75 cm (4¼ × 29½ in). (Finished width of the ties: 4.5 cm [1¾ in].) Measurements for casings and ties include a 1 cm (⅜ in) seam allowance all round. See cutting layout for placement of casings and ties.

**Sewing:** Same as the instructions for the short apron, with the following exceptions:
*Self-lined patch pockets:* fold each pocket piece in half on the fold, with right sides together. Stitch round the raw edges, leaving an opening for turning. Turn to right side, sew opening

shut. Topstitch the pockets on to the apron front as shown, before stitching the side seams.
*Ties:* with right sides facing, seam the short ends of one long and one short tie strip together; press open. Repeat for the two remaining strips. Complete ties as for short apron.

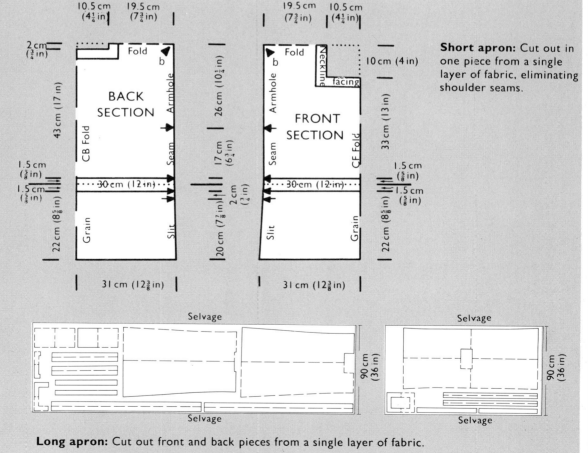

Patterns for the short and long aprons are shown in reduced size. Enlarge the measurements given (in centimetres or inches) to full size. The dotted lines are guidelines, notably the waistline. To draw pattern, measure out from the waistline. Measure half the casing width from waist upwards, then measure the same width downwards.

**Short apron:** Cut out in one piece from a single layer of fabric, eliminating shoulder seams.

BACK SECTION

FRONT SECTION

**Long apron:** Cut out front and back pieces from a single layer of fabric.

# 12

## Totally Tea-towel Kitchen

*Tips for sewing with tea-towels (dish towels):* purchase towels which are uniform in size and pattern. The edges should be as straight as possible and all sides should match in design. Wherever possible, make use of tea-towel hems on the outer edges of your project.

**Curtains:** Each side is made out of two linen tea-towels which have been seamed across their width. Use a seam ripper to unpick the seams where they are to be joined, then clean-finish the raw edges and stitch the towels together, with right sides facing and patterns (if any) matching. Press seams open. (Re-stitching in this way reduces bulk and makes the curtains hang better.) To finish, either stitch on a curtain tape (for use with hooks or rings) or simply make a casing for use with a curtain wire or rail (rod). (NOTE: these curtains can be made to fit any size window. To determine how many tea-towels you need, follow these rules of thumb: fabric width must be at least 1½ times the width of the curtain rail and curtain length should fall either just above or below the windowsill. Remember to add on for the heading or casing at the top. No side or bottom hems are necessary if towels are used whole.)

**Cushion cover:** (To fit a 40 × 40 cm [16 × 16 in] unboxed [knife-edged] cushion pad [pillow form]): This is a pillowcase-style cushion cover. To make it, cut out the back cover 40 cm (16 in) square and the front according to pattern diagram (see top right), adding 1 cm (⅜ in) seam allowance to each. Cut both pieces so that the lower edge of each is a finished tea-towel hem. Match fabric plaids or patterns, if necessary. Place front and back together, matching top edges and with right sides together. Now fold the 20 cm (8 in)-wide flap portion of the cushion front over on to the back cover, matching

points **b** and **c**. (Finished edge of cushion front is now sandwiched between front and front flap.) Stitch the pieces together round the three raw edges. Finish the raw edges and turn the cushion right side out. Press. Slip in the cushion pad. (NOTE: this pattern can easily be adapted to fit square unboxed [knife-edged] cushions of all sizes. Simply cut a square of the appropriate size for the back piece and enlarge the cushion front pattern proportionately, adding 1 cm (⅜ in) seam allowance to each.)

**Tablecloth:** Ours is made from four tea-towels, each measuring 58 × 58 cm (22¾ × 22¾ in). To determine the size of your tablecloth, measure the tabletop, then add 50 cm (20 in) to both the length and the width. (This results in a 25 cm [10 in] overhang on all sides.) Now, measure your chosen tea-towel and calculate how many are required to make up the tablecloth dimensions. It may be necessary to use partial tea-towels. Wherever possible, use tea-towel hems along outer edges of cloth.
*Sewing:* to reduce bulk, open all the interior seams which are to be sewn together, clean-finish the edges and stitch them together (as for curtains). If four tea-towels are to be joined, stitch two pairs of two towels together, then stitch the centre seam. If more towels are to be joined, stitch them together row by row.

**Serviette** (napkin): (Size: approx. 30 × 30 cm [12 × 12 in], depending on size of towel). Try to cut four serviettes out of one towel (reduce size, if necessary). Fold edges under twice and stitch a narrow hem.

**Tea-Cosy:** Cut out the enlarged tea-cosy pattern (see top right) twice, adding 1 cm (⅜ in) seam allowance all round. (It will be necessary to join small towels together. Seam them along the pattern fold line.) Using the top portion of the cosy pattern (above the fold), cut out two pieces of synthetic wadding (batting)

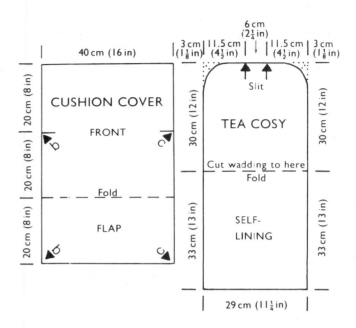

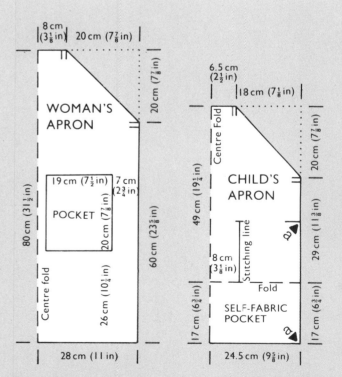

Patterns for the cushion cover front, tea-cosy and aprons are shown in reduced size. Enlarge the measurements given (in centimetres or inches) to full size. The dotted lines are guidelines.

without seam allowance. With right sides facing, stitch the tea-cosy pieces together, leaving top slit and bottom edges open. Topstitch all round top slit opening and clean-finish seam allowances, including bottom edges, with machine zigzag. Press seams. Turn cosy right side out. Oversew (overcast) the edges of the two wadding pieces together by hand, leaving top slit and bottom edges open. Slip the wadding into the top portion of the cosy, then turn the self-lining under along the fold and draw the edges through the slit. Fan out the edges.

**Butcher-Style Aprons** (To fit woman's sizes 10–18 [8–16 U.S.] and a child of about six): Enlarge pattern pieces to full size and join tea-towels as necessary to make up fabric pieces of the required sizes. Cut out the woman's and the child's apron on the fold, adding 1 cm (⅜ in) seam allowance to all edges. (IMPORTANT: make child's apron from fully reversible towels.) For patch pocket on woman's apron, use a remnant from the tablecloth or one of the other tea-towel projects.

*Ties:* for woman's apron, cut four pieces of white 12 mm (½ in)-wide twill tape, each 65 cm (26½ in) long. For child's apron, cut four pieces of twill tape, each 50 cm (20 in) long. You will also need 1.3 m (1½ yd) of 12 mm (½ in)-wide bias binding (enough for both aprons).
*Sewing:* stitch binding along the diagonal apron edges. Turn full width of binding on to the wrong side, press. Turn binding ends under and stitch the free edge down.
*Woman's apron:* stitch patch pocket on to apron at marked position. Narrow-hem seam allowances (turn under twice and stitch). Sew on the ties at the neck and waist corners, knotting the ends to prevent fraying.
*Child's apron:* Fold hem allowance twice on to *right* side of fabric and stitch. Clean-finish side edges. Turn up the self-fabric pocket along fold line, matching point **a**. Stitch along pocket stitching lines, to form pocket. Narrow-hem apron sides, catching in the side edges of pocket. Narrow-hem the top edge of apron. Sew on ties and knot ends, as for woman's apron.

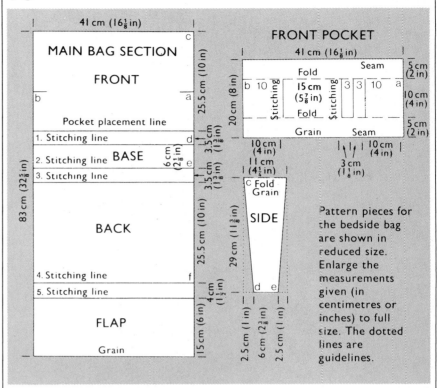

## Bedside Bag

**Size:** approx.
41 × 25.5 × 11 cm
(16 × 10 × 4 in)

**Materials:** 1.4 m (1⅝ yd) of 90 cm (36 in)-wide cotton fabric. Four pieces of card (cardboard): for the front section 40.5 × 24.5 cm (16 × 9⅝ in), for the base 40.5 × 5.5 cm (16 × 2⅛ in), for the back section 40.5 × 25 cm (16 × 9¾ in), for the flap 40.5 × 15 cm (16 × 5½ in). Matching sewing thread.

**Cutting out:** Cut out the bag main section twice and the front pocket once. Cut out the side section twice on the fold. Add a 1 cm (⅜ in) seam allowance to all seams.

**Sewing:** The bag is sewn in a double layer of fabric. Place the two main sections of the bag together with right sides facing and stitch only the two sides of the flap as far as the fourth

marked stitching line (point **f**). Cut into the seam allowance at point **f**. Turn bag right side out; press flap seams.
*Front pocket:* stitch the lengthwise seam and press open. A tube is formed. Turn right side out, centring the seam on pocket back; press. Stitch along the upper pocket edge, making a narrow seam. Baste the pocket on to one bag section, positioning it as shown. Stitch pocket along vertical stitching lines, forming pocket divisions.
*Finishing:* with wrong sides facing and raw edges matching, baste the main sections of the bag together. Now stitch the front pocket along the placement line, through all thicknesses. Stitch both bag sections together along the first, second and third stitching lines, leaving the sides open. Insert the card for the base. Fold the side section in half as shown, with wrong sides together. Baste the side section

together and treat it as a single layer of fabric. With right sides together, stitch side section to bag front, matching side **c-d**. Cut into the corner of the front section seam allowance at point **d**. Stitch the base seam from **d** to **e**, cutting into bag seam allowance at point **e**. Then stitch side section on to back section along side **e-f**. Stitch on other side section in same way. Turn bag right side out. Insert the card for the front section into the top opening. Insert the card for the back opening into the open edge of the flap, then slide it into its proper position. Stitch the bag back section along the fourth and fifth stitching lines, through both fabric layers. Fold under the seam allowances along the upper edge of the front section and stitch them together close to the folded edges. Finally, insert the card for the flap. Tuck under the seam allowances along the opening and stitch them together close to the edges.

# 14

## Patchwork Quilt in Mixed Plaids and Checks

**Size:** approx. 0.9 m (35½ in) wide × 1.8 m (71 in) long, including frill (ruffle)

**Materials:** *Quilt top:* assorted plaid and checked cotton fabrics, enough for thirty-six 20 cm (8 in) squares.
*Backing:* 1.9 m (2⅛ yd) of 90 cm (36 in)-wide plaid cotton fabric.
*Frill:* 1.6 m (1¾ yd) of 90 cm (36 in)-wide plaid cotton fabric.
*Filling:* 3.3 m (3⅝ yd) of 150 cm (58–60 in)-wide synthetic wadding (batting). Matching sewing thread.

**Cutting out:** For quilt underside cut out a 180 × 80 cm (72 × 32 in) piece of plaid backing fabric, adding a 1 cm (⅜ in) seam allowance all round. For the frill, cut out 10 cm (4 in)-wide strips of fabric, measuring a total length of 11 m (12 yd), plus 1 cm (⅜ in) seam allowance all round. Make a 20 cm (8 in) square cardboard template. Using the template as a guide cut out 36 squares from the assorted plaid fabrics, adding a 1 cm (⅜ in) seam allowance all round each. Again using the template, cut out 108

squares of wadding without seam allowance (each square has three layers of wadding). (NOTE: the quilt can be made in any size by varying the number of squares. When planning quilt and calculating fabric requirements, remember that each square loses approximately 2 cm [¾ in] in length and width due to the bulk of the filling. Frill length = 2½–3 times the quilt circumference. Also remember that each square contains three layers of wadding. For large quilts, it will be necessary to seam the backing fabric.)

**Sewing:** Sort the fabric squares according to pattern and colour, then place them in a pleasing arrangement. Stitch the squares together in rows of four, with right sides together. Press seams open. Next, stitch the rows together lengthwise, matching seams carefully and with right sides together. Press seams open. Sandwich the quilt top and backing together, with wrong sides facing. Baste the two fabric layers together using large diagonal stitches moving across row 1 of the squares. Stitch the top width of the quilt together, seaming close to raw edges. Stitch all vertical lines (marked red on diagram) to the bottom of row 1 of

squares. Remove basting. Fill each pocket in row 1 with three layers of wadding. To seal in the wadding, stitch the quilt horizontally (green on diagram) above row 2 of the squares. Baste, stitch and fill each successive row of squares in the same way. (NOTE: a quilter guide-bar sewing machine attachment is helpful for stitching regularly spaced lines, such as these.)
*Frill:* with right sides facing, stitch the short ends of the strips together and join them to form a ring. Press seams open. Press under the seam allowance 5 mm (¼ in) twice on one long edge and stitch to form a narrow hem. Gather the other side to fit the quilt circumference. (To gather: run two parallel rows of machine basting 6 and 12 mm [¼ and ½ in] from edge. Carefully draw up the threads.) Pin the frill to the quilt top, distributing gathers evenly and with raw edges even and right sides together. Stitch the frill to quilt top, then clean-finish the seam allowances together. Turn the frill to the right side. On wrong side of quilt, lightly press seam allowance towards the frill. Edgestitch through frill and seam allowance, just inside frill seamline.

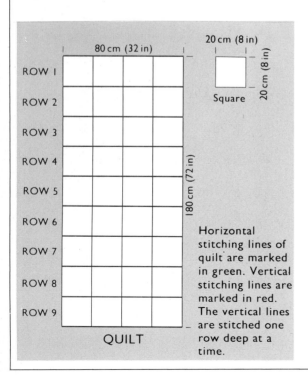

ROW 1
ROW 2
ROW 3
ROW 4
ROW 5
ROW 6
ROW 7
ROW 8
ROW 9

80 cm (32 in)

20 cm (8 in)

20 cm (8 in)

Square

180 cm (72 in)

QUILT

Horizontal stitching lines of quilt are marked in green. Vertical stitching lines are marked in red. The vertical lines are stitched one row deep at a time.

# 15

## Soft Toys with a Jungle Theme

### Giraffe

**Size:** approx. 60 cm (24 in) high × 22.5 cm (9 in) long

**Materials:** 0.6 m (¾ yd) of 150 cm (58–60 in)-wide synthetic fur. Synthetic filling (stuffing), as needed. Colourful scraps of printed fabric (for ears and soles of feet). Small amount of black and white felt (for eyes). Brown embroidery thread (for mouth). Matching sewing thread.

**Cutting out:** Enlarge pattern pieces to full size, adding 1 cm (⅜ in) seam allowance to all pieces. Lay out the pattern pieces with pile running downwards. Cut out the body and inside leg piece twice each, the head inset once and each ear twice from both fur and printed fabric. For soles of feet, cut out four 3 cm (1⅛ in)-diameter circles from printed fabric. From fur, cut out two 3 × 4 cm (1⅛ × 1½ in) strips for the horns and one 4 × 16 cm (1½ × 6¼ in) strip for the tail. For each eye, cut out one circle of felt in white (2 cm [¾ in]-diameter) and one in black (15 mm [⅝ in]-diameter).

**Sewing:** Stitch seams in the direction of the pile. Baste seams before stitching. With right sides together, stitch the top edge of the two inside leg pieces together, leaving a slit approx. 12 cm (5 in) long for turning and filling. With right sides together, stitch the inside leg pieces between the leg section of the body pieces, matching points C and D. With right sides together, stitch the head inset in between the body pieces, matching points A and B. Stitch the back seam, then the neck seam. Trim fur from seam allowance to reduce bulk, if necessary. Turn giraffe right side out. Fill the toy firmly and sew up the slit. Pick out any hairs caught in the seams with a needle. Ears: with right sides facing, stitch each ear together, backing fur with printed fabric and leaving an opening for turning.

Turn to right side, sew opening shut. With fur side outwards, fold the bottom edge of each ear to meet in the centre of the bottom edge on the printed side. Baste in place. Sew each ear to head at the position marked on diagram and facing as shown in photo. Tightly roll up the strips for horns and tail, with fur to inside. Sew each roll together along its length, fluffing out the ends of the horns and turning the last 3 cm (1⅛ in) of the tail to the right side. Sew them to the body, as shown. Sew on the eyes and embroider mouth.

### Elephant

**Size:** approx 30 cm (12 in) high × 47.5 cm (19 in) long

**Materials:** 0.8 m (⅞ yd of 150 cm (58–60 in)-wide synthetic fur. Synthetic filling, as needed. Colourful scraps of printed fabric (for ears and soles of feet). Small amount of black and white felt (for eyes). Matching sewing thread.

**Cutting Out:** Enlarge pattern pieces to full size, adding 1 cm (⅜ in) seam allowance to all pieces. Lay out the pattern pieces with the pile running downwards. Cut out the body and inside leg piece twice each, the back panel and the trunk once each and each ear twice from both fur and printed fabric. For soles of feet, cut out four 6 cm (2¼ in)-diameter circles from printed fabric. From fur, cut a 5 × 18 cm (2 × 7 in) strip for the tail. For each eye, cut out one circle of felt in white (3 cm [1⅛ in] diameter) and one in black (2 cm [¾ in] diameter).

**Sewing:** Stitch seams in the direction of the pile. Baste seams before stitching. With right sides together, stitch the back panel between the body pieces, matching points A and B. Then stitch the top edge of the two inside leg pieces facing, with right sides together and leaving a slit approx. 12 cm (5 in) long for turning and filling. With right sides together, stitch this piece between the leg section of the body pieces, matching points **B** and **C** and leaving soles open. With right sides together, stitch the trunk on to the underside of the body pieces, matching points **C** and **D**. Next, stitch the trunk top seam to point **A**. With right sides together, sew on soles of feet. Trim fur from seam allowance to reduce bulk, if

necessary. Turn elephant right side out. Fill it firmly and sew up the slit. Pick out any hairs caught in the seams with a needle. With fur to inside, tightly roll up the tail strip and sew it together. Sew the tail on to elephant as shown, turning the last 3 cm (1⅛ in) to right side. With right sides facing, stitch each ear

together, backing fur with printed fabric and leaving an opening for turning. Turn to right side, sew opening shut. Baste the ear pleats in place, matching **X** to **O**. Sew ears on to head at position marked on diagram and facing as in photo. Sew on eyes.

## Crocodile

**Size:** approx. 12.5 cm (5 in) high × 85 cm (35 in) long

**Materials:** 0.7 m (⅞ yd) of 150 cm (58–60 in)-wide synthetic fur. Synthetic filling, as needed. Scrap of plain red fabric (for jaws). White and black felt (for teeth and eyes). Matching sewing thread.

**Cutting out:** Enlarge pattern pieces to full size, adding 1 cm (⅜ in) seam allowance to all pieces. Lay out pattern pieces with the pile running downwards. Cut out the tummy panel once, the top/side panel twice and the foot eight times. Cut out the jaws once on the fold, from red fabric. For each eye, cut out one circle of felt in white (2.5 cm [1 in]-diameter) and one in black (2 cm[¾ in]-diameter). Cut out eight white felt triangles for the teeth.

**Sewing:** Stitch seams in the direction of pile. Baste seams before stitching.

With right sides together, stitch the two top/side panels together along the top seam. Stitch four pairs of feet together, with right sides facing. Turn each foot right side out, trim fur from seams and fill firmly. Baste across the top edge of each foot. With right sides together, stitch the tummy panel to the bottom edges of the top/side panel, beginning at point **A** and catching feet in the seams as shown on diagram. (Insert feet so that they protrude inside the body section, matching raw edges and points **C**.) Leave a slit approx. 12 cm (5 in) long in one side for turning and filling. With right sides together, stitch on the jaws as shown, matching points **A** and catching teeth in the seam. (Point teeth inside body and space them as shown in photo.) Trim fur from seam allowance to reduce bulk. Turn crocodile right side out. Fill firmly and sew up the slit. Pick out any hairs caught in the seams with a needle. Sew on the eyes.

Each box of the grid measures 5 cm (2 in) square. To enlarge patterns, draw grid to scale on paper. Copy each design line into exactly the same position in the corresponding box of the full-size grid.

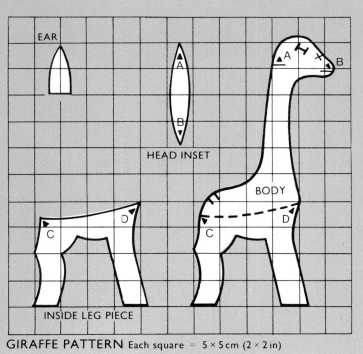

**ELEPHANT PATTERN** Each square = 5 × 5 cm (2 × 2 in)

**GIRAFFE PATTERN** Each square = 5 × 5 cm (2 × 2 in)

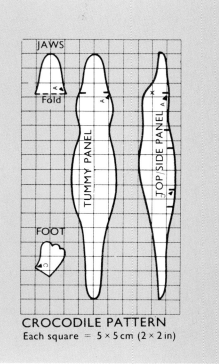

**CROCODILE PATTERN** Each square = 5 × 5 cm (2 × 2 in)

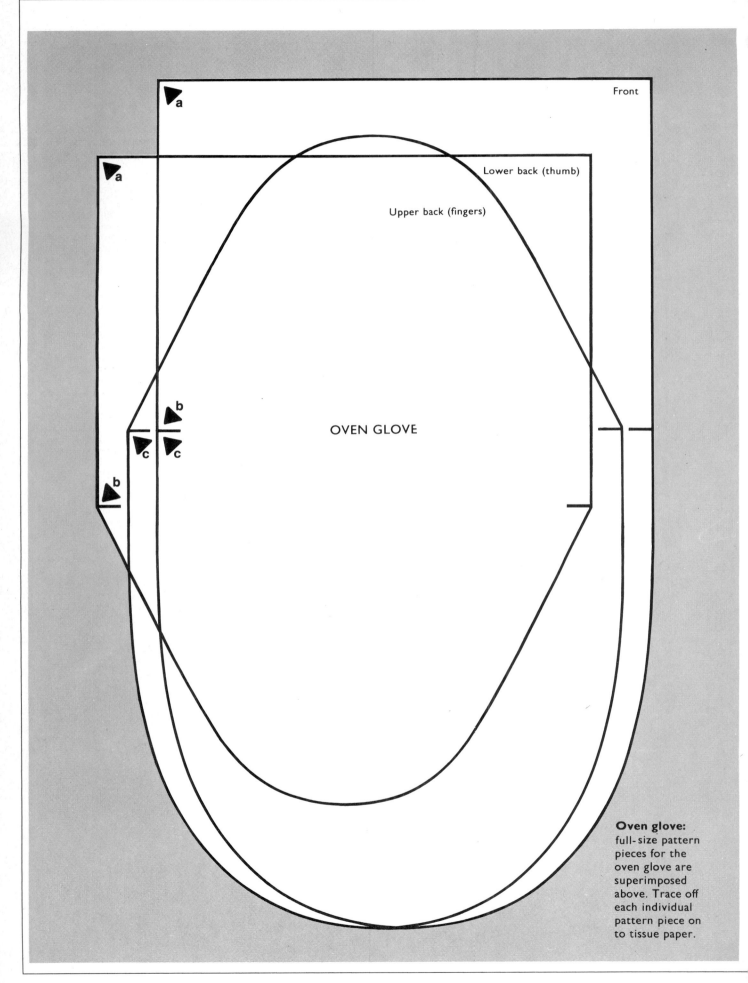

Front

a

a

Lower back (thumb)

Upper back (fingers)

b

c c

OVEN GLOVE

b

**Oven glove:** full-size pattern pieces for the oven glove are superimposed above. Trace off each individual pattern piece on to tissue paper.

# 16
## Oven Gloves

**Size:** approx. 13 × 22.5 cm (5 × 9 in)

**Materials:** *For one glove, you need:* remnant of colourful fabric and a thick piece of cotton or synthetic wadding (batting), each measuring 15 × 80 cm (6 × 31½ in).
*For binding:* 3 × 45 cm (1¼ × 18 in) strip of contrasting fabric or 45 cm (18 in) of 12 mm (½ in)-wide bias binding. Matching sewing thread.

**Cutting out:** Trace off each of the three pattern pieces on to tissue paper, adding 5 mm (¼ in) seam allowance all round each. Lay pattern pieces vertically on wadding; cut out one of each. Cut the pattern pieces out again in fabric. *Binding:* if a wide binding is preferred (finished width 15 mm [⅝ in]), use a strip of contrasting fabric (dimensions above). For a narrower finish, use purchased 12 mm (½ in) bias binding (finished width 5 mm [¼ in]). Cut the binding strip into a 28 cm (11 in)-long piece and a 14 cm (5½ in)-long piece (for hanging loop).

**Sewing:** Place each piece of fabric face up on its corresponding piece of wadding. Stitch the layers together along the seam allowance, using large stitches. With right sides facing, stitch the side seams of the front and lower back pieces together, from point a to point b. Fasten off the thread ends securely. With right sides together, place upper back piece on top of the front piece and stitch them together round the curved finger section, from point c to point c, taking care not to catch in the lower back piece. Now stitch the thumb seam together, joining the upper back piece to the lower back piece. Clean-finish the raw edges together.
*Apply binding to glove opening:* with wrong sides together, press under one long edge of binding strip 15 mm (⅝ in), then turn back short ends of binding 1 cm (⅜ in). Pin binding to glove opening, with right side of binding to wadding, with long edges of binding even with glove edges and with folded binding ends at a side seam. Stitch binding to glove 15 mm (⅝ in) from glove edge. (If using bias binding, apply in a similar manner. The lengthwise seam will be narrower.) Turn the glove right side out. Fold binding up and over the raw edge of glove, so that the folded edge slightly overlaps stitching line on the right side of the fabric. Baste binding in place, then carefully edge-stitch it. The short ends of the binding remain open at the side seam.
*Hanging loop:* fold long edges of the strip to meet in centre, fold in half lengthwise, then stitch together close to edge. Insert loop into the open side seam of the binding. Sew the opening shut by hand, catching in the loop.

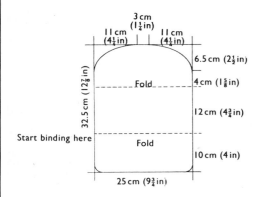

**SERVIETTE POUCH**

Reduced size pattern for serviette pouch. Enlarge the measurements given (in centimetres or inches) to full size.

# 17
## Serviette (Napkin) Pouch with Matching Serviette

**Size:** *Pouch:* approx. 25 × 12 cm (9¾ × 5 in), folded
*Serviette:* 40 × 40 cm (16 × 16 in), unfolded

**Materials:** 0.7 m (⅞ yd) each of 90 cm (36 in)-wide plain and printed cotton fabrics. 0.3 m (⅜ yd) of iron-on interfacing (necessary for lightweight fabrics only). Matching sewing thread.

**Cutting out:** *Pouch:* enlarge pouch pattern as directed. Cut pouch out twice from printed fabric and once from iron-on interfacing (if necessary), without seam allowance. For pouch binding, cut a 5 × 110 cm (2 × 43½ in) bias strip from plain fabric.
*Serviette:* cut out a 40 cm (16 in) square from plain fabric. Round off the corners. For serviette binding, cut a 5 × 160 cm (2 × 64½ in) bias strip from printed fabric.

**Sewing:** *Pouch:* iron interfacing on to the wrong side of the outside piece, if necessary. Baste both pouch pieces together round edges, with the wrong sides together. Bind the pouch edges to a width of 12 mm (½ in)
*To apply binding:* press under long edges of binding 12 mm (½ in), wrong sides together. Turn back one short end, wrong sides together. With right sides together, pin binding all round the pouch piece, with raw edges even. For an inconspicuous join, start with the folded end of the binding at the lower pouch fold (arrow on diagram). Work binding round, then lap the remaining short end of binding over this. Stitch all round binding, 12 mm (½ in) from pouch edges. Fold binding up and over pouch edges, so that it meets the stitching line on the other side. Slipstitch the binding to the stitching line. To finish: fold pouch up along the lower fold line; slipstitch the sides together.
*Serviette:* bind edges as for pouch. Fold into quarters and insert into pouch.

# 18
## Raggedy Laundry Bags

**Size:** approx. 97 cm (38 in) high × 60 cm (24 in) wide

**Materials:** To make each bag, you need: 0.9 m (1 yd) of 90 cm (36 in)-wide linen (used, if possible). Remnants of printed cotton fabric. Embroidery thread (for features). Matching sewing thread.

**Cutting out** (for each bag): Referring to the photo, cut out all pattern pieces twice from the appropriate fabrics, adding 1 cm (⅜ in) seam allowance all round.
*Hanging loop:* cut a 10 cm × 12 cm (4 × ½ in) strip from printed fabric.
*Neckband:* cut a 50 × 6 cm (20 × 2¼ in) strip from printed fabric.

**Sewing:** Turn under and stitch a narrow hem along pocket tops. Turn under and press seam allowances on the remaining pocket sides. Edge-stitch the pockets on to the bag front, as shown. Stitch shoe-leg seam, if applicable. Stitch each pair of leg pieces together with right sides together, leaving tops open. Turn right side out. With right sides together, stitch the front and back laundry bag together, leaving the top open and catching the legs in the seam. (Pin legs at bottom markings with raw edges even, toes pointing outwards and legs protruding inside the bag.) Turn bag right side out. Cut a 30 cm (12 in) slit in the centre back and clean-finish the edges.
*Head:* with right sides together, stitch the interior seams of the head (stitch on hair or cap, as applicable). Embroider the facial features, as shown. Use satin stitch for the eyes and chain stitch elsewhere. Fold under the long edges of the hanging loop strip; then stitch them together close to the edge. Fold the strip into a loop, then pin it, loop downwards, to centre top of head (see arrow on diagram). With right sides facing, stitch head pieces together, catching loop in the seam and leaving neck open. Pleat the neck edge of the bag, adjusting fullness to fit the neck opening of the head. Baste the pleats in place. Turn under seam allowance at the neck opening of head. Slip the neck opening over the pleated seam allowance of the bag; baste all layers together. Stitch neck seam close to edge, through all layers. With wrong sides together, fold neckband in half lengthwise and stitch 5 mm (¼ in) from raw edges, leaving an opening for turning. Turn to right side, sew up the opening. Fasten neckband as shown, concealing the neck seam. Sew the neckband in place.

Laundry bag pattern(s) are shown in reduced size. Enlarge the measurements given (in centimetres or inches) to full size. The broken lines are guidelines.

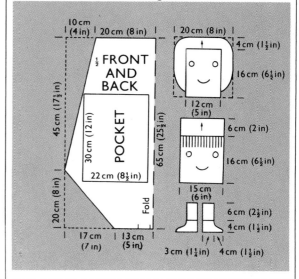

19

## A Double Life: Reversible Quilted Jacket

This quilted jacket is lightweight, yet warm. It makes a suitable outer layer on a grey and chilly autumn day. Its squarish cut leaves plenty of room for chunky sweaters underneath. We have selected seasonal colours that are muted but not dreary. The jacket's Mandarin collar, tie closures and basic styling give it an Oriental ambience.

The noteworthy feature of this quilted jacket is that it is fully reversible. Its chameleon-like nature is a great advantage, from a fashion standpoint. Turn it inside out to suit your mood or match your outfit.

We have backed plain fabric with plaid, for two very different effects. A plaid or striped fabric is a particularly good choice, because it provides natural guidelines for quilting. For a dramatic contrast, back a plain fabric with a patterned one. Remember, though, to select colours that complement each other, so that the turn-back cuffs provide a pleasing accent.

You can quilt the jacket from scratch, or make it up in reversible quilted fabric to save time. We give instructions for both methods. The jacket's special construction utilizes bound edges and flat-fell seams for a double-sided finish.

Instructions for the quilted jacket are on pages 60 and 61

# 20

## Spacious Sailor Bag

Often when you go away for a short break, a weekend trip or even on a journey to a far-off country, you don't have the right kind of bag – one that is spacious and comfortable to carry. The versatile duffel shown is lightweight and is made from sturdy striped canvas. It's an ideal choice.

Our duffel is so handy, you won't want to limit its use to travel. It is roomy and attractive enough for daily use.

You can fit an incredible amount of things inside our bag. Take it on shopping expeditions, to keep-fit classes or to the swimming pool. Make it up in differerent colour combinations to match your wardrobe. Pretty soon, your family and friends will all be clamouring for one of their own.

Our bag has matching webbing straps with easy-grip cushioned handles. An additional strap is sewn on to one round end of the bag to enable you to carry it over the shoulder, as a sailor does. It has a convenient outer pocket for holding maps, magazines or odds and ends. The edges of the zip opening are bound for extra durability. Wise choice of fabric teamed with functional design make this roomy

bag virtually indestructible. To keep it fresh-looking, spray the bag with a protective fabric finish to retard soiling and make it moisture-resistant.

Instructions for the duffel bag are on page 61.

## Smocks: Casual Yet Chic

Our smocks with their wide cut and casual appearance are an attractive, comfortable creation. Pop them on over a blouse or pullover and trousers and you will look elegant and well-dressed, effortlessly.

The festive folkloristic smocks on this page are made from jeans fabric. They have no fastenings and the arms are cut in one with the body. The bouncy little pleats and the side slits provide width and an easy-going air. The boldly coloured rickrack gives these garments their youthful character.

The overjacket in brightly striped woollen blanketing is a classically simple design. The style has no fastenings, so its wide cut skims the body. A boat neck, dropped shoulders and high side slits are additional sophisticated touches. The large muff-type patch pocket emphasizes the sportiness of the garment. It's just the thing for a country weekend or a stroll on a crisp autumnal day.

Instructions for these smocks are on pages 62 and 63.

23

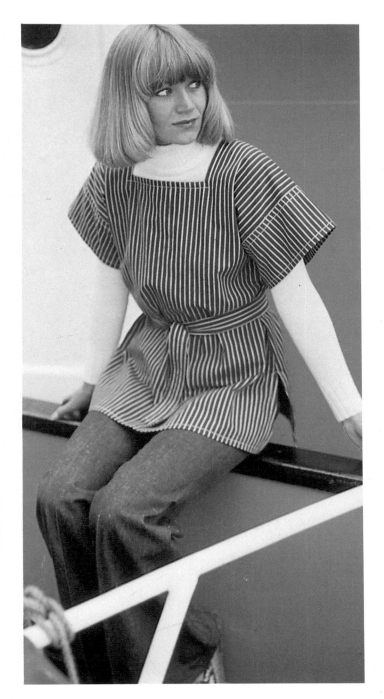

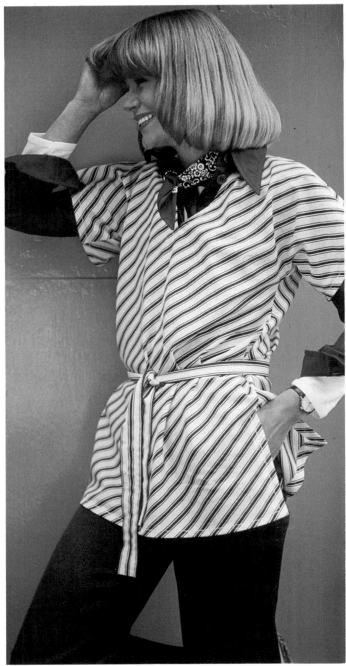

## Wide-cut Tops in Sporty Stripes

These tops are a practical and comfortable creation from the world of fashion. You'll find them over and over again in many different designs in fashion magazines and in the shops. This comes as no surprise because they always look smart. On cooler days you can wear a blouse or pullover underneath. When it's hot, you just wear the top on its own.

These kimono-sleeved tops are best worn with trousers. On these pages, we show you three different styles in casual-looking striped fabrics. Vertical stripes are a fashion favourite because they are striking and slimming. For a professional finish, take care to match the stripes perfectly when you are cutting the pattern pieces out.

These tops can also be made up as 'special occasion' overblouses. Select a lustrous material which drapes in soft folds, for example, silk or jersey. The bias-cut top on the right looks particularly flattering this way. Worn over a plain long-sleeved T-shirt with elegant trousers, the evening versions of our tops are quite chic. Sew sequins or small pearls around the neckline to add a stunning accent.

Instructions for these tops are on pages 64 and 65.

# 24

## Attractive Curtains for a Fine Outlook

Pretty curtains give a room warmth and cosiness. A window without curtains looks bare and uninviting. You can create an intimate atmosphere by using unlined, decorative fabric which hangs well and matches the colours of your wallpaper or furnishings.

When choosing your material,

remember that, if it is for the kitchen or bathroom, you don't want to shut out the daylight. Choose sheer fabric that lets through plenty of light or thin, lightweight fabric which can be drawn back without bulk. You can see both options in our photos.

On these pages, we've cleverly brightened up plain fabrics which sometimes tend to be a little bit dull.

The red and white cotton curtains are hanging in the kitchen but they can be used elsewhere. The bold diagonal stripes are joined together from pieces of plain fabric. The wooden curtain rail (rod) and the large curtain rings go very well with this design.

The delicate floor-to-ceiling net (sheer) curtains are decorated with velvet ribbons. This element is picked up again in the same colour sequence on the valance. The combination of light and dark green ribbons is, of course, only a suggestion which you can adapt to suit your own colour scheme.

Instructions for these curtains are on pages 65 and 66.

# 25

## A Medley of Cuddly Cushions . . . In All Shapes, Sizes and Colours

A sofa or armchair can often look very stark on its own, even if it is clad in attractive loose covers (slipcovers). Empty spaces like these cry out for cheerful cushions in an array of shapes, sizes and colours. On lawn furniture, such as a chaise longue or a bench like ours, a cluster of cushions is a delightful, unexpected luxury.

It's easy to learn the knack of mixing patterns and colours. To create a harmonious total effect, choose colours that are similar in weight and value and patterns of a like character and scale. As you can see from our photos, we have combined lots of different patterns and colours, but they all work together to create a unified composition.

The summery cushions on this page are made from flowered cotton prints in sweetshop colours. Narrow pastel ribbons applied in delicate lattice-like designs complete the romantic mood. Our cushions contain machine-washable synthetic filling, to make them practically carefree.

What gives the cushions on the right-hand page their lively appeal? It comes from the extravagant mixture of floral and geometric patterns in vibrant primary colours. An abundance of frills and gathers contributes to their festive appearance. The cushions contain fibrefill. The firmer you pad them, the more the ruffles stand out.

Instructions for the ribbon-trimmed cushions are on pages 66 and 67; those for the frilly cushions are on pages 68 and 69.

## 27 A Cavalcade of Mixed-fabric Cushions

Cushions made from odd scraps of fabric can be planned to blend in with any decor and to suit any taste. Furthermore, they are economical to make, which is a blessing when you have mischievous children about.

Kids love playing with cushions. They often borrow the living room cushions for use in a cushion fight or to build a cushion fortress. Why not provide your children with cushions of their own, made from materials selected for durability and washability? They will stimulate your children's imagination and creativity. Let your children participate in making up the cushions. They'll eagerly select the patterns and assist.

All the remnants we used had a green and white colour scheme, which created a refreshing garden-like effect. We have designed our cushions with a variety of attractive design features, which makes them fascinating to sew. Two of them have stylish flanged borders, one of which is scalloped. Two others are button-tufted, to emphasize their plump fillings (don't make these for very young children). All are created from fashionable mixed prints and have inner fabric shells enclosing the filling.

Instructions for these mixed-fabric cushions are on pages 68 and 69.

# 19

## Reversible Quilted Jacket

**Size:** 12–14 (10–12 u.s.)

**Materials:** *Machine-quilted jacket:* 2.5 m (2¾ yd) each of 115 cm (44–45 in)-wide plain (solid-coloured) and plaid cotton fabrics. 1.5 m (1¾ yd) of 150 cm (58–60 in)-wide synthetic wadding (batting).
*Pre-quilted jacket:* 2.5 m (2¾ yd) of 115 cm (44–45 in)-wide reversible quilted fabric.
*For both:* 5.4 m (6 yd) of 24 mm (1 in)-wide matching bias binding (6.8 m [7½ yd] for pre-quilted jacket). Matching sewing thread.

**Cutting out:** Enlarge the pattern pieces. If you are quilting the jacket yourself, cut out the following pieces from plain fabric, plaid fabric and wadding, leaving about 5 cm (2 in) of extra fabric around each piece: cut out two jacket fronts (reverse the pattern piece before the second cutting), one jacket back and two sleeves. Match plaid as best you can. If you are using pre-quilted fabric, cut out the same pieces adding the following seam allowances: 2 cm (¾ in) seam allowance on front shoulder and side seams, on the sleeve head (sleeve cap) placement line (round sleeve head, from **c** to **c**) and to one under-sleeve seam (below point **c**) on each sleeve. Add a 1 cm (⅜ in) seam allowance to back shoulder and side seams, to jacket armhole edges and underarm seams (line **b-c**), to front and back neck and to the remaining under-sleeve seam on each sleeve. Remaining edges are without seam allowance. Cut out the collar once in a triple layer of fabric (or one layer of pre-quilted fabric), adding 1 cm (⅜ in) seam allowance to neck edge.

*Patch pockets:* if you are quilting, cut out four plain fabric pockets, adding 1 cm (⅜ in) seam allowance all round. If using pre-quilted fabric, cut out two pockets without seam allowance.
Cut bias binding as follows:
*Sleeve hems:* one 50 cm (20 in) strip for each.
*Jacket fronts (from end of collar to side seam):* one 90 cm (36 in) strip for each.
Back hem: one 55 cm (22 in) strip.
*Collar:* one 45 cm (18 in) strip.
*Tie fastenings:* eight 20 cm (8 in) strips.
*Patch pockets (for pre-quilted jacket, only):* one 70 cm (27½ in) strip for each.

**Machine quilting:** Place the three layers of each jacket piece together with the wrong sides of fabric facing and the wadding sandwiched in between. Baste the layers together using long hand stitches.

Baste in a starburst pattern, starting at the centre of each piece with stitching lines radiating out to the edges. To quilt, machine stitch through all fabric layers, following the vertical stripes of the plaid as your stitching lines (select lines at regularly spaced intervals). To reduce bulk as you sew, roll up the quilted portion of each piece under the sewing machine arm. When quilting is completed, lay each pattern piece on top of the corresponding piece of fabric. Trim each piece to the correct size, adding the necessary seam allowances.

**Sewing:** To make the jacket fully reversible, it is constructed using flat-fell seams. The interior jacket seam allowances have been pre-trimmed for felling. To make a flat-fell seam: with wrong sides together, place the narrow seam allowance 1 cm (⅜ in) below the edge

of the wider one. Stitch the seam on the right side of the garment, taking a 2 cm (¾ in) seam allowance. Remove wadding from both seam allowances, then press seam with the wider allowance on top (usually towards garment back). Fold under the edge of the top allowance and stitch it down along the folded edge. Seam the jacket on the plain side of the fabric, always remembering to match plaids on the reverse.

*Jacket assembly:* join front to back at shoulders with a flat-fell seam. Stitch sleeve head into armhole along line **b-b**, leaving sleeve head seam allowances free. Do not complete the flat-fell seam. Join the side seams using a flat-fell seam.
*Underarm seams:* stitch each line **b-c**, from corner to jacket side seam at centre. Do not complete the flat-fell seam. Clip jacket seam

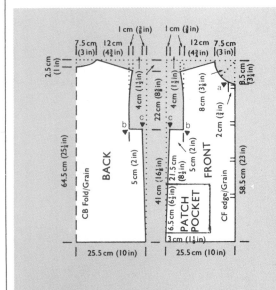

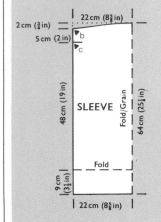

The jacket pattern is shown in reduced size, at left. Enlarge the measurements given (in centimetres or inches) to full size. The dotted lines are guidelines. Make a separate pattern piece for the patch pocket.

**Cutting layouts (right):**
Above is the jacket in plain fabric. Cut out four pocket pieces in plain fabric, only. Below is the layout for plaid fabric. Pay attention to the direction of the plaid. If using a pre-quilted fabric, follow the plain fabric layout, but cut the pocket piece out twice only.

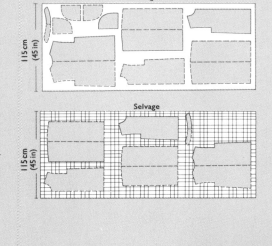

The jacket collar is shown in slightly reduced size, below. Very precise measurements (in millimetres or inches) are given to enable you to copy the shape accurately. Enlarge it to full size in the usual way.

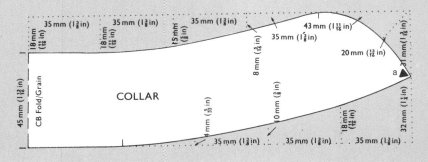

allowances at underarm corners diagonally to the last stitch. Next, join each under-sleeve seam with a flat-fell seam, slipstitching each seam down by hand. Now make a continuous flat-fell seam all round each sleeve head placement line, completing the seams started previously. Cut off the triangular flaps of jacket seam allowance at each underarm corner. Trim the 2 cm ($\frac{3}{4}$ in) sleeve head seam allowances diagonally across the corners, to a width of 1 cm ($\frac{3}{8}$ in). Press seams towards jacket body and stitch the flat-fell seam, pivoting the machine needle at corners.
*Machine-quilted collar:* baste the collar wadding on to the wrong side of one collar piece. Stitch these, with right sides together and raw edges even, on to the neck edge of the same fabric, matching points **a**. With right sides together and raw edges even, pin the neck edge of the remaining collar piece on to the neck edge of the reverse side of the jacket, also matching points **a**. Stitch the seam through all thicknesses, along the previous seamline. Trim the neck seam. Press both sides of the collar upwards and baste them together.
*Pre-quilted collar:* unpick the quilting from one side of the collar seam allowance. Seam collar to the neck edge, taking care not to get

the free seam allowance caught up. Trim seam; press it upwards. On the reverse side, trim the free seam allowance, then fold it under and slipstitch it over the seamline.
*Tie fastenings:* fold under one end of each tie strip, then fold it in half lengthwise and stitch close to the folded edges. Pin ties to the placement markings on the front edges of jacket at 14 cm ($5\frac{1}{2}$ in) intervals, with raw edges even and each tie pointing inwards. Apply the pre-cut binding strips to the corresponding edges as follows: open out one folded edge of binding. Pin right side of binding to plaid side of jacket, with raw edges even. Stitch binding along the foldline, then fold it over to meet the seamline on the reverse side. Slipstitch the binding to the seamline. Turn under binding ends and mitre corners as necessary. Catch ties in seam when binding jacket front. Bind the edges of the pre-quilted pockets.
*Pockets:* with right sides facing, stitch together two pairs of patch pocket pieces, leaving an opening for turning. Turn each pocket right side out; slipstitch opening shut. Topstitch the plain or pre-quilted pockets on to one side of the jacket, with pocket openings at side seams, as shown.
*Finishing:* to wear jacket, turn up cuffs.

# 20
## Two-way Duffel Bag

**Size:** 60 cm (24 in) long × 28.5 cm (11$\frac{1}{4}$ in) wide

**Materials:** 1.25 m (1$\frac{1}{2}$ yd) of 90 cm (36 in)-wide striped canvas.
*Straps:* 2.7 m (3 yd) of 5 cm (2 in)-wide canvas webbing (available at upholstery shops).
One 50 cm (20 in) zip. 1.1 m (1$\frac{1}{4}$ yd) of 12 mm ($\frac{1}{2}$ in)-wide bias binding. Foam rubber remnants (a kitchen sponge cloth is ideal). Size 110(18) sewing machine needle (canvas-weight). Matching heavy-duty sewing thread. Sailmaker's needle (optional; may be necessary for hand sewing).

**Cutting out:** Enlarge the pattern pieces to full size. Cut out the main bag section and the patch pocket once each and the circular side pieces twice. Add 1 cm ($\frac{3}{8}$ in) seam allowance all round each piece, except to the long sides of the patch pocket which are without seam allowance. Pay close attention to the pattern grain markings.
*Straps:* cut two lengths of webbing for the straps, one piece 240 cm (91 in) long and another piece 30 cm (12 in) long.

**Sewing:** *Patch pocket:* clean-finish the raw edges on the short sides of the pocket piece, then press the seam allowances under and stitch them close to each folded edge. Pin pocket into position (see diagram), then stitch in place close to each long raw edge. Now stitch across the pocket width 20 cm (8 in) 'down' from each pocket top (short side). These pocket bottom seams prevent the contents from slipping through from one pocket to the other.
*Straps:* press under the ends of both the long and short strap pieces 15 mm ($\frac{5}{8}$ in). Baste the long strap piece on to the main bag section so that it forms a continuous loop beginning and ending on the base of the bag. (Make sure that the ends lie flat at the join.) Position the strap so that it conceals the raw pocket edges. Stitch the strap on to the bag, seaming along both long pocket edges and machining just inside both strap edges. Stitch a cross (for decoration and reinforcement) at the patch pocket ends, as shown. Pin the short strap piece on to one bag side piece, with each strap end 4.5 cm (1$\frac{3}{4}$ in) from the edge. Stitch a cross at either end of this handle. Pad the straps with foam rubber to make them comfortable to grip: cut out one 5 × 10 cm (2 × 4 in) piece of flat sponge cloth

for the short strap, and two 5 × 15 cm (2 × 6 in) pieces for the other two. Roll up each piece of sponge into a lengthwise tube, sewing a few stitches to secure it. To complete the handles, fold each strap round the appropriate piece of sponge and stitch the webbing edges together using machine zigzag (see photo on page 49).
Next, pin together the short sides (bag top) of the main bag section, with right sides together. Stitch the short seams at either end as far as the slit marks. Cut out a rectangular zip slot by trimming 5 mm ($\frac{1}{4}$ in) from either side of the zip opening on bag top. Bind the slit with bias binding to a width of 5 mm ($\frac{1}{4}$ in), mitring at corners (for how to apply binding, see Mother Goose Waistcoat, page 21). Centre the zip beneath the slot and baste it in place. Stitch zip to bag along the binding placement seam.
*Finishing:* with right sides together and zip open, pin a circular side piece to each end of the bag main section, matching the placement marks. Stitch each end on, then finish the raw edges with zigzag stitching. Turn bag right side out.

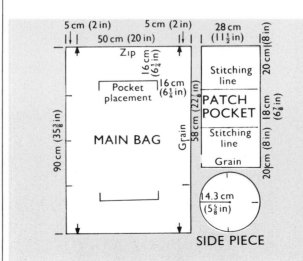

The duffel bag pattern is shown in reduced size. Enlarge the measurements given (in centimetres or inches) to full size.

# 21
## Rickrack-trimmed Smocks

## Woman's Smock

**Size:** 12–14 (10–12 U.S.)

**Materials:** 2 m (2¼ yd) of 150 cm (58–60 in)-wide poplin or lightweight denim. (NOTE: if you can't find these fabrics in wider widths, substitute a suitable furnishing cotton). 2 cm (¾ in)-wide rickrack: 8.2 m (9 yd) of red, 3.1 m (3½ yd) of yellow. Matching sewing thread.

**Cutting out:** Enlarge pattern pieces. Following the pattern layout, cut out one smock front, one back, one front facing and one back facing from a single layer of fabric. Add a 2 cm (¾ in) seam allowance to the lower sleeve/side seam, tapering to 5 mm (¼ in) at the underarm curve. Add a 4 cm (1½ in) allowance for the sleeve hems and hem. Elsewhere, add a 1 cm (⅜ in) seam allowance. Mark the pleats on the wrong side of the smock front as directed below.

**Sewing:** Stitch the smock front pleats from the wrong side. Press each group of pleats towards the centre front. On right side of the garment, stitch rickrack on top of each of the middle pleat seams (see photo on page 50 for colour placement), leaving the two end pleat seams untrimmed. Turn under the raw ends of the rickrack at the bottom of each pleat seam. With right sides together, stitch front to back along the shoulder/sleeve top seam; press open and clean-finish seam

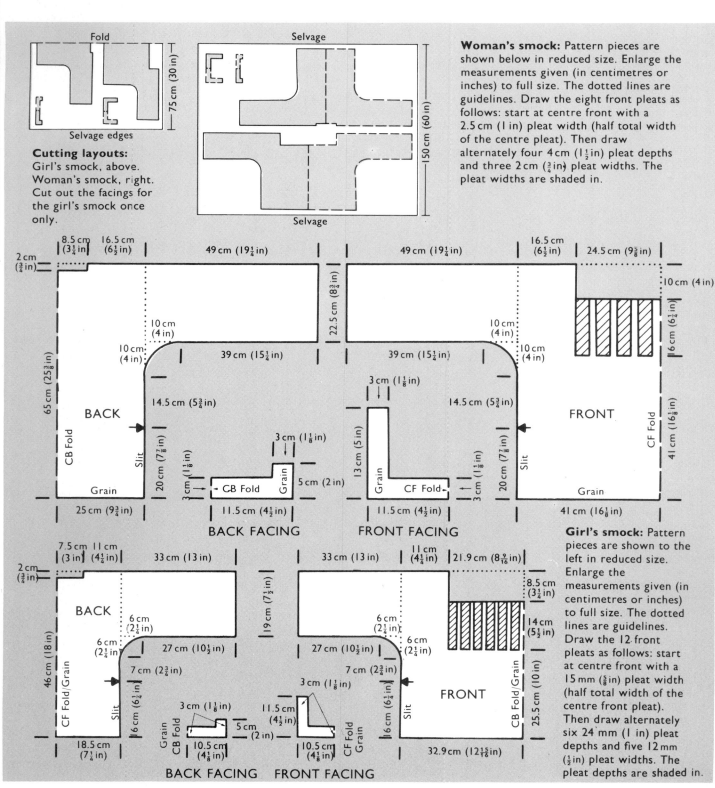

**Cutting layouts:** Girl's smock, above. Woman's smock, right. Cut out the facings for the girl's smock once only.

**Woman's smock:** Pattern pieces are shown below in reduced size. Enlarge the measurements given (in centimetres or inches) to full size. The dotted lines are guidelines. Draw the eight front pleats as follows: start at centre front with a 2.5 cm (1 in) pleat width (half total width of the centre pleat). Then draw alternately four 4 cm (1½ in) pleat depths and three 2 cm (¾ in) pleat widths. The pleat widths are shaded in.

**Girl's smock:** Pattern pieces are shown to the left in reduced size. Enlarge the measurements given (in centimetres or inches) to full size. The dotted lines are guidelines. Draw the 12 front pleats as follows: start at centre front with a 15 mm (⅝ in) pleat width (half total width of the centre front pleat). Then draw alternately six 24 mm (1 in) pleat depths and five 12 mm (½ in) pleat widths. The pleat depths are shaded in.

allowances. Stitch red rickrack over each shoulder/sleeve top seam. With right sides together, stitch the front neck facing to the back facing at shoulder seams, then press seams open and clean-finish them. With right sides together, stitch neck facing to smock, matching shoulder seams and with raw edges even. Clip into the facing seam allowances at the corners. Turn facing to inside; press. Now apply rickrack, starting at one untrimmed pleat seam, working round the back neckline (mitring at corners) and finishing at the remaining untrimmed pleat seam. Stitch three rows of rickrack above front and back hem and above each sleeve hem (see photo for colour sequence). With right sides together, stitch each lower sleeve/side seam to the side seam slit mark. Clean-finish seam allowances, clip seams at underarm curves and press seams open (including slit edges). Stitch red rickrack along the back slits, then stitch red rickrack along the front slits, continuing up each side/lower sleeve seam. Turn up and sew the hem and sleeve hems.

## Girl's Smock

**Size:** To fit a 4–5 year old (height: 116–122 cm [46–48 in])

**Materials:** 1.2 m (1⅜ yd) of 150 cm (58–60 in)-wide poplin or lightweight denim (or a suitable furnishing cotton). 1 cm (⅜ in)-wide rickrack: 2.3 m (2½ yd) of green, 2.3 m (2½ yd) of yellow, 5.5 m (6 yd) of white. Matching sewing thread.

**Cutting out:** Same as for woman's smock with these exceptions: cut out smock front and back on the fold and the front and back facings from a single layer of fabric (see cutting layout).

**Sewing:** Follow the instructions for the woman's smock, except stitch four rows of rickrack on to hem and sleeve seams (see photo for colour sequence).

## 22
## Woollen Overjacket with Muff-style Pocket

**Size:** 12–14 (10–12 u.s.)

**Materials:** 1.4 m (1⅝ yd) of 150 cm (58–60 in)-wide striped woollen fabric. Matching sewing thread.

**Cutting out:** Enlarge pattern pieces. Referring to cutting layout and placing stripes on grain as indicated, cut out one front, one back, one pocket and two sleeves from a single layer of fabric. Add a 2 cm (¾ in) seam allowance to each side seam, tapering to 5 mm (¼ in) at the underarm curve. Add 15 mm (⅝ in) all round pocket and a 4 cm (1½ in) allowance to hem and sleeve hems. Elsewhere, add a 1 cm (⅜ in) allowance. Using the pattern as a guide, draw 3 cm (1⅛ in)-wide front and back neck facings. Cut them out as shown, adding a 1 cm (⅜ in) seam allowance to the neck and shoulder edges.

**Sewing:** With right sides together, stitch front to back at shoulder seams; clean-finish seam allowances. Press seams open and topstitch the width of the machine foot on either side. With right sides together, stitch front and back neck facings together at shoulder seams.

Press seams open. Stitch the facing on to the overjacket neckline with right sides together, shoulder seams matching and raw edges even. Clip into the curves along the seam allowance. Press facing to inside, then topstitch the width of the machine foot all round neck opening. Clean-finish facing edges and catch-stitch them to the inside of the garment. Trim diagonally across pocket corners to reduce bulk. Finish pocket seam allowances, press them under, then baste them in place. Topstitch each short pocket side the width of the machine foot. Pin pocket on to garment front as indicated, matching points

**b.** Seam pocket to garment by topstitching the width of the machine foot along top and bottom edges. Next, stitch the crosswise seam joining each sleeve to the overjacket main section, with right sides together. Press each sleeve seam towards the main section and topstitch through all thicknesses. With right sides together, stitch each sleeve/side seam to the side seam slit mark. Clean-finish seam allowances and press open. Blindstitch the slit seam allowances to the garment. Press under and sew the hem and the sleeve hems, then topstitch them the width of the machine foot.

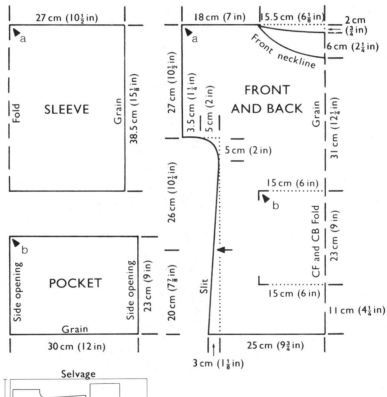

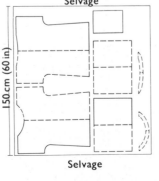

The overjacket pattern pieces are shown in reduced size. Enlarge the measurements given (in centimetres or inches) to full size. The dotted lines are guidelines. Front and back pattern pieces are superimposed. They are identical except for the lower neckline curve in front. To save time, draw the enlarged main section pattern only once, copying both necklines. Cut out the back first, then the front.

# 23

## Three Striped Overblouses

**Size:** 10 or 14 (8 or 12 U.S.)

### STYLE 1
(square-necked top with shoulder interest)

**Materials:** 2.5 m (2¾ yd) of 90 cm (36 in)-wide striped cotton fabric. 0.2 m (¼ yd) of 90 cm (36 in)-wide iron-on interfacing. Matching sewing thread.

**Cutting out:** Enlarge the Style 1 pattern pieces. Cut out the front and back pieces once each, as far as the Style 1 yoke line. Centre the CF and CB folds over a prominent stripe. Add a 2 cm (¾ in) seam allowance to each side seam until 10 cm (4 in) above the slit, then taper to 5 mm (¼ in) round the underarm curve. Add a 2 cm (¾ in) hem allowance and a 1 cm (⅜ in) seam allowance elsewhere. Cut out the Style 1 yoke once on the fold, with stripes running horizontally across the shoulders and adding 1 cm (⅜ in) seam allowance. *Neckline facing:* using the pattern pieces as your guide, draw a 3 cm (1¼ in)-wide one-piece facing to surround the front and back neckline, adding a 1 cm (⅜ in) seam allowance to all edges. The facing is shaped like a rectangular window. Cut it out once each from fabric and interfacing. Trim 5 mm (¼ in) from inner and outer interfacing edges, then iron it, centred, on to the wrong side of the facing. *Tieband;* cut two strips, each measuring 10 × 77 cm (3¾ × 30 in), including seam allowance (finished width: 4 cm [1½ in]). Cut out the tieband pieces with stripes running lengthwise.

**Sewing:** With right sides together, stitch the yoke on to the front and back pieces, matching points **a**. Clean-finish seam allowances together and press them towards the yoke. Clean-finish the outer edges of the neckline facing, then stitch it on to the neckline with right sides together and raw edges even. Press the facing to the inside, then topstitch all round the neckline 1 cm (⅜ in) from the edge. With right sides together, stitch each underarm/side seam to the slit mark. Clean-finish the seam allowances separately until 15 cm (6 in) above each slit, then finish them together. Topstitch round each slit, 1 cm (⅜ in) from the edges.

Turn up and stitch the hem. Fold the lower sleeve edges under twice and stitch a narrow hem. *Tieband:* with right sides together, stitch short ends together to make one long strip. With right sides facing, fold the strip in half lengthwise and stitch it together, leaving an opening for turning. Turn to right side, slipstitch opening shut and topstitch all round. If you wish, make thread loop belt carriers at waist level on each side seam.

### STYLE 2
(square-necked top with sleeve bands)

**Materials:** 2 m (2¼ yd) of 90 cm (36 in)-wide striped cotton fabric. 0.2 m (¼ yd) of 90 cm (36 in)-wide iron-on interfacing. Matching sewing thread.

**Cutting out:** Enlarge the Style 2 pattern pieces. Butt the front and back pattern pieces together along the shoulder seams to form an all-in-one pattern piece. Cut this piece out once, centring CF and CB over a stripe. Cut out the sleeve band twice on the fold, with stripes running from side to side (see photo on page 53). For seam allowances, neckline facing and tieband, see Style 1 instructions.

**Sewing:** Apply the neckline facing and topstitch as for Style 1. With right sides together, stitch each sleeve band on to main garment, matching point **b**. Clean-finish the sleeve band seam allowances together, press them towards the band, then topstitch through all thicknesses, 1 cm (⅜ in) from the seamline. To complete the overblouse, stitch the side seams, hems and tieband according to Style 1 instructions.

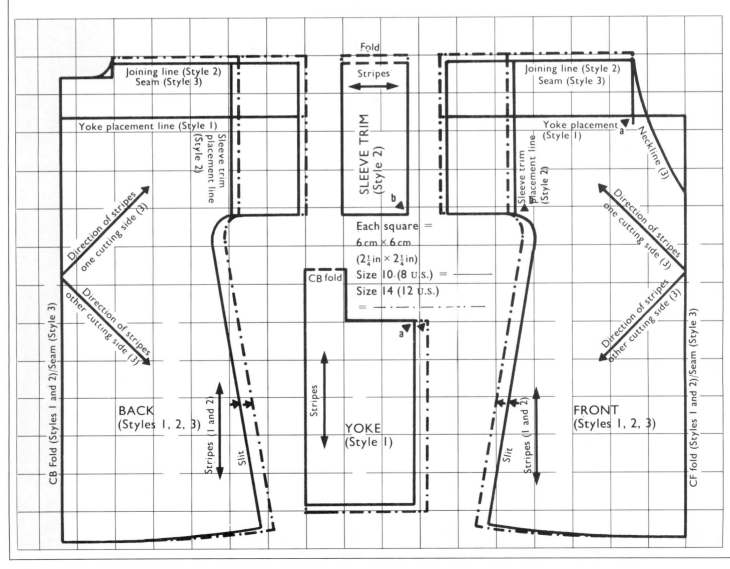

STYLE 3
(bias-cut V-necked top)

**Materials:** 3.2 m ($3\frac{1}{2}$ yd) of 90 cm (36 in)-wide striped cotton fabric. 0.2 m ($\frac{1}{4}$ yd) of 90 cm (36 in)-wide iron-on interfacing. Matching sewing thread.

**Cutting out:** Enlarge the Style 3 pattern pieces, taking care to copy the front V-neckline and the back neckline curve. Note that the centre front, centre back and shoulders are seamed. Cut out the front and back pieces twice each on the bias, from a single layer of fabric. Reverse each pattern piece before the second cutting. Make sure that the diagonal stripes along the centre front and back seams meet and continue running in the same direction (see diagram arrows and photo on page 53). Match stripes carefully along the side and shoulder seams (here, they will chevron). For seam allowances, tieband and neckline facing, see Style 1 instructions. In this case, the neckline facing is a teardrop-shaped window.

**Sewing:** To prevent the bias-cut fabric from stretching, stitch the seams using a small, flat zigzag stitch. With right sides together, stitch centre front, centre back and shoulder seams. Clean-finish the edges separately and press seams open. Apply the neckline facing and topstitch, as for Style 1. To complete the overblouse, stitch the side seams, hems and tieband according to Style 1 instructions.

# 24

## Curtains with Diagonal Stripes

**Size:** Made-to-measure

**Materials:** Make up pattern, calculate fabric requirements, then buy the following: equal quantities of red and white cotton fabric. Standard cotton curtain tape (length = twice that of the curtain rail [rod]). Matching sewing thread.

**How to make the pattern:** To make a curtain pattern to fit your own window dimensions, you need a ruler, a set square (right triangle) and paper.
Refer to our diagram as a guide. For each *side* of the curtain, draw a rectangle measuring the *full length* of the curtain rail by the desired finished height from top of rail to bottom of windowsill. Draw a diagonal line from the top left to the bottom right corner. Divide the length of the rectangle into thirds; mark these points on the top and bottom edges. Use the set square to draw line a–b, which is at a right angle to the centre diagonal and which starts at the first division on the bottom line (see diagram). Measure line a–b. Draw a line from each of the points on the top and bottom edges to the adjacent side of the rectangle. Each of these lines must be parallel to the centre diagonal and distance a–b wide. The rectangle is now divided into six equal diagonal stripes.
Divide the pattern into alternating red and white stripes (see diagram for the left side of the curtain). The pattern for the right side of the curtain is the same, but with the order of the stripes reversed (see diagram). Notice that when the left and right sides of the curtain meet, the stripes are continuous and unbroken.
*Seam allowances:* add 2 cm ($\frac{3}{4}$ in) to the sides and top edge and 4 cm ($1\frac{1}{2}$ in) to the hem. When pattern pieces are cut apart into separate diagonal stripes (see below), add a 5 mm ($\frac{1}{4}$ in) seam allowance to each long edge.

**Cutting out:** Make colour-coded tissue paper pattern pieces for each side of the curtain, cutting the pattern into diagonal stripes and adding the seam allowances specified above. Pin these to the fabric so that the lengthwise grain runs parallel to the selvage. You should get two lengths from one width of fabric (with seam allowances in between). For the most economical use of fabric, butt the diagonals end to end (also with seam allowances in between). To calculate fabric requirements: cut up the pattern piece for one curtain side into individual stripes. Place these side to side and end to end, with seam allowances in between, as described. Measure the length and the width (to the nearest standard width). Buy this amount of each colour.

**Sewing:** For each side of the curtain: pin, then stitch all the stripes together, with right sides together and following the correct colour and size sequence. Clean-finish seam allowances together using machine zigzag, then press towards the darker colour (here red). The fabric is cut on the bias, so take care not to stretch it during stitching. Fold under the side edges of the curtains twice, 1 cm ($\frac{3}{8}$ in) each time; stitch close to inner fold. Turn under the hem twice, 2 cm ($\frac{3}{4}$ in) each time; stitch. Cut the curtain tape into two equal pieces, one for each side. Turn under the top edge of each curtain 2 cm ($\frac{3}{4}$ in). Baste the curtain tape over the raw edge on each curtain, turning the tape under 5 mm ($\frac{1}{4}$ in) at each end. To reduce bulk, cut the tape so that the ends fall 5 mm ($\frac{1}{4}$ in) short of each side seam. Stitch on the curtain tape along both edges. Hang the curtains, inserting curtain hooks and drawing each curtain side across half the width of the rail. Knot the ends of the curtain tape drawstring. *Do not cut the drawstring off* because the curtains will be opened to full width for laundering.

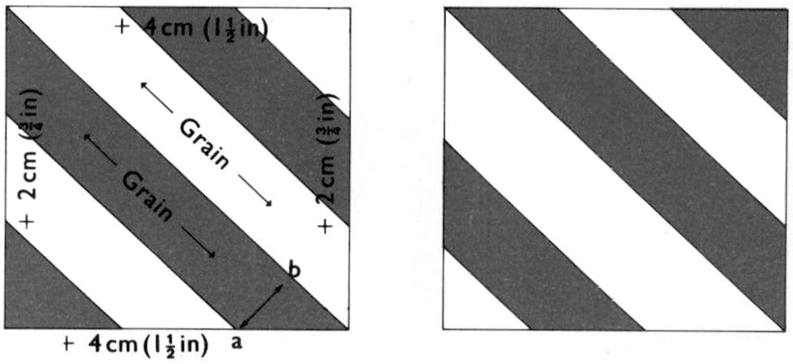


Use these diagrams as guides for drawing your own made-to-measure curtain patterns. The instructions tell you how.

# 25

## Net (Sheer) Curtains

**Size:** Made-to-measure

**Materials:** Measure up carefully as described below, then buy the necessary quantities of the following: synthetic curtain net (tulle). Standard synthetic curtain tape. Rayon velvet ribbon: 2.5 cm (1 in)-wide medium green, 15 mm ($\frac{5}{8}$ in)-wide dark green. Matching polyester thread.

**Measuring up:** Follow these instructions to calculate your fabric requirements:
*Curtains:* width: sheer curtains are very full. For each *side* of the curtains, you will need *four times* the width of *half* the curtain rail (rod). *Length:* measure the desired finished length from top of curtain rail to hem edge.
*Valance:* width: *twice* the width of the curtain rail. Length: the valance should be long enough so that a sufficient amount is visible beneath the pelmet (cornice), but not long enough to get in the way when the window is opened or shut. If your valance is going to be narrow, turn up a shorter hem than specified (see below). Ribbons and curtain tape: purchase enough to go across the width of each of the two curtain sides and the valance. Add on 30 cm (12 in) to the total length of each of the two ribbon strips and the tape. Seam allowances (for curtains and valance): add a 5 cm (2 in) hem allowance, 2 cm ($\frac{3}{4}$ in) to the sides and top edge. If you are using a hanging method other than standard tape and hooks, allow enough fabric at the top so that the curtain fittings (fastenings) are concealed. A casing for a curtain rail or wire requires two equal turnings of fabric.

**Purchasing the fabric:** Net curtaining is often sold in fixed lengths. Purchase the length closest to the one you need. The required *width* is then measured off. If you cannot obtain this special curtain fabric,

*Continued overleaf*

purchase tulle as regular dressmaking fabric (the usual narrower width, with *length* measured off the bolt). If this is the case, do not join several lengths to achieve the necessary width. The seams will show through and be unsightly. Instead, sew several individual curtains. When these are hung side by side, the edges will be concealed by the folds, creating the illusion of one continuous curtain.

**Sewing:** The curtains and the valance are all made the same way. Turn up the hem edges of each curtain side and the valance on to the *right side* of the fabric. Place a piece of wide green velvet ribbon over the raw edges of each piece of net, cutting the ribbon with 5 cm (2 in) extra at each end. Baste the ribbon in place with a diagonal tacking stitch, using a fine needle and sewing thread. Now cut the narrow dark green ribbon to size and baste it 2 cm (¾ in) above each wide green band. Trim the ends of the ribbon even with the side edges of the fabric after basting is completed. Now adjust your sewing machine to

maximum stitch length and loosen the tension. Stitch the ribbons on along both selvages. If the fabric slips beneath the machine foot, sew through strips of tissue paper. Afterwards, these tear away easily. Next, fold under the side edges of the curtains and valance twice, 1 cm (⅜ in) each time. Baste in place, then stitch sides close to each inner folded edge.

*Attach the curtain tape:* cut the tape into three pieces, one for each curtain side and one for the valance. Fold under the allowance along the top edge of each piece of net. Baste the curtain tape over the raw edges of the net, turning the tape under 5 mm (¼ in) at each end. To reduce bulk, cut the tape so that the ends fall 5 mm (¼ in) short of each side seam. Stitch on the curtain tape along both edges.

*Hang the curtains:* insert curtain hooks and draw each curtain side across half the width of the rail, the valance across the full width of the rail. Knot the ends of the curtain tape drawstring but *do not cut it off* because the curtains will be opened to full width for laundering.

# 26
## Ribbon-trimmed Cushions

**Finished sizes:** *Round cushion:* 42.5 cm (16¼ in)-diameter
*Heart-shaped cushion:* 45 cm (18 in) high × 52.5 cm (20½ in) at widest point
*Rectangular cushion:* 40 × 50 cm (16 × 20 in)
*Square cushions:* 40 × 40 cm (16 × 16 in) each
*Oval cushion:* 40 × 50 cm (16 × 20 in)

**Materials:** Flowered cotton fabrics and 1 cm (⅜ in)-wide woven-edge taffeta ribbon as follows:
*Round cushion:* 0.5 m (½ yd) of 90 cm (36 in)-wide lilac-coloured fabric. 2 m (1⅞ yd) of lilac-coloured ribbon.
*Heart-shaped cushion:* 0.6 m (⅝ yd) of 90 cm (36 in)-wide light blue fabric. 4.5 m (5 yds) of light blue ribbon.

*Rectangular cushion:* 0.6 m (⅝ yd) of 90 cm (36 in)-wide blue fabric. 2.6 m (2⅞ yd) of blue ribbon.
*Square cushions:* 0.5 m (½ yd) of 90 cm (36 in)-wide pink fabric each. 3 m (3⅜ yd) of pink ribbon per cushion.
*Oval cushion:* 0.6 m (⅝ yd) of 90 cm (36 in)-wide yellow/blue fabric. 4 m (4½ yd) of yellow ribbon.
You will also need synthetic filling and matching sewing thread for each cushion.

**Enlarging the patterns:** The cushion patterns are shown in reduced size at a ratio of 1:5. They are simple shapes and are easily enlarged by referring to both the diagrams and the measurements given above. To find out what a cushion dimension is at any given point, measure it and multiply by five. Use these short-cuts to draw the

more difficult shapes:
*Heart:* draw the heart by inscribing it in a 45 cm (18 in)-high × 52.5 cm (20½ in)-wide rectangle.
*Oval:* draw a 40 × 50 cm (16 × 20 in) rectangle and round it off as shown.

**Cutting out:** Cut out one front and one back piece for each cushion, adding 1 cm (⅜ in) seam allowance all round.

**Sewing:** Baste ribbons to each cushion front, following the placement diagram. Overlap or fold the ribbons exactly as shown. Edge-stitch the ribbons on to the fabric. With right sides together stitch cushion back to cushion front, leaving an opening for turning. Turn right side out. Fill the cushion, then slipstitch the opening shut by hand.

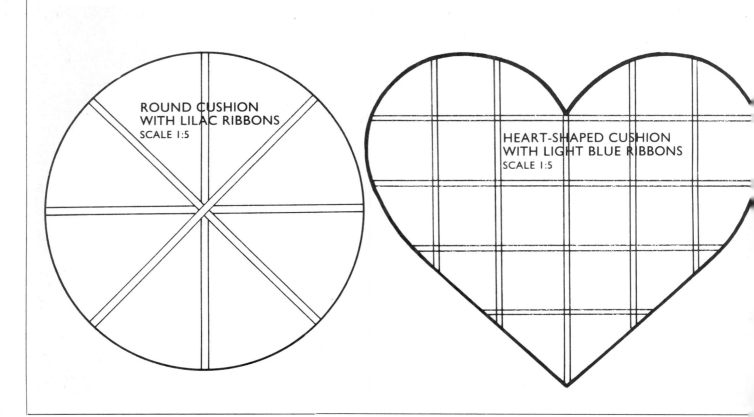

ROUND CUSHION
WITH LILAC RIBBONS
SCALE 1:5

HEART-SHAPED CUSHION
WITH LIGHT BLUE RIBBONS
SCALE 1:5

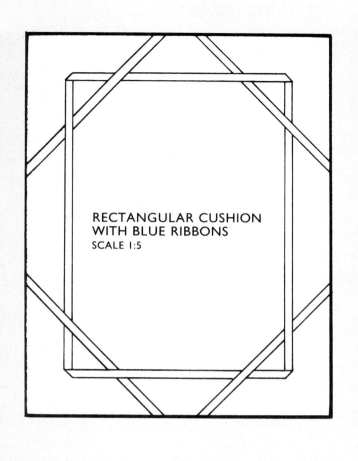

RECTANGULAR CUSHION
WITH BLUE RIBBONS
SCALE 1:5

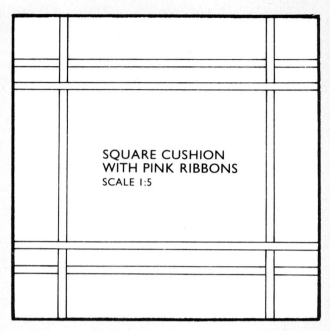

SQUARE CUSHION
WITH PINK RIBBONS
SCALE 1:5

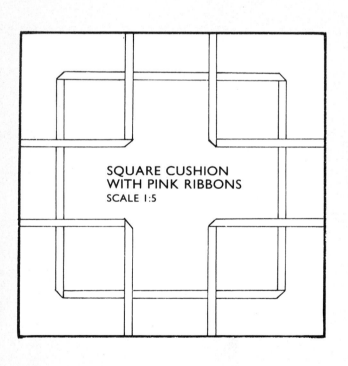

SQUARE CUSHION
WITH PINK RIBBONS
SCALE 1:5

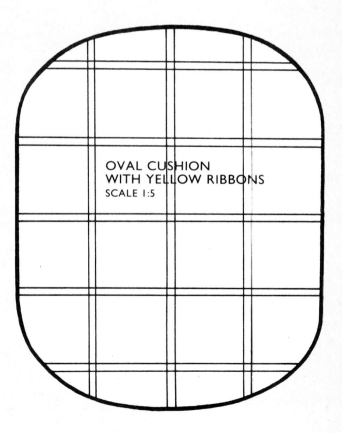

OVAL CUSHION
WITH YELLOW RIBBONS
SCALE 1:5

# 27

## Mixed-Fabric Cushions

### General instructions

All of these cushions contain made-to-measure cushion pads (pillow forms), consisting of padding with a covering of unbleached calico (unbleached muslin). Each pad is cut larger than its outer fabric cover in order to fill it completely. For each cushion, cut out five layers of synthetic wadding (batting), adding 2 cm ($\frac{3}{4}$ in) all round to the finished measurements of the basic cushion shape (size without border or frill). Stack the wadding layers on top of each other, then overcast their edges together. Cut out the two pieces for the pad cover to the same dimensions as the pad. Stitch the pad cover together taking a 1 cm ($\frac{3}{8}$ in) seam allowance. Leave an opening of 20–25 cm (8–10 in) in both the cushion pad cover and the fabric cushion cover. This can then be slipstitched shut by hand. For best results, make up a paper pattern for each cushion cover with a seamed front.

*Cushions 1–3 on page 57, anti-clockwise from top right:*

## Cushion 1 *(round cushion with ruched border)*

**Finished size:** 46 cm (18 in)-diameter

**Materials:** *For cushion pad:* 1 m (1$\frac{1}{8}$ yd) of 150 cm (58–60 in)-wide synthetic wadding.
*For pad cover:* 0.5 m ($\frac{5}{8}$ yd) of 115 cm (44–45 in)-wide unbleached calico.
*For cushion cover:* Border: 0.3 m ($\frac{1}{4}$ yd) of 115 cm (44–45 in)-wide striped fabric. Circles: 0.3 m ($\frac{1}{4}$ yd) of 90 cm (36 in)-wide flowered fabric. 1.3 m (1$\frac{1}{2}$ yd) of elastic cord. Matching sewing thread.

**Cutting out:** Cut out two 20 cm (8 in)-diameter flowered fabric circles, adding 1 cm ($\frac{3}{8}$ in) seam allowance all round. Join together the striped fabric as necessary to make two border strips, each measuring 13 × 190 cm (5 × 75 in), adding 1 cm ($\frac{3}{8}$ in) seam allowance all round.

**Sewing:** With right sides together, join each border strip to form a ring. Fold one raw edge of each border strip under twice to form a casing, leaving an opening for elastic insertion. Thread the elastic through each casing, gather it to fit round the edges of each flowered circle, then stitch the elastic ends together and sew the opening shut. Pin the gathered edges of each border strip on top of the seam allowance of each circle, with wrong side of strip to right side of circle. Stitch in place, using machine zigzag.
*Finishing:* with right sides together, stitch cushion front to back, leaving an opening for turning. Turn to right side, insert cushion pad and slipstitch the opening shut.

## Cushion 2 *(square cushion with surface ruffle)*

**Finished size:** 46 × 46 cm (18 × 18 in)

**Materials:** *For cushion pad and cover:* 1 m (1$\frac{1}{8}$ yd) of 150 cm (58–60 in)-wide wadding. 0.6 m ($\frac{5}{8}$ yd) of 115 cm (44–45 in)-wide unbleached calico.
*For cushion cover:* 0.6 m ($\frac{5}{8}$ yd) of 115 cm (44–45 in)-wide patterned fabric.
*Ruffle:* 0.15 m ($\frac{1}{4}$ yd) of 115 cm (44–45 in)-wide flowered fabric. Matching sewing thread.

**Cutting out:** Cut out two 46 cm (18 in) patterned fabric squares, adding 1 cm ($\frac{3}{8}$ in) seam allowance.
*Ruffle:* join the flowered fabric to make a strip measuring 7 × 210 cm (2$\frac{3}{4}$ × 83 in), without seam allowance.

**Sewing:** Join the ruffle strip to form a ring. Clean-finish the raw edges of the ruffle with machine zigzag. Run a gathering thread (machine basting) along the centre of the ruffle strip (see photo). Carefully draw up the gathers, then pin the ruffle to the cushion front, forming a rounded square with outer edges approx. 5 cm (2 in) from the cushion edges. Distribute the gathers evenly, then stitch the ruffle in place along the centre basting. Stitch cushion front to back, completing as for cushion 1.

## Cushion 3 *(round cushion with frill)*

**Finished size:** 43 cm (17 in), without frill

**Materials:** *For cushion pad and cover:* 1 m (1$\frac{1}{8}$ yd) of 150 cm (58–60 in)-wide wadding. 0.5 m ($\frac{5}{8}$ yd) of 115 cm (44–45 in)-wide unbleached calico.
*For cushion cover:* 0.45 m ($\frac{1}{2}$ yd) of 90 cm (36 in)-wide flowered fabric.
*Ruffle:* 0.15 m ($\frac{1}{4}$ yd) of 115 cm (44–45 in)-wide gingham. Matching sewing thread.

**Cutting out:** Cut out two 43 cm (17 in)-diameter flowered fabric circles, adding 1 cm ($\frac{3}{8}$ in) seam allowance.
*Frill:* join the gingham to make a strip measuring 5 × 240 cm (2 × 95 in), adding a 1 cm ($\frac{3}{8}$ in) seam allowance to one long edge.

**Sewing:** Join the frill strip to form a ring. Clean-finish one raw edge of frill with machine zigzag. Gather the other edge of the frill to a circumference of approx. 135 cm (53$\frac{1}{2}$ in). With right sides together and raw edges even, pin the gathered edge of the frill to the cushion front, distributing the gathers evenly. Baste in place. Stitch cushion front to back, completing as for cushion 1.

*Cushions 4–8 on pages 58 and 59, anti-clockwise from centre top:*

## Cushion 4 *(button-tufted square cushion)*

**Finished size:** 46 × 46 cm (18 × 18 in)

**Materials:** *For cushion pad and cover:* 1 m (1$\frac{1}{8}$ yd) of 150 cm (58–60 in)-wide wadding. 0.6 m ($\frac{5}{8}$ yd) of 115 cm (44–45 in)-wide unbleached calico.
*For cushion cover:* 0.6 m ($\frac{5}{8}$ yd) of 115 cm (44–45 in)-wide plaid fabric. Remnant of printed fabric for square appliqué (dimensions below). One button. Matching sewing thread.

**Cutting out:** Cut out two 46 × 46 cm (18 × 18 in) plaid fabric squares, adding 1 cm ($\frac{3}{8}$ in) seam allowance.
*Appliqué:* cut out one 26 × 26 cm (10 × 10 in) printed fabric square, adding 1 cm ($\frac{3}{8}$ in) seam allowance.

**Sewing:** Press under the seam allowances of the appliqué. Centre it on the cushion front. Baste in place. Stitch the appliqué to the cushion front close to its folded edges. Stitch cushion front to back, completing as for cushion 1.
*Finishing:* position the button in cushion centre and sew it on, taking the needle through all thicknesses.

## Cushion 5 (square cushion with flanged border)

**Finished size:** 51 × 51 cm (20 × 20 in), including border

**Materials:** *For cushion pad and cover (45 × 45 cm [17¾ × 17¾ in], without border).* 1 m (1⅛ yd) of 150 cm (58–60 in)-wide wadding. 0.5 m (⅝ yd) of 115 cm (44–45 in)-wide unbleached calico. *For cushion cover:* 0.5 m (⅝ yd) of 115 cm (44–45 in)-wide printed fabric A. *Border:* 0.1 m (⅛ yd) of 115 cm (44–45 in)-wide printed fabric B. Matching sewing thread.

**Cutting out:** Cut out two 45 cm (17¾ in) squares from printed fabric A, adding 1 cm (⅜ in) seam allowance all round. For border, cut out eight strips from printed fabric B, each measuring 5 × 53 cm (2 × 20⅞ in), seam allowance included (finished width of border: 3 cm [1⅛ in]).

**Sewing:** *Border:* stitch two sets of four strips together to form a square, mitring the corners; press seams open. With right sides together, stitch the outer edges of the border together.
*Cushion:* with right sides together, seam the outer edges of the cushion front to the raw inner edges of one side of the border. (It will be necessary to clip the border seam allowances diagonally into each corner.) Next, seam the cushion back piece to the remaining inner border edges in the same way, but leaving an opening for turning. Press seams. Turn cushion right side out, insert cushion pad, then slipstitch opening shut. Centre the cushion cover over the pad, then baste through all thicknesses round the border seamline. Stitch all round cushion, through the border seamline.

## Cushion 6 (rectangular cushion with triangles)

**Finished size:** 58 × 40 cm (23 × 16 in)

**Materials:** *For cushion pad and cover:* 1.1 m (1¼ yd) of 150 cm (58–60 in)-wide wadding (cutting layout: place two rectangles lengthwise, three crosswise). 0.6 m (¾ yd) of 115 cm (44–45 in)-wide unbleached calico. *For cushion cover:* 0.7 m (¾ yd) of 115 cm (44–45 in)-wide printed fabric A (for cushion back and one front triangle). Remnants of printed fabrics B,C and D (for remaining front triangles). Matching sewing thread.

**Cutting out:** For cushion back, cut out one 58 × 40 cm (23 × 16 in) rectangle, adding 1 cm (⅜ in) seam allowance all round. For cushion front, divide the rectangle into four triangles as shown. Cut out one triangle from each of printed fabrics A,B,C and D, adding 1 cm (⅜ in) seam allowance all round each.

**Sewing:** *Cushion front:* with right sides facing, stitch two pairs of two triangles together; press seams open. With right sides facing, stitch the two larger triangles together along the diagonal seam. Press seam open.
*Finishing:* stitch cushion front to back, completing as for cushion 1.

## Cushion 7 (rectangular cushion with scalloped border)

**Finished size:** 66 × 42 cm (26 × 16½ in), including border (52 × 32 cm [22 × 12½ in], without border)

**Materials:** *For cushion pad and cover:* 1.2 m (1⅜ yd) of 150 cm (58–60 in)-wide wadding. 0.6 m (¾ yd) of 115 cm (44–45 in)-wide unbleached calico. *For cushion cover:* 0.6 m (¾ yd) of 115 cm (44–45 in)-wide flowered fabric. *Border:* 0.5 m (⅝ yd) of 115 cm (44–45 in)-wide gingham. Matching sewing thread.

**Cutting out:** Cut out two 56 × 32 cm (22 × 12½ in) rectangles, adding 1 cm (⅜ in) seam allowance all round. For scalloped border (finished width 5 cm [2 in], at widest point of scallop), cut out four gingham strips measuring 6 × 68 cm (2⅜ × 26¾ in) and four strips measuring 6 × 46 cm (2⅜ × 17¼ in), necessary seam allowance included. For the scallop template, draw a 2 cm (¾ in)-diameter semicircle on a piece of card.

**Sewing:** *Border:* Stitch together two short and two long gingham strips to form a rectangle, mitring the corners and with right sides together. Press seams open. Repeat for the remaining four strips. With wrong sides together and raw edges even, baste the two rectangular windows together. Mark the scalloped edges all round the border, using the template to a depth of 15 mm (⅝ in). Embroider the scallops using machine satin stitch (closely spaced zigzag), then trim fabric close to stitching. Remove basting and complete, following the cushion portion of cushion 5 instructions.

## Cushion 8 (button-tufted round cushion)

**Finished size:** 48 cm (19 in)-diameter

**Materials:** *For cushion pad and cover:* 1.6 m (1¾ yd) of 150 cm (58–60 in)-wide wadding. 0.55 m (⅝ yd) of 115 cm (44–45 in)-wide unbleached calico. *For cushion cover:* 0.55 m (⅝ yd) of 90 cm (36 in)-wide printed fabric A (for cushion back and ½ front). 0.3 m (¼ yd) of 90 cm (36 in)-wide printed fabric B.

**Cutting out:** For cushion back, cut out one 48 cm (19 in)-diameter circle from printed fabric A, adding 1 cm (⅜ in) seam allowance all round. Divide the cushion front into quarters, as shown. Cut out two pieces from printed fabric A and two from printed fabric B, adding 1 cm (⅜ in) seam allowance all round each.

**Sewing:** With right sides facing, stitch two identical pairs of fabric A and B pieces together; press seams open. With right sides together, stitch the centre seam; press open. Finish as for cushion 1, then sew on button as for cushion 4.

**28**

### Waiting in Style

During pregnancy, light, comfortable clothing is essential. If you are expecting a baby in the summertime you want dresses, blouses and trousers to be airy. You feel proud when you think of this forthcoming event and you naturally want to look pretty.

Pregnancy is a very important stage in a woman's life.

However, the anticipated new arrival means lots of baby gear to buy, so you may decide to do without some of the things you yourself wanted. Choose a few attractive maternity clothes which are easy to care for and can be mixed and matched successfully. When you sew them yourself, you're creating exactly the styles you want and cutting costs, too.

On these two pages, you will find designs which fulfil these wishes completely. The little smock on this page can be worn with your maternity trousers. Select a colour to coordinate with your trousers so you have the right combination for the summer. The shirred panel in the front and back of this top gives it its fullness. The fine gathering is achieved with elastic sewing thread, which controls the fit flexibly and does not bind.

Narrow topstitched released tucks in the front and back give this dress its easy fit. You can adjust the width to suit your own measurements; the instructions tell you how. All the edges are bound with blue bias binding. The straps are criss-crossed at the back and buttoned at the front.

Both these versatile styles will make the transition into your everyday wardrobe after the big event.

Instructions for both maternity styles are on page 80.

29

30

## Warm Fur for Cold Days

The cold days come round more quickly than you think, so it's a good idea to have some suitable warm clothing ready. Of course, nothing can compare with the warmth and luxury of real fur. On these pages, we show you two attractive designs which are simple to make.

The glamorous cap is made up of six equal-sized pieces. You will find the full-size pattern in the instruction section. Cutting out the pelts is slightly complicated, but the actual sewing is very easy. It's a good introduction to the furrier's art and an excellent way to salvage an old fur coat.

The sleeveless jackets for mums and kids are made from washed sheepskin. The leather is worn on the outside and the sheepskin pile is visible along the seams. These waistcoats, which are cut quite long, look best worn with trousers and casual clothing. Little boys like wearing them, too.

Instructions for the hat and jackets are on pages 81 and 82.

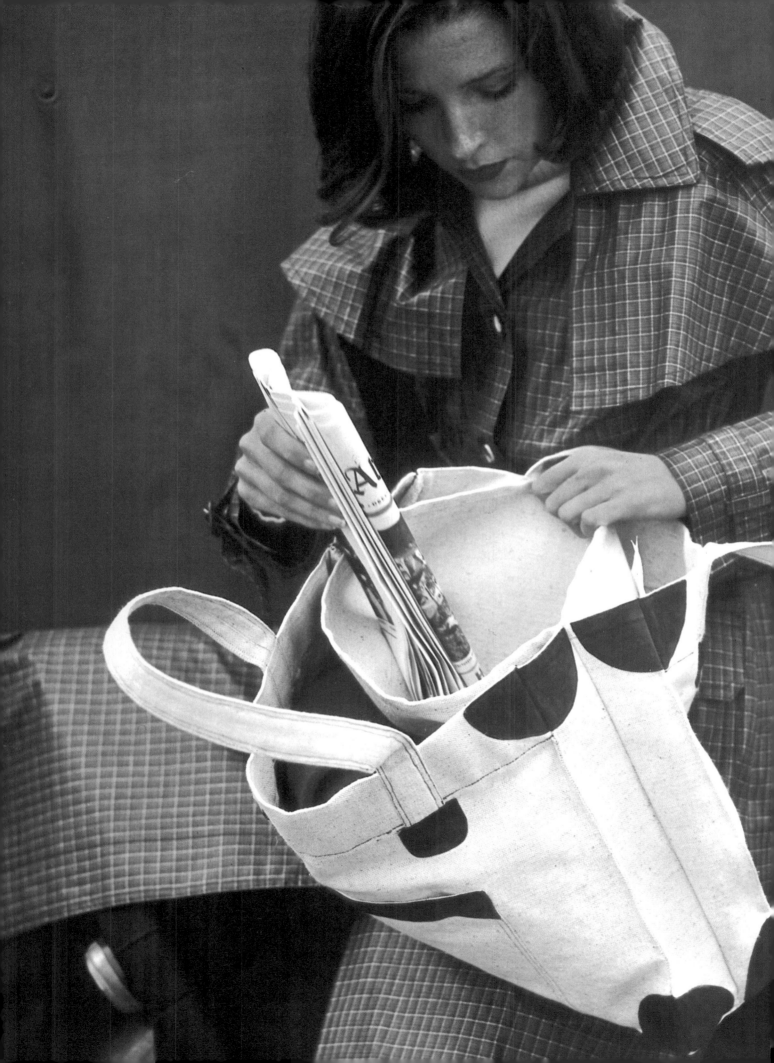

**Common-sense Carryalls: Lots of Pockets and Lots of Space**

Large sporty-looking leather or fabric bags have always been fashionable, but they're not always well-designed.

You've probably had the frustrating experience of standing parcel-laden at the front door, unable to find the key anywhere. Of course, it's always tucked away at the bottom of your bag. Our wisely-planned

bags remedy that situation. They've got plenty of pockets in plain sight, to put an end to all that rummaging. The handles of the left-hand style are long enough for over-the-shoulder use, to leave your hands free.

Instructions for making five different bags are on pages 83, 84 and 85.

**31**

**32**

33

## Carefree Rainwear for Cyclists

'There's no such thing as bad weather, just unsuitable clothing', so the saying goes. The cyclists on these pages are protected from head to toe against the wet. They're appropriately kitted out, whether for a short trip to school or a refreshing countryside bike ride through the autumn rain.

The little girl's yoked raincapes (left) are made out of water-repellent poplin. The women's raincapes (right) are made from waterproof oilcloth. The cape styling allows freedom of movement and they're short enough to clear the bicycle pedals safely.

We've designed these raincapes with a choice of fastening. The blue capes have a zip closure, the yellow ones have snap fasteners. The girl's raincapes come in hooded (blue) and unhooded (yellow) versions. The cheerful colours will brighten up the gloomiest day. These raincapes are so stylish and practical, pedestrians will want them, too.

Instructions for these raincapes are on pages 86, 87 and 88.

# 35

## A Winning Combination: Patchwork plus Crochet

Keen needleworkers always keep a large stock of fabric remnants on hand in anticipation of future projects. Follow our suggestion here to put them to beautiful use.

The patchwork bedspread looks delicate and summery because it is made up entirely of fabrics with a light-coloured background. The crocheted joins create an almost filigreed effect. As an added feature, the cover is reversible: one side is made up of floral-patterned fabrics, as shown; the other side is made up of patches in geometric designs. You may wish to use dark-ground prints on the flip side, for a striking contrast in mood. We explain how to make the reversible patchwork squares in the instructions section.

The cover consists of 187 squares, all of which are interfaced to give shape and stability. It measures approximately 150 × 250 cm (60 × 99 in), which is just right for a single bed. Since it is made square by square, the size can easily be enlarged at will. Two covers can be joined together to make a quilt for a five-foot bed. To fit a standard double bed, make up enough squares for one and a half covers.

There's also a matching cushion cover which we've designed in slightly scaled-down squares. It's a nice finishing touch, particularly in rooms you not only sleep in but also use as day space.

This isn't a 'just for show' bedspread. It's practical and washable in the all-cotton version shown. Substitute soft woollen remnants for the cotton ones, and you'll have a cuddly winter afghan to snuggle up in.

Instructions for the bedspread and cushion cover are on page 89.

Details of abbreviations and American equivalents are on page 236.

# 28
# Maternity Dress and Top

**Sizes:** 12 (14 and 16), (10 [12 and 14] U.S.)

**How to enlarge the patterns:** The patterns for both dress and blouse are given in reduced form for size 12 (10). Enlarge the measurements given (in centimetres or inches) to full size. The patterns can easily be enlarged to fit size 14 (12) or 16 (14). On the dress front and back piece, leave the tucked panel as it is but widen the side areas from 14.5 to 15.5 cm (5¾ to 6⅛ in) for size 14 (12) or to 16.5 cm (6½ in) for size 16 (14). The additional width runs the full length of the pattern piece. Adjust the size of the blouse in the same way, leaving the shirred panel untouched.

## DRESS

**Materials:** 2.4 m (2⅝ yd) of 90 cm (36 in)-wide printed cotton fabric. One 16 cm (7 in) zip. 3.25 m (3⅝ yd) of 25 mm (1 in)-wide matching bias binding. Four buttons. Matching sewing thread.

**Cutting out:** Enlarge the appropriate pattern pieces, adjusting the size as instructed above, if necessary. Cut out the dress front and back using the same pattern piece. Add the following seam allowances: 2 cm (¾ in) to the side seams, 4 cm (1½ in) for the hem and cut the top edge without seam allowance. Cut out the shoulder strap twice with a 1 cm (⅜ in) seam allowance at the slanted back end, none elsewhere. Round off the front shoulder strap corners (see photo on page 71). Cut out patch pocket twice without seam allowance.

**Sewing:** Make the released tucks on the right side of the fabric: place X on top of O and then topstitch close to the folded edge. Stitch the side seams with right sides together, sewing only as far as the slit mark on the left side seam; clean-finish seam allowances. Apply bias binding to the top edge of the dress: open out one folded edge of the

binding. Pin binding to fabric with right sides together and binding foldline 1 cm (⅜ in) from edge of fabric. Stitch along binding foldline. Fold binding over to wrong side of fabric, so that its remaining folded edge slightly overlaps the seamline. Baste in place. On the right side, stitch just above the lower edge of the binding, taking care to catch in all layers. Next, insert the zip with a lapped application in the left side seam.

*Straps:* bind the straps (except the back ends) and make two machine buttonholes in the front end of each (see diagram). Finish the back ends of each strap, then stitch them on to the top edges of the dress back with slanted ends level with the binding seam (see photo), so that they criss-cross. Sew buttons on to front, as marked. Turn under the hem allowance twice and stitch. Bind all edges of the pockets and stitch each on to dress front as indicated, stitching along the binding seam.

## TOP

**Materials:** 1.15 m (1¼ yd) of 115 cm (44–45 in)-wide lightweight printed fabric. Elastic sewing thread (for shirring). Matching polyester sewing thread.

**Cutting out:** Enlarge the appropriate pattern pieces, adjusting the size as instructed above, if necessary. Cut out the front and back using the same pattern piece, adding 2 cm (¾ in) seam allowance at the side seams and top edge and 4 cm (1½ in) at the hem. Cut out the strap twice and the in-seam pocket four times with 1 cm (⅜ in) seam allowance all round.

**Sewing:** Clean-finish the top edges and press the seam allowance to the wrong side.
*Shirred panel:* within the area marked on the front and back pieces, work rows of shirring parallel to the top edges and 1 cm (⅜ in) apart. Catch in the seam allowance of the top edge in the uppermost row of

stitching. (To shirr: wind elastic thread on to the bobbin by hand, stretching it slightly and winding with even tension. Thread the top of the machine with polyester sewing thread. Set the machine for the longest straight stitch possible. Stitch from the right side of the fabric, pulling fabric taut as you do so. To distribute gathers evenly, stretch the previous rows as you stitch each successive row. Knot thread ends securely.) When the shirring is complete, stitch a narrow pin tuck over each group of knots on

either side of the panel, on the wrong side of the fabric. (These pleats stay the shirring.)
*Straps:* clean-finish the strap ends and press the seam allowances under. Shirr the strap in the lengthwise direction, stitching close to each edge and twice along the middle.
*Pockets:* clean-finish the straight edge of each pocket piece. With right sides together and straight edges even, stitch each pocket piece between the slit markings on the front and back pieces. Press pocket and side seam allowances

outwards. With right sides together, stitch front to back at side seams, starting from the lower edge and continuing round the pocket curve (leave the pocket opening unstitched). Press pockets towards the front and clip the pocket back seam allowance diagonally into the corners.
*Finishing:* turn the hem up twice and stitch. Stitch straps on as marked.

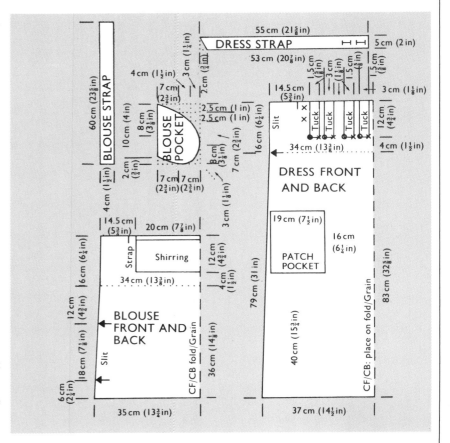

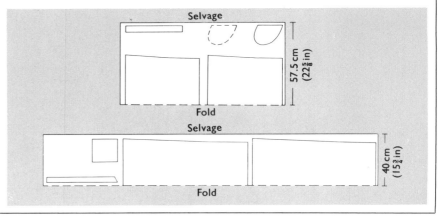

# 29

## Fur Hat

**Size:** To fit an average-sized head: head circumference 56 or 58 cm (22 or 22¾ in)

**Materials:**

*Fur:* take the pattern along when you buy the pelts. Place the pattern on the fur to determine how much you need. Enough fur for six crown sections and one brim strip measuring 4 × 56 (or 58)cm (1½ × 22 [or 22¾]in) is required. *You also need:* 4.2 m (4⅝ yd) of 12 mm (½ in)-wide twill tape or seam binding (extra is needed if you are piecing pelts). 0.3 m (⅜ yd) of 150 cm (58–60 in)-wide lightweight synthetic wadding (batting). 0.3 m (⅜ yd) of 90 cm (36 in)-wide taffeta lining fabric. 0.6 m (¾ yd) of 3 cm (1⅛ in)-wide millinery petersham (grosgrain ribbon). One single-edged razor blade. One size 7 glover's needle. Strong waxed thread. Matching sewing thread (for lining).

**Sewing with fur:** Fur is a material which requires special handling. Follow these tips for best results: fur is sewn by hand, using a spear-pointed glover's needle and strong waxed thread. Always sew from the skin side, piercing only the skin.
*Seams:* to reinforce the fur, sew a strip of twill tape flush along each of the two edges to be joined, using a long hand zigzag stitch. With fur sides facing and edges even, sew the seam using a small, close overhand stitch, catching in the tape as well as the skin. Keep the seam edges pressed flatly together and avoid stretching or pulling the fur as you stitch. Sew only as far into the fur as is necessary to keep it from coming apart. Pick out any hairs caught in the seam with a needle. To finish, stroke the seam edges flat with a scissor handle.

**Cutting out:** Cut out one full crown section and make a pattern piece for the brim.
*Fur:* cut out six crown sections and one brim. On the crown section, add a 5 mm (¼ in) seam allowance to the brim placement line

only. The brim is cut out without seam allowance. To select the best parts, place pattern pieces on the fur side of the pelts. Adjacent pieces must be uniform in colour, pile height and direction of pile (the pile runs clockwise round our hat; see photo on page 72).
(It may be necessary to piece the pelts in order to make up a fur area of sufficient size. In this case, match the fur pieces as described, then sew them together as follows: using strong waxed thread and a glover's needle, join pelts together using an overhand stitch. Sew from the skin side, piercing only the skin. To reinforce the seam, sew twill tape over it, with running stitches along the edges.) Outline each pattern piece with pins, piercing the skin. Remove pattern and turn to the skin side. Using a light-coloured felt-tipped pen, draw the pin-marked pattern outline. Cut the fur from the skin side, using a single-edged razor blade. Cut along the pattern outline, lifting the fur to avoid slicing the hairs. Work over a protected surface. Padding insert: cut out the wadding pieces for the six crown sections and the brim without seam allowance and 1–2 mm (1/16–⅛ in) narrower all round than the fur.
*Lining:* cut out pieces for the six crown sections only, adding 5 mm (¼ in) all round. Millinery petersham (grosgrain ribbon): cut a length to head circumference + 1 cm (⅜ in).

**Sewing:** *Hat assembly:* join the six fur crown sections together, then join the brim strip to form a ring. Do not sew brim to crown yet. Padding insert: machine-overcast the wadding crown sections together, using a zigzag stitch. Stitch each seam from bottom to peak. Slip the insert over the skin side of the hat, so that it fits exactly, with seams aligned. Anchor padding to skin with diagonal tacking (loose stitches made by inserting the needle crosswise at 20–40 mm [¾–1½ in] intervals). Next, join the wadding strip to the skin side of the brim along both edges.

*Brim:* fold under the 5 mm (¼ in) seam allowance on one edge of the brim and secure the fur to the wadding using herringbone stitch (catchstitch). Now sew the ribbed band over the turned-up fur edge using small overhand stitches. Hand-sew the brim on to the crown, with fur sides facing. Reinforce the seam edges with twill tape, as directed. Turn hat right side out.
*Lining:* with right sides facing, machine-stitch the lining crown sections together. Turn under the lower seam allowance and slip lining into hat, with wrong sides together and aligning seams. Slipstitch the lining to the ribbed band.

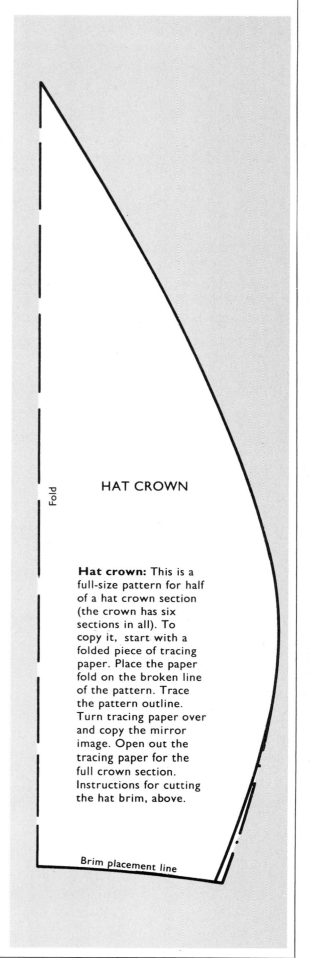

Fold

## HAT CROWN

**Hat crown:** This is a full-size pattern for half of a hat crown section (the crown has six sections in all). To copy it, start with a folded piece of tracing paper. Place the paper fold on the broken line of the pattern. Trace the pattern outline. Turn tracing paper over and copy the mirror image. Open out the tracing paper for the full crown section. Instructions for cutting the hat brim, above.

Brim placement line

# 30

## Sleeveless Sheepskin Jacket for Mother and Child

**Sizes:** *Woman's jacket:* 14–16 (12–14 U.S.)
*Child's jacket:* to fit a 3–4 year old (112–116 cm [44–46 in]) (finished length of jacket: 49 cm [19 in])

**Materials:** *Sheepskin:* take the pattern along when you buy the skins. To determine quantity, place each pattern piece on the suede side, with nap running lengthwise.
*You also need:* one single-edged razor blade. One size 7 glover's needle. Matching button- or heavy-duty thread.

**Cutting out:** Enlarge the pattern pieces. Cut out the front and back pieces twice each, reversing each pattern piece before the second cutting. Cut out the front/back yoke piece once. Add the following seam allowances: 5 mm (⅛ in) to the centre back seam of the left back piece, to the back side seams, to the yoke

placement lines on both back pieces and to the yoke placement line of each front piece. Add a 2 cm (¾ in) seam allowance to all other edges of the woman's jacket and a 1 cm (⅜ in) allowance to the remaining edges of the child's jacket. Cut out each pattern piece separately. Inspect the skin for flaws; avoid these when positioning pattern pieces. Lay each pattern piece on the suede side of the sheepskin with the nap running downwards in the lengthwise direction. Weight or tape the pattern piece in place, then cut it out using a single-edged razor blade. Work on a protected surface.

**Sewing:** *Seams:* sew jacket seams with a spear-pointed glover's needle and strong thread. With suede side up, lap the wide seam allowance over the narrow one, with seamlines matching. Stitch the seamlines together by hand, using a running stitch (diagram 1). Fold the wide seam allowance over, so that the pile side of the sheepskin is face up. Still on the suede side of the

jacket, stitch down the edge of the seam allowance by hand, using a small overcasting stitch (diagram 2).
*Jacket assembly:* sew the centre back seam first. Next, seam the yoke on to the back, matching points **a.** Now seam the front edges of the yoke on to each jacket front, matching points **b.** Sew the side seams. Trim diagonally across the seam allowance on each lower front corner. To finish, turn the seam allowances of the armhole, neck, hem and front edges over, so that the sheepskin pile is showing. Sew these seam allowances down in the same way as for the seams. The trimmed front corners will form a neat mitre when this is done.

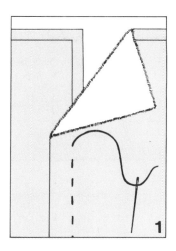

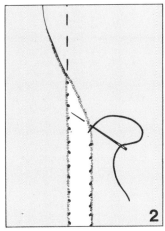

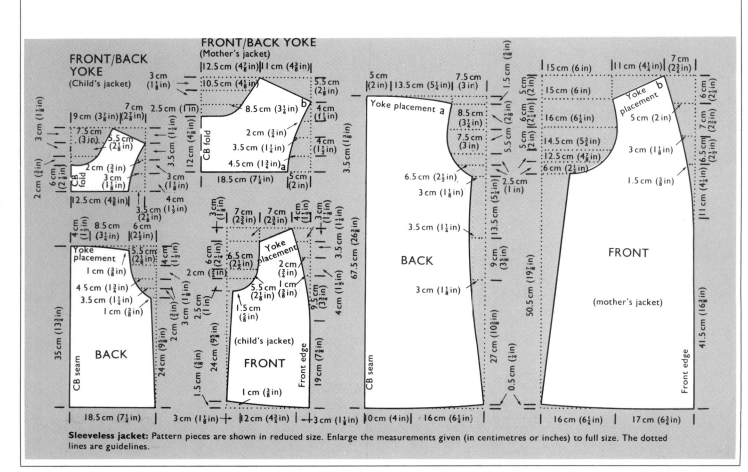

**Sleeveless jacket:** Pattern pieces are shown in reduced size. Enlarge the measurements given (in centimetres or inches) to full size. The dotted lines are guidelines.

# 31

## Canvas Bags

**Finished size:** 32.5 × 45 cm ($12\frac{3}{4} \times 17\frac{3}{4}$ in)

**SUEDE-TRIMMED BAG**

**Materials:** 1.5 m ($1\frac{3}{4}$ yd) of 90 cm (36 in)-wide natural-coloured canvas. Suede remnants. Heavy-duty sewing thread (to match suede). Leather adhesive (rubber solution [rubber cement]). Size 90 (14) sewing machine leather needle (for use on canvas and suede trim).

**Cutting out:** Enlarge the appropriate pattern piece to full size. Cut out the main bag section and the patch pocket once each, the inner section and the handle twice. Add a 2 cm ($\frac{3}{4}$ in) seam allowance to the top edges of the main bag section and a 1 cm ($\frac{3}{8}$ in) seam allowance to all other pieces. Cut out the following pieces from suede, without seam allowance: cut out the bag corner 16 times, the handle end tab four times and the pocket trim once.

**Sewing:** The bag is sewn with contrasting thread (to match suede), for a decorative effect.

*Make the inner section first:* with wrong sides together, stitch the middle 45 cm ($17\frac{3}{4}$ in) of the base seam, leaving 6 cm ($2\frac{1}{4}$ in) unstitched at each end. Tie the thread securely at both ends of this seam. Trim the seam allowances. Clip diagonally into the beginning and end of this seam, then turn the inner section inside out. Now turn the seam allowances along the top edges of the inner section to the outside, then fold the edges under and stitch a narrow hem. Glue the first eight suede corners on to the corner seamlines of the inner section, on the right side of the fabric (see photo, page 74). It will be necessary to trim them to fit. Remember to leave the seam allowances uncovered. Stitch each corner in place, close to the edges. Next, stitch the two interior side seams of the inner section, with right sides together (see diagram: seam).

*Now make the main bag:* fold under the seam allowances on the top edge of the bag, and stitch them 5 cm (2 in) from the top. Glue the remaining eight suede corners on to the corners of the bag front and back (no trimming necessary) and stitch in place.

*Patch pocket:* turn under the seam allowances. Glue on the leather trim and stitch it down. Stitch the pocket on to the bag front so that it is 2 cm ($\frac{3}{4}$ in) from the base fold and 9 cm ($3\frac{1}{2}$ in) from each side.

*Handles:* trim each handle piece diagonally across the corners, then turn under the seam allowances. Press each handle under along the lengthwise folds, so that the long edges meet in the centre, on the back. Stitch the lengthwise edges of each handle close to the edge. Baste the ends of each handle to the bag in the position shown (see diagram). Stitch each handle down with a continuous seam, simultaneously topstitching all round the handle the width of the machine foot. Glue the suede tabs in place, concealing the handle ends; then stitch them down. Next, edgestitch a narrow lengthwise tuck in the middle of the base, from the inside. (A small ridge is formed inside the bag.) With right sides together and points **a** matching, stitch the side seams of the front section to the side seams of one piece of the inner section. Next, stitch the cross seams joining the front half of the bag base to the unstitched (6 cm [$2\frac{1}{4}$ in]) portions of the corresponding inner section seams. Turn the bag on to the other side and join the bag back to the remaining inner section piece in the same way.

*Finishing:* edgestitch the bottom edges and the side seams of the bag front and back from the right side, so that these form ridge-like tucks (see photo on page 74).

**BROWN BAG WITH TOPSTITCHING**

**Materials:** 1.5 m ($1\frac{3}{4}$ yd) of 90 cm (36 in)-wide brown canvas. Heavy duty contrasting sewing thread. Size 110 (18) sewing machine needle (for stitching the heavy canvas).

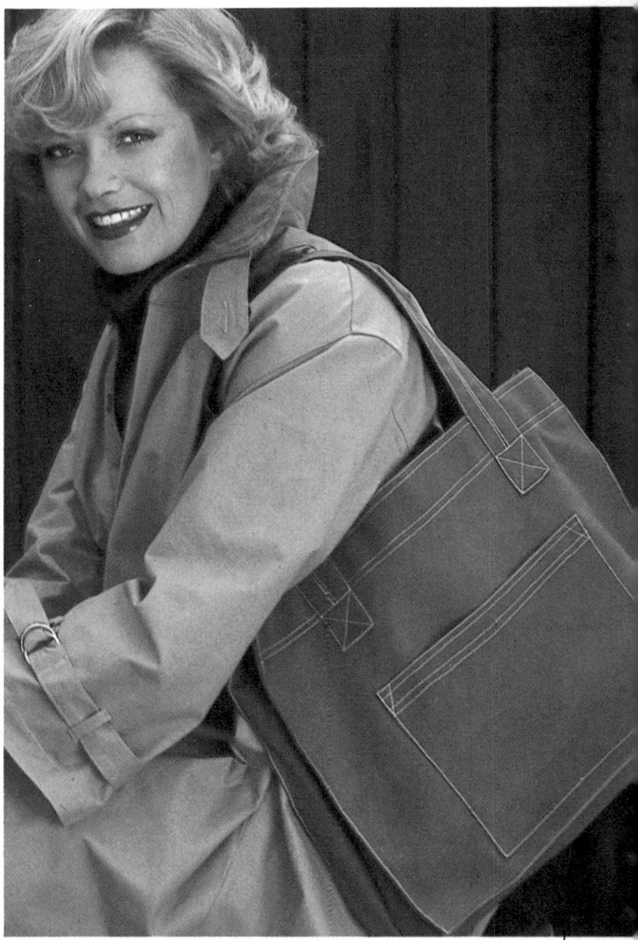

**Cutting out:** Enlarge the appropriate pattern pieces to full size. Cut out the main bag section and the patch pocket once each, the inner section and the handle twice. Add a 2 cm ($\frac{3}{4}$ in) seam allowance to the top edges of the main bag section, a 3 cm ($1\frac{1}{8}$ in) seam allowance to the top edge of the patch pocket and a 1 cm ($\frac{3}{8}$ in) seam allowance elsewhere.

**Sewing:** Assemble the bag according to the instructions for the suede-trimmed bag, omitting the suede trim and adding decorative topstitching as follows: topstitch each part of the bag at a logical stage in the bag's construction, using contrasting thread and referring to the photo on this page. Topstitch twice along the top edge of the bag, first stitching close to the edge and then the width of the machine foot. Repeat 4 cm ($1\frac{1}{2}$ in) below the top edge of the bag. Topstitch another double seam along the top edge of the patch pocket; repeat 2 cm ($\frac{3}{4}$ in) below the pocket edge. Stitch pocket on to bag as directed, stitching a small angled seam (for reinforcement and decoration) at each top pocket corner (see photo above). Stitch a cross (for reinforcement and decoration) on each handle end, through all thicknesses (see photo).

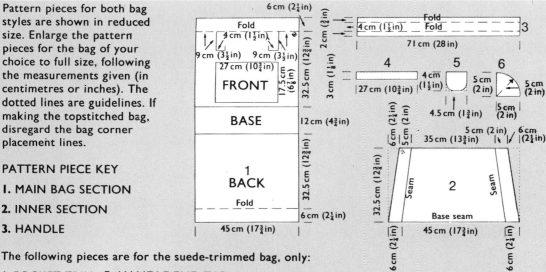

Pattern pieces for both bag styles are shown in reduced size. Enlarge the pattern pieces for the bag of your choice to full size, following the measurements given (in centimetres or inches). The dotted lines are guidelines. If making the topstitched bag, disregard the bag corner placement lines.

PATTERN PIECE KEY

1. MAIN BAG SECTION
2. INNER SECTION
3. HANDLE

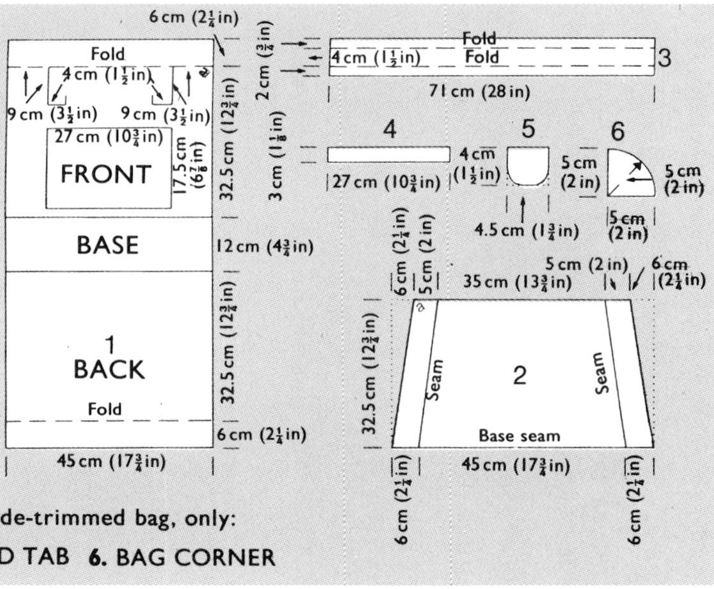


The following pieces are for the suede-trimmed bag, only:

**4.** POCKET TRIM **5.** HANDLE END TAB **6.** BAG CORNER

# 32

## Multi-pocketed Bags

**Finished size:** 30 × 42 cm ($11\frac{3}{4} \times 16\frac{1}{2}$ in)
*Style 1:* Green bag with patch pocket
*Style 2:* Orange bag with zip
*Style 3:* White bag with bound slit pocket

**Materials:** *For each bag, you need:* 1.25 m ($1\frac{3}{8}$ yd) of 115 cm (44–45 in)-wide canvas in the appropriate colour. Size 110 (18) sewing machine needle (for stitching heavy canvas).
*Style 1:* white mercerized cotton thread (size 30).
*Style 2:* 25 cm (10 in) zip, white mercerized cotton thread (size 30).
*Style 3:* 55 cm ($21\frac{1}{2}$ in) of 12 cm ($\frac{1}{2}$ in)-wide blue bias binding, blue mercerized cotton thread (size 30).

**Cutting out:** Enlarge the pattern pieces for the style of your choice. The pattern pieces are numbered for easy identification (see diagram). For each bag, cut out the bag front/back (1) and the handle pieces (8) twice. Cut out the side/base panel (2), the small patch pocket (4) and pocket flap (5), the pen pocket (6) and the mini-pocket (7) once each. For Style 1, cut out a large front patch pocket, using the bag front/back piece (1) as far as line AB. For Styles 2 and 3, cut out a pocket pouch (3) and also mark the position of the zip/binding slit on the bag front.
*Seam allowances:* add a 4 cm ($1\frac{1}{2}$ in) seam allowance to the top edges of the front, back and side/base pieces and to the top edge of the large patch pocket on Style 1. Elsewhere, add a 1 cm ($\frac{3}{8}$ in) seam allowance.

**Sewing:** Clean-finish all the raw edges except those on the handles. Turn under the seam allowances on the top edges (including the Style 1 large patch pocket) and stitch 3 cm ($1\frac{1}{8}$ in) below the edge. To reduce bulk, trim diagonally across the corners of all the pattern piece seam allowances. *Then press under the seam allowances on all the pattern pieces.* (IMPORTANT: Remember that the seam allowances have been folded under as you follow the subsequent instructions.)
*Small front pockets:* on Style 1, these are stitched on top of the large patch pocket (see photo, page 75); on Styles 2 and 3 these are stitched directly on to the bag front. Accordion-pleat the sides of the small patch pocket (4), then edgestitch the uppermost folds (see photo). Pin this pocket in place, matching points **d**. Stitch on the pocket sides, catching in only the bottom layer of pocket fabric (see photo). Then stitch across the lower edge of the pocket, sewing over the side folds.
*Pocket flap* (5): fold flap in half lengthwise, with wrong sides together, then topstitch round the folded seam allowance edges as shown (see photo). Next, stitch the lengthwise fold of the flap in place, 5 mm ($\frac{1}{4}$ in) above the small patch pocket (see photo).
*Double pen pocket* (6): topstitch 8 mm ($\frac{5}{16}$ in) below the top edge, then pin pocket in place, matching point **e**. Stitch down the pen pocket, making a small pinch pleat in the centre of each of the two pen compartments, on the bottom edge (see photo). Then stitch the centre dividing line.
*Mini-pocket* (7): topstitch 8 mm ($\frac{5}{16}$ in) below the top edge and stitch it in place, matching point **f**.
*Handles:* fold each handle in half lengthwise, with wrong sides together, and topstitch all round as shown. Stitch one handle on to the bag front and the other one on to the bag back, matching points **g** and **h** and stitching a cross (for decoration and reinforcement) at each handle end (stitch in the direction of the arrows).

**FINISHING:**

**Style 1:** The large patch pocket runs across the full width of the bag front. Baste the pocket to the bag front with wrong side of pocket to right side of bag and with raw edges even. Press under the seam allowances once more and treat as a single layer of fabric.
*Finishing:* with wrong sides together, pin the side/base panel between the bag front and back pieces, matching points **c**; baste in place. Stitch the side and base seams from the right side of the fabric, through all thicknesses (see photo). Pivot the sewing machine needle at each base corner.

**Style 2:** Slash open the centre portion of the zip slit, leaving about 1 cm ($\frac{3}{8}$ in) uncut at each end; then cut diagonally into the corners. Turn under the seam allowances and centre the zip beneath the opening, so that it is visible. Stitch the zip in place. On the wrong side of the bag, stitch the upper and lower edges of the pocket pouch on to the corresponding seam allowances above and below the zip. Stitch the side seams of the pocket pouch together.
*Finishing:* stitch the side/base panel between the bag front and back pieces, following the Style 1 instructions.

**Style 3:** Bound slit pocket: cut the bias binding into two 27.5 cm ($10\frac{3}{4}$ in) strips. Open out one folded edge of each strip. With right sides together, baste a binding strip on either side of the marked slit line, with the long raw edges of the binding meeting at the centre slit. On the wrong side of the bag front, pin the lower edge of the pocket pouch piece to the marked slit line. Stitch along each binding foldline, as far as the slit end markings. Slash open the centre portion of the slit, leaving about 1 cm ($\frac{3}{8}$ in) uncut at either end; then cut diagonally into the corners. Turn the binding to the inside and slipstitch the remaining folded edge of each binding strip to a seamline. Carefully stitch the cross seams of the slit. On the wrong side of the bag, sew the upper edge of the pocket pouch to the upper edge of the top binding strip, by hand. Stitch the side seams of the pocket pouch together, catching in the slit cross seams.
*Finishing:* stitch the side/base panel between the bag front and back pieces, following the Style 1 instructions.

**All styles:** To reinforce the base of the bag, insert a piece of card (cardboard) cut to size and covered with fabric.

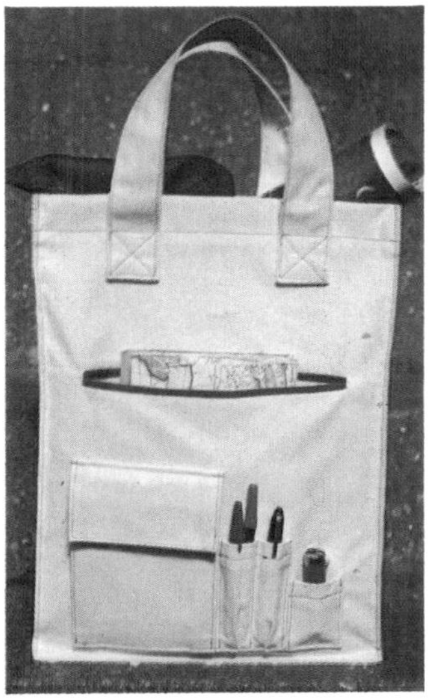

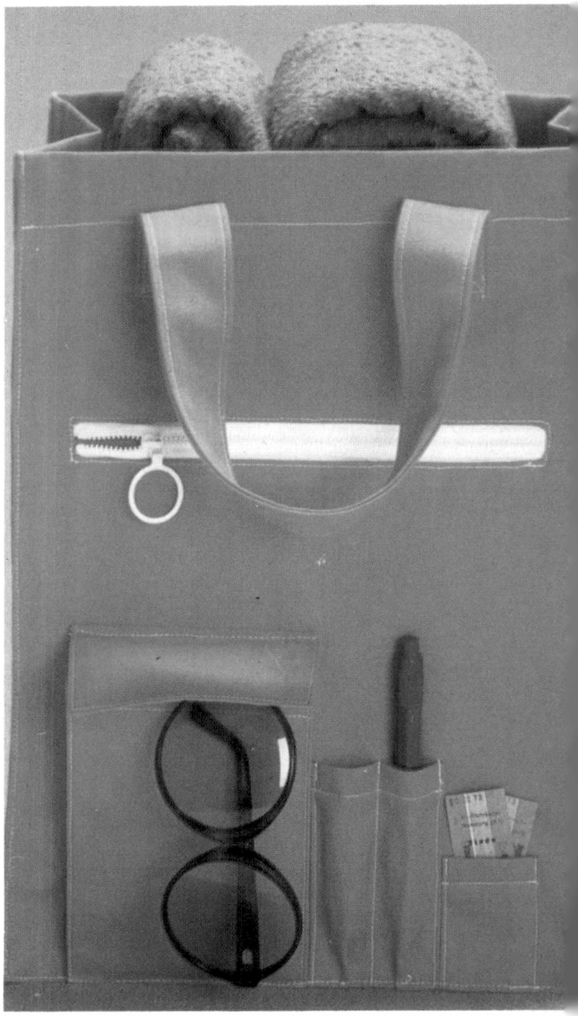

**Pattern Piece Key**

1. **BAG FRONT/BACK PIECE:** The back piece for all three styles is the same. Front: Style 1: cut out once completely and a second time only as far as line AB (for the large patch pocket). Styles 2 and 3: cut out the front piece once, marking the position of the zip/ binding slit.

2. **SIDE/BASE PANEL** (one piece)

3. **POCKET POUCH** (for Styles 2 and 3)

4. **SMALL PATCH POCKET** (with side folds)

5. **POCKET FLAP** (for small patch pocket)

6. **DOUBLE PEN POCKET** (with dividing stitching line)

7. **MINI-POCKET**

8. **HANDLE**

**3**

24.5 cm (9¾ in)

Fold

24.5 cm (9¾ in)

**4**

Pleat

Pleat

17 cm (6¾ in)

12 cm (4¾ in)

2 cm (¾ in) 2 cm (¾ in) 2 cm (¾ in) 2 cm (¾ in)

d d

**5**

Fold

7 cm (2¾ in)

12.5 cm (4⅞ in)

**7**

f

6.5 cm (2½ in)

5 cm (2 in)

**6**

Stitching line

11.5 cm (4½ in)

e

4 cm (1½ in) 4 cm (1½ in)

7 cm (2¾ in)

5 cm (2 in)

g

h

Handle placement

14.5 cm (5¾ in)

2.75 cm (1⅛ in)

24.5 cm (9¾ in)

2.75 cm (1⅛ in)

A

1.2 cm (½ in)

Zip/Bias binding

B

**1**

2.75 cm (1⅛ in)

2.75 cm (1⅛ in)

2.75 cm (1⅛ in)

d

e

f

c

27.5 cm (10¾ in)

30 cm (11¾ in)

50 cm (19¾ in)

Fold

**8**

g

h

4 cm (1½ in)

**How to enlarge the bag patterns:** Pattern pieces for all three styles are given in reduced size. Enlarge the measurements given (in centimetres or inches) to full size. Take care to copy the correct pattern pieces for the style of your choice.

42 cm (16½ in)

15 cm (6 in)

c

**2**

Side

Bag base

Fold

16 cm (6¼ in)

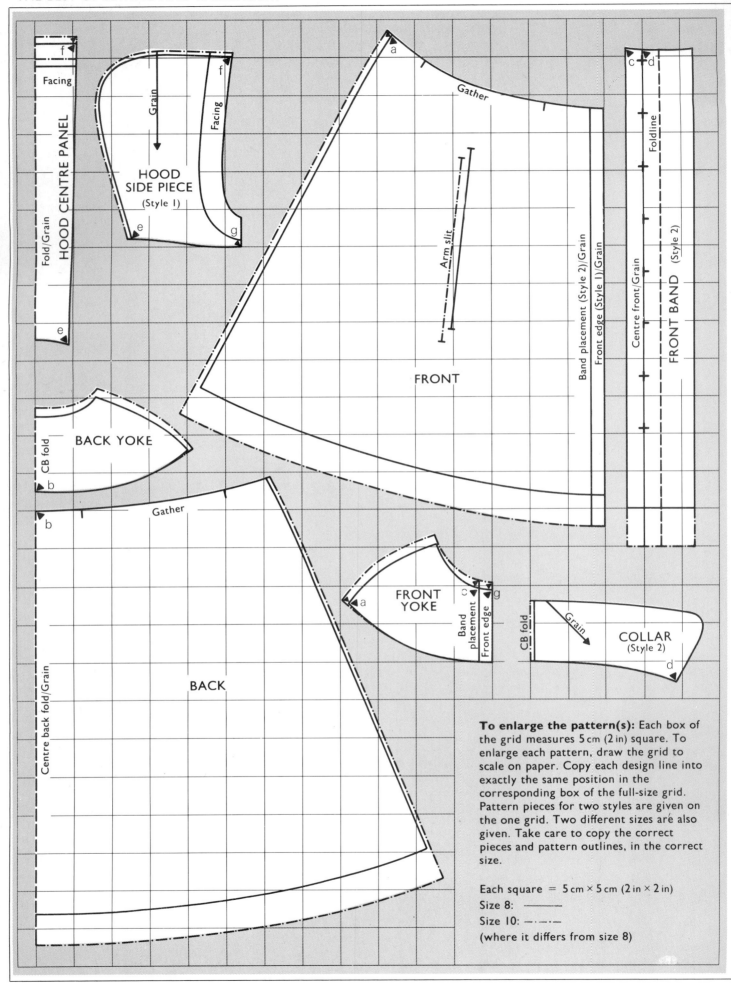

Facing

f

HOOD CENTRE PANEL

Fold/Grain

e

HOOD
SIDE PIECE
(Style 1)

Grain

Facing

f

e

g

a

Gather

Arm slit

FRONT

Band placement (Style 2)/Grain

Front edge (Style 1)/Grain

Centre front/Grain

Foldline

FRONT BAND (Style 2)

c d

BACK YOKE

CB fold

b

b

Gather

a

FRONT
YOKE

Band placement

Front edge

c

g

CB fold

Grain

COLLAR
(Style 2)

d

BACK

Centre back fold fold/Grain

**To enlarge the pattern(s):** Each box of the grid measures 5 cm (2 in) square. To enlarge each pattern, draw the grid to scale on paper. Copy each design line into exactly the same position in the corresponding box of the full-size grid. Pattern pieces for two styles are given on the one grid. Two different sizes are also given. Take care to copy the correct pieces and pattern outlines, in the correct size.

Each square = 5 cm × 5 cm (2 in × 2 in)

Size 8: ———————

Size 10: —·—·—·—

(where it differs from size 8)

# 33

## Girl's Raincapes

**Sizes:** To fit an 8- or 10-year-old child (height: 128 or 140 cm [50½ or 55 in])

**Style 1**
(blue cape with hood and zip)

**Materials:** Water-repellent poplin or gaberdine:
*Size 8:* 1.2 m (1⅜ yd) of 150 cm (58–60 in)-wide fabric.
*Size 10:* 1.3 m (1½ yd) of 150 cm (58–60 in)-wide fabric.
*You also need:* one 60 cm (24 in) zip and two 25 cm (10 in) zips. 1.1 m (1¼ yd) of cotton cord. Matching sewing thread.

**Cutting out:** Enlarge the Style 1 pattern pieces. Cut out the cape back, the back yoke and the hood centre panel once each, on the fold. Cut out the cape front, the front yoke and the hood side section twice each. Using the pattern outlines as your guide, draw a 3 cm (1⅛ in)-wide one-piece facing for the hood front (remember to include the width of the centre panel).
*Seam allowances:* add 3 cm (1⅛ in) to each front edge, 2 cm (¾ in) to the side seams and 1 cm (⅜ in) elsewhere. For the arm slit facings, cut out two fabric strips, each measuring 6 × 28 cm (2¼ × 11 in), seam allowance included. Mark the position of each arm slit on the cape fronts, but do not cut them out.

**Sewing:** Gather the cape fronts and back between the markings, so that each piece fits the corresponding yoke edge (for how to gather, see Summer dress with place mat yoke, page 116). With right sides facing and raw edges even, stitch each cape front to a front yoke, matching points **a** and distributing gathers evenly. Stitch the cape back on to the back yoke in the same manner, but

matching point **b**. Press seam allowances towards each yoke and clean-finish them together. Topstitch each yoke through all thicknesses, 8 mm (5/16 in) above the seamline.
*Arm slits:* with right sides together, centre each slit facing strip over a marked slit line and baste in place. Stitch a rectangular window 1 cm (⅜ in) wide round each slit, pivoting the machine needle at the corners. Cut the centre slit through both fabric layers, then clip diagonally into each corner. Turn each facing to the inside; press. Clean-finish the facing edges. Centre a zip beneath each slit opening and stitch in place. Next, stitch the side seams, with right sides together. Clean-finish them separately and press open.
*Hood:* with right sides facing, stitch hood centre panel to the side sections along seamlines e–f. Finish the seam allowances together. Press under the short seam allowances on the lower front edges of the hood. Press under the short ends of the hood facing. With right sides together, stitch the facing on to the front edge of the hood, then clean-finish the outer edge of the facing. With right sides together and raw edges even, stitch hood on to the neck edge of the cape, matching points **g**. Clean-finish the hood seam allowances together, press them towards the cape and edgestitch through all thicknesses, just below the seamline. To form a drawstring casing, topstitch along the hood front 8 mm (5/16 in) from the edge.
*Finishing:* fold the hem under twice and stitch. Press under the seam allowances on the front edges and insert the zip underneath, with a centred application. To finish, thread the cord through the hood casing, then knot each end to prevent fraying.

STYLE 2
(yellow cape with Peter Pan collar and snap fasteners)

**Materials:** Water-repellent poplin or gaberdine:
*Size 8:* 1.4 m (1⅝ yd) of 150 cm (58–60 in)-wide fabric.
*Size 10:* 1.5 m (1¾ yd) of 150 cm (58–60 in)-wide fabric.
*You also need:* eight snap fasteners and insertion tool. Matching enamel paint (optional). Matching sewing thread.

**Cutting out:** Enlarge the Style 2 pattern pieces. Cut out the cape back and the back yoke once each, on the fold. Cut out the cape front, the front yoke and the front band twice each. Cut the collar out twice, on a fold on the bias.
*Seam allowances:* add a 2 cm (¾ in) seam allowance to the side seams and hem and a 1 cm (⅜ in) seam allowance elsewhere. For the arm slit binding, cut out four strips, each measuring 4 × 28 cm (1½ × 11 in), seam allowance included. Mark the position of each arm slit on the cape front, but do not cut them out.

**Sewing:** Gather, join and topstitch the cape front and back sections to the front and back yoke sections, same as for Style 1. With wrong sides together, fold each front band in half lengthwise and press. With right sides together and long edges even, stitch one side of a front band on to each cape front edge, matching points **c**. Clean-finish the remaining long raw edge of each band.
*Collar:* stitch the collar pieces together, with right sides together and edges even. Turn the collar right side out. Staystitch the neck edge of the cape (including front bands) along the seamline. With

right sides together, stitch one collar layer on to the neck edge of the cape, matching points **d**. Fold the top portion of each front band on to the right side along the foldline, sandwiching the collar end in between. Stitch the short seams at each band top, from point **d** to the band fold, taking care not to catch in the collar. Clip all layers of the seam allowances at point **d** to the stitching. Grade the seam allowances along the seamed collar edge. Turn under the free collar edge and the neck edge seam allowances, including the unstitched part of each band top. Slipstitch the collar to the neck edge seamline. Topstitch the collar 8 mm (5/16 in) from the edge. With right sides together, stitch across the hem edge of each front band. Turn each band under again to the wrong side and topstitch 8 mm (5/16 in) from the edge.
*Arm slits:* press each binding strip in half lengthwise, with wrong sides together. Open out each strip. With right sides together baste one strip on either side of the marked arm slit line, with the long raw edge of each strip on the line. Stitch along each binding foldline, as far as the slit end markings. Cut each slit, then cut diagonally into the corners. Fold the binding under, press and stitch the cross seams. Clean-finish the raw edges, then topstitch round each slit, just outside the seamlines and through all thicknesses.
*Finishing:* punch the snap fasteners into the front bands as marked, following the manufacturer's instructions. If you wish, paint them with enamel paint in a colour to match the cape.

# 34

## Women's Raincapes

**Size:** One size fits 12–16 (10–14 u.s.)

**Materials:** Oilcloth or plasticized fabric (coated on the outside, textile on the inside):
*Style 1* (blue cape with zip): 2.5 m (2¾ yd) of 150 cm (58–60 in)-wide fabric. One 90 cm (36 in) zip. Four medium-sized snap fasteners and insertion tool. Matching sewing thread.
*Style 2* (yellow cape with snap fasteners): 2.6 cm (2⅞ yd) of 150 cm (58–60 in)-wide fabric. Ten medium-sized snap fasteners and insertion tool. Matching sewing thread.

**Cutting out** (both styles): Pins leave permanent holes in coated fabric, so either weight or tape pattern pieces in place when cutting them out. Enlarge the pattern pieces for the style of your choice. Following the pattern layout, cut the following pieces from a single layer of fabric: cut out two cape fronts, one hood back and one hood side section. Cut out one cape back with a snap fastener underlap at either side.
*Seam allowances:* add 2 cm (¾ in) to the front edge of the hood, 1 cm (⅜ in) elsewhere. If you wish, the outer edges of the cape can be cut out without seam allowance and left unfinished.

**Sewing** (both styles): Coated fabrics require a few special sewing techniques: the coated side tends to stick beneath the sewing machine foot. To prevent this, stitch through sheets of tissue paper whenever you sew with the shiny side outwards. Afterwards, the tissue paper tears away easily. To avoid making holes, use paper clips or tape to hold pieces together and secure folded seam allowances when you are sewing. Pins can be used, but only within seam allowances. It is best to avoid ironing, since melting can occur. If absolutely necessary, press with a warm dry iron, on the

*Continued overleaf*

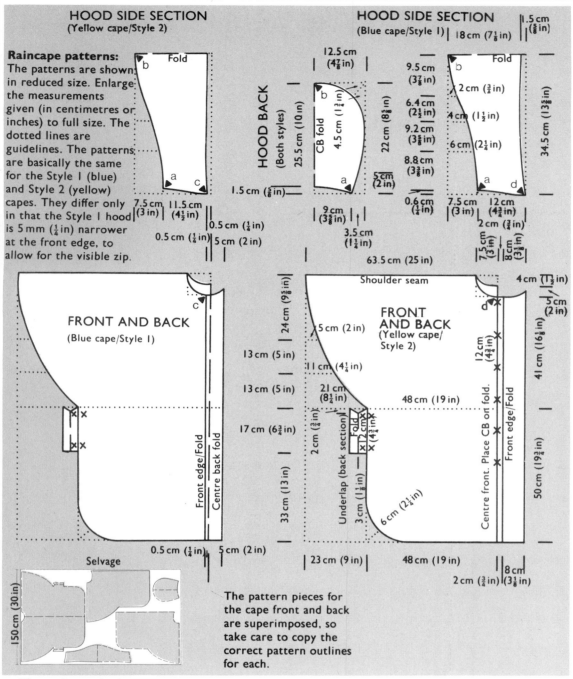

### HOOD SIDE SECTION
(Yellow cape/Style 2)

**Raincape patterns:**
The patterns are shown
in reduced size. Enlarge
the measurements
given (in centimetres or
inches) to full size. The
dotted lines are
guidelines. The patterns
are basically the same
for the Style 1 (blue)
and Style 2 (yellow)
capes. They differ only
in that the Style 1 hood
is 5 mm (1/4 in) narrower
at the front edge, to
allow for the visible zip.

Fold — b

7.5 cm (3 in)    11.5 cm (4 1/2 in)
0.5 cm (1/4 in)    0.5 cm (1/2 in)    5 cm (2 in)

### HOOD SIDE SECTION
(Blue cape/Style 1)    18 cm (7 1/2 in)    1.5 cm (5/8 in)

HOOD BACK (Both styles)    25.5 cm (10 in)

12.5 cm (4 7/8 in)
CB fold    4.5 cm (1 3/4 in)
22 cm (8 5/8 in)
1.5 cm (5/8 in)
9 cm (3 5/8 in)
3.5 cm (1 1/2 in)
5 cm (2 in)
63.5 cm (25 in)

9.5 cm (3 3/8 in)
6.4 cm (2 1/2 in)
9.2 cm (3 5/8 in)
8.8 cm (3 3/8 in)
0.6 cm (1/4 in)
7.5 cm (3 in)    12 cm (4 1/2 in)
2 cm (3/4 in)
7.5 cm (3 in)    8 cm (3 1/8 in)

Fold — b
2 cm (3/4 in)
4 cm (1 1/2 in)
6 cm (2 1/4 in)
34.5 cm (13 5/8 in)

### FRONT AND BACK
(Blue cape/Style 1)

24 cm (9 5/8 in)
5 cm (2 in)
13 cm (5 in)
13 cm (5 in)
17 cm (6 3/4 in)
33 cm (13 in)

Front edge/Fold    Centre back fold

0.5 cm (1/4 in)    5 cm (2 in)

### FRONT AND BACK
(Yellow cape/Style 2)

Shoulder seam    4 cm (1 1/2 in)
5 cm (2 in)
11 cm (4 1/4 in)
21 cm (8 1/4 in)
48 cm (19 in)
12 cm (4 3/4 in)
41 cm (16 1/8 in)
Underlap (back section)
2 cm (3/4 in)    Fold    12 cm (4 3/4 in)
3 cm (1 in)
6 cm (2 1/4 in)
Centre front. Place CB on fold    Front edge/Fold
50 cm (19 5/8 in)

23 cm (9 in)    48 cm (19 in)
2 cm (3/4 in)    8 cm (3 1/8 in)

Selvage

150 cm (30 in)

**Cutting layout for both styles.**

The pattern pieces for
the cape front and back
are superimposed, so
take care to copy the
correct pattern outlines
for each.

wrong side. Iron a test
scrap first.
*Cape assembly:* Hood: with
right sides facing, stitch the
hood sections together,
matching points **a** and **b**.
Finger-press the seam
allowances towards the
front and topstitch the
width of the machine foot,
through all thicknesses.
Fold the hood front seam
allowance to the inside;
topstitch the edge the width
of the machine foot. On the
cape back, fold each snap
fastener underlap in half
lengthwise, with right sides
together. Stitch the short
seams on each underlap,
then clip the seam

allowances to the stitching
at the edges nearest the
cape. Turn the underlaps
right side out. With right
sides together, stitch back
to fronts at the shoulder
seams. Finger-press the
seam allowances towards
the cape front and topstitch
the width of the machine
foot, through all
thicknesses. Turn under the
seam allowances on the
hem, the sides and the
lower sleeve edges and
stitch them down. Pull the
curved edges to ease them
while sewing.
*Style 1* (blue cape with zip):
staystitch the neck edge of
the cape along the seamline

(including the self-facings).
With right sides together,
stitch the hood on to the
neck edge, matching points
**c**. Clip the neck edge to the
stitching at point **c**. Fold
under the top edge of
each front facing, clipping
the curve. Finger-press the
neck/hood seam
downwards, then fold the
top of each front facing to
the inside, sandwiching the
front edges of the hood in
between. Edgestitch the
neck edge through all
thicknesses, just below the
seamline. Turn each front
facing to the inside along
its full length. Apply the zip
under the front edges,

inserting it so that it is
visible and turning under
top edges of the zip tape.
*Style 2* (yellow cape with
snap fasteners): apply the
hood to the neck edge in
the same manner as for
Style 1, only matching
hood and then clipping the
neck edge at points **d**. Turn
each front facing to the
inside along its full length,
then topstitch each front
edge the width of the
machine foot.
*Both capes:* punch in the
snap fasteners at the
marked positions, following
maker's instructions. (On
Style 2, lap the right front
over the left front.)

## 35

### Reversible Patchwork/ Crochet Bedspread plus Matching Cushion Cover

**CUSHION COVER**

**Size:** approx. 60 × 60 cm
(23 1/2 × 23 1/2 in)

**Materials:** Assorted
flowered cotton fabric
remnants, enough for
twenty-five 10 × 10 cm
(4 × 4 in) squares. 0.7 m
(7/8 yd) of 90 cm (36 in)-wide
white cotton fabric (for
cushion underside). 0.4 m
(1/2 yd) of 82 cm (32 in)-wide
sew-in non-woven
interfacing, a chenille
needle size 24, a tapestry
needle size 18, a Millwards
crochet hook size 4.50 mm
(size G/U.S.), matching
sewing thread, a
50 × 50 cm (20 × 20 in)
square cushion pad
(without gusset). We used
Twilleys Lyscordet no. 5
cotton for stitching round
each square and Twilleys
Pegasus for the crochet.
The amount required will
vary according to the size.
NOTE: U.S. crochet terms
are given in parentheses.

**Instructions:** *Cushion top:*
cut out 25 10 × 10 cm
(4 × 4 in) squares from the
flowered fabric remnants.
Cut the interfacing into 25
8 × 8 cm (3 1/8 × 3 1/8 in)
squares. Centre an
interfacing square on the
wrong side of each fabric
square, then fold under and
baste down the edges of
each fabric square (photo
No. 1). Make sure that the
corners are formed
correctly and that the
fabric lies flat. Using a
chenille needle and
Lyscordet, work blanket
stitch around each square,
spacing the stitches 5 mm
(1/4 in) apart (photo No. 2).
Make sure each side has
the same number of
stitches. Remove basting.
Mark the four corner
stitches.
*Crochet edging 1st rnd:* using
Pegasus and with right side
facing attach yarn to any
stitch along side. 1 dc (1
sc) into same place as join,
* 1 dc (1 sc) into each
stitch along side until
marked stitch is reached (1
dc [1 sc], 1 ch, 1 dc [1 sc])

into marked stitch; repeat from * ending with 1 dc (1 sc) into each stitch, 1 dc (1 sc) into first dc (sc).
*2nd rnd:* * 1 dc (1 sc) into each dc (sc) (1 dc [1 sc], 1 ch, 1 dc [1 sc]) into 1 ch sp at corner; repeat from * ending with 1 dc (1 sc) into each dc (sc), 1 ss (sl st) into first dc (sc). Fasten off. Crochet all 25 squares in this way. Arrange the completed squares in five rows of five, placing the various patterned fabrics in a pleasing order. Join the squares together side-to-side to form each row, then join the rows together lengthwise. Overcast the squares together edge-to-edge, using a tapestry needle threaded with Lyscordet cotton.
*Crochet border 1st rnd:* using Pegasus and with right side facing attach yarn to 1 ch sp at any corner, 3 ch, ** * 1 tr (1 dc) into each sp between dc (sc) along side of square, 1 tr (1 dc) into 1 ch sp before join, 1 tr (1 dc) into 1 ch sp after join on next square; repeat from * until last square of side is reached; end with 1 tr (1 dc) into each sp between dc (sc) (2 tr [2 dc], 1 ch, 2 tr [2 dc]) into corner 1 ch sp,** repeat from ** to ** 3 times more omitting 1 tr (1 dc) at end of last repeat, 1 ss into 3rd of 3 ch.
*2nd rnd:* 1 ss (sl st) into next sp between tr (dc), 3 ch, * 1 tr (1 dc) into each sp between tr (dc) (2 tr [2 dc], 1 ch, 2 tr [2 dc]) into corner 1 ch; repeat from * 3 times more ending with 1 ss (sl st) into 3rd of 3 ch. Repeat 2nd round 3 times more. Fasten off.
*Finishing:* cut a square of white cotton fabric to the dimensions of the cushion top minus the border, then add 1 cm ($\frac{3}{8}$ in) seam allowance all round. Press under the seam allowances. With wrong sides together, slipstitch the cushion underside to the cushion top, leaving the fourth side open. Insert the cushion pad and slipstitch the opening shut.

**REVERSIBLE BEDSPREAD**

**Size:** To fit a single bed (approx. 150 × 250 cm [60 × 99 in])

**Materials:** Assorted cotton fabric remnants in floral and geometric prints, enough for one-hundred and eighty-seven 12 × 12 cm ($4\frac{3}{4} × 4\frac{3}{4}$ in) squares of each. 4.7 m ($5\frac{1}{4}$ yd) of 82 cm (32 in)-wide sew-in non-woven interfacing. A chenille needle size 24, a tapestry needle size 18, a Millwards crochet hook size 4.50 mm (size 7/U.S.), matching sewing thread. We used Twilleys Lyscordet no. 5 cotton for stitching round each square and Twilley's Pegasus for the crochet. The amount required will vary according to the size. NOTE: U.S. crochet terms are given in parentheses.

**Instructions:** Make the squares as shown in photos 1–4. Cut out 187 12 × 12 cm ($4\frac{3}{4} × 4\frac{3}{4}$ in) squares from the floral fabrics and the same number from the geometric fabrics. Cut out 374 10 × 10 cm (4 × 4 in) interfacing squares. Centre an interfacing square on the wrong side of each fabric square, then fold under and baste down the edges of the fabric square (photo 1). Make sure that the corners are formed correctly and that the fabric lies flat. With wrong sides facing, back each floral square with a geometric square; baste them together with edges even. Using a chenille needle and strong embroidery thread, work blanket stitch all round each square, spacing the stitches 5 mm ($\frac{1}{4}$ in) apart (photo 2). Make sure each side has the same no. of stitches. Remove basting. Mark the four corner stitches. *Crochet edging 1st rnd:* using Pegasus and with right side facing attach yarn to any stitch along side, 3 ch, * 1 tr (1 dc) into each stitch until marked stitch is reached (1 tr [1 dc]. 1 ch, 1 tr [1 dc])into marked stitch; repeat from * 3 times more ending with 1 tr (1 dc) into each stitch, 1 ss (sl st) into 3rd of 3 ch.
*2nd rnd:* 1 ss (sl st) into next sp, 3 ch, * 1 tr (1 dc) into each sp between tr (dc) until 1 ch sp is reached (2 tr [2 dc], 1 ch, 2 tr [2 dc]) into 1 ch sp; repeat from * 3 times more ending with 1 tr (1 dc) into each sp between tr (dc), 1 ss into

3rd of 3 ch. Fasten off. (See photo 3). Crochet all 187 squares in this way. Place the completed squares, floral side up, in 17 rows of 11, making a pleasing arrangement of the various patterned fabrics. (The geometric side will have a random order.) Join the squares together side-to-side to form each row, then join the rows together lengthwise. Overcast the squares together edge-to-edge, using a tapestry needle threaded with crochet cotton (photo 4).
*Crochet border 1st rnd:* using Pegasus and with right side facing attach yarn to 1 ch sp at any corner, 3 ch, ** * 1 tr (1 dc) into each sp between tr along side of square, 1 tr (1 dc) into 1 ch sp before join, 1 tr (1 dc) into 1 ch sp after join on next square; repeat from * until last square of side is reached, end with with 1 tr (1 dc) into each sp between tr (dc) (2 tr [2 dc], 1 ch, 2 tr [2 dc]) into corner 1 ch sp,** rep from ** to ** 3 times more omitting 1 tr (1 dc) at end of last repeat, 1 ss (sl st) into 3rd of 3 ch.
*2nd rnd:* 1 ss (sl st) into next sp between tr (dc), 3 ch, * 1 tr (1 dc) into each sp between tr (dc) (2 tr [2 dc], 1 ch, 2 tr [2 dc]) into corner 1 ch sp; repeat from * 3 times more ending with 1 ss (sl st) into 3rd of 3 ch. Fasten off.

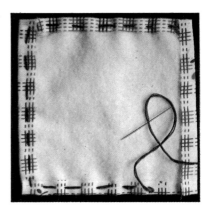

1

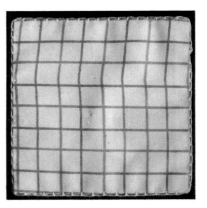

2

3

4

## Wraparound Aprons for Girls: Pretty Cover-ups for Indoors or Out

You know from experience how quickly children forget what's going on around them when they are playing; that's when they get dirty. One minute your daughter is clean and tidy, the next thing you know, she's upset milk down her sweater or soiled her skirt by sitting on the pavement. Minor mishaps like these always seem to happen just when you're about to go out visiting or shopping. But such times are over because now these smock-style aprons protect your child's clothes.

These little aprons are ideal for playing in the house or garden. They're sweet and feminine, with butterfly sleeves and a bow in back. Best of all, the front and back of each apron overlap to provide complete coverage. The three small photos on the left-hand page show you how to put the apron on: first tie the back apron-strings at the front (far left), then tie the front apron-strings at the back (lower left).

Patterns are given for three different sizes, each with lots of growing space. Five styles are shown, each differing only in minor details (large or small kangaroo or patch pockets, self-fabric or commercial bias binding). Make them up in colourful cotton, wipe-clean plasticized fabric or washable velveteen and each will have a character all its own.

Instructions for these aprons are on pages 98 and 99.

## A Keepsake and a Party-make: Sleepyhead Doll and Star-shaped Tablecloth

The charming little baby doll on the left-hand page will be cherished by children and admired by grown-ups. Who can resist such a cuddly creation swaddled in a lace-trimmed gown? Attention to detail makes it special.

The star-shaped satin tablecloth adds a festive touch to any gathering. You can make it up at the last minute because there's practically no sewing involved. The silver lamé ribbon is simply ironed on using adhesive web. We also tell you how to make matching place mats. Your guests will be dazzled.

Instructions for the doll and tablecloth/ place at set are on pages 99, 100, 101 and 102.

**38**

## Children's Costumes for Party- or Playtime

Children enjoy dressing up at playschool and at home; and of course, there's the occasional fancy dress (costume) party which crops up. Play-acting helps to develop young imaginations and it's so much more fun for children if they're dressed for the part. Buying costumes is expensive, though, so what's the solution? The four simple costumes on these pages show how a drop of ingenuity can produce fantastic results without much trouble.

The seemingly elaborate fringed 'buckskin' costumes of the Indian chief and squaw can be whipped up in a jiffy out of felt, braid and a few feathers. Fabric glue speeds up the making. The squaw's sandals are a cleverly disguised pair of flip-flops, with felt thonging criss-crossed up the legs.

We devised the pirate and clown get-ups from cast-off clothing, with just a few alterations and a generous sprinkling of patches sewn on.

Instructions for the costumes are on pages 102, 103 and 104.

**42**

## Quick-sew Jackets for Children

Every mum likes to dress her children in style, but it costs a fortune to outfit a growing child. When it comes to outerwear, the outlay is especially steep. The alternative is to take out the sewing machine, but few mothers have as much time as they'd like to spare.

We've designed the windcheaters (windbreakers) and the furry jacket on these pages using clever short-cuts which will please the busy mum and the inexperienced sewer alike. Put aside any apprehensions you may have about making up an outer garment. These designs are truly easy to sew.

The fuzzy pile jacket is warm, cuddly and comfortable to wear. The hook and eye fastenings are easy for children to manage. There's a stand-up collar and ample patch pockets, too.

The jacket is a straight-sew project which can easily be completed in one sitting. All the edges are bound with knitted braid, so there are no facings to contend with.

There are no darts either.

The hooded windcheaters have a centre front seam which eliminates some tricky stitching at the neck opening. The seam is artfully concealed by a whimsical kangaroo pocket that children will adore. There's elastic at the wrists and side slits to give plenty of room to grow.

Instructions for the jackets are on pages 104, 105 and 106.

# 36

## Wraparound Aprons for Girls

**Sizes:** To fit a child aged:
5/6 (height: 110–116 cm [42–46 in])
7/8 (height; 122–128 cm [48–51 in])
9/10 (height: 134–140 cm [53–55 in])

**General instructions**
Measure the height of your child to determine which size you should make. Apron width is adjusted by using the tiebands.

**How to enlarge the patterns:** Pattern pieces for the aprons are shown in reduced size. All three sizes of the one-piece apron body are superimposed on the one grid. The front and back necklines are shown together on each apron body piece. Pocket pieces are given for three different apron styles. Take care to copy the correct pieces and pattern outlines, in the correct size.
Each box of the grid measures 3.5 cm (1¼ in)

square. To enlarge each pattern, draw the grid to scale on paper. Copy each design line into exactly the same position in the corresponding box of the full size grid.

**Cutting out:** *All styles:* one quarter of the full apron body pattern is given, as are one half of the Style 1,

3 and 4 pocket pieces. Enlarge the appropriate pieces to full size, then cut them out double from paper by placing the CF/CB line on a fold. One half of the apron body and full pocket pieces result.
*Apron body:* cut this from a double layer of fabric with the fold running crosswise. Place the shoulder lines of

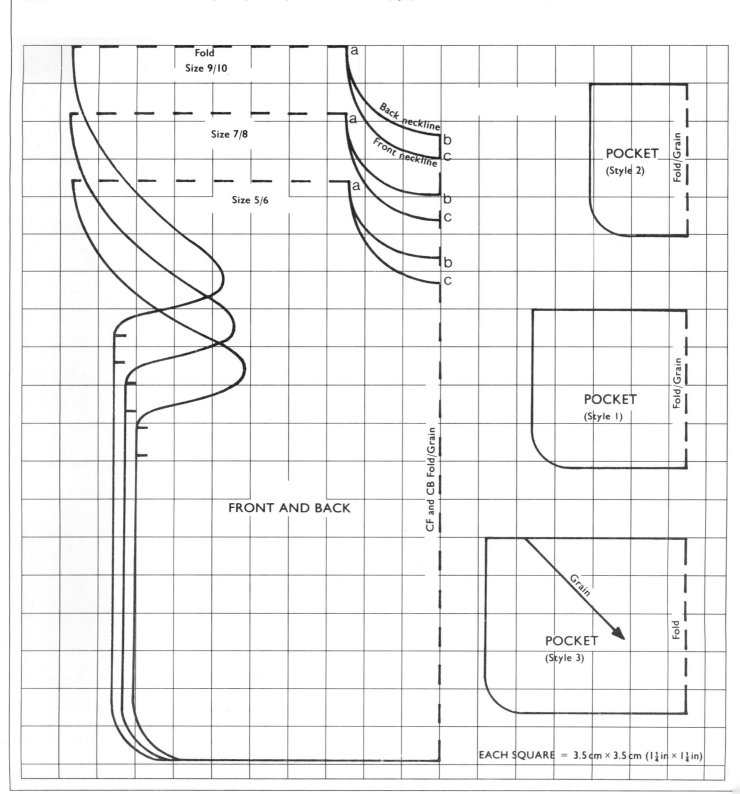

the paper pattern along the fabric fold. Cut out the apron body in one piece, with seam allowances as specified for each style.
*Tiebands:* for each apron, cut out two front tieband strips measuring 5 × 60 cm (2 × 24 in) each and two back tieband strips measuring 5 × 45 cm (2 × 18 in) each. Add a 1 cm (⅜ in) seam allowance all round each (finished width of tieband: 1 in [2.5 cm]).
*Pockets and binding:* cut out as specified for each style.

**Styles 1–5 on page 91, from left to right:**

**STYLE 1**
(Red apron in plasticized fabric)

**Size:** 7/8 (height: 122–128 cm [48–51 in])

**Materials:** 1.3 m (1½ yd) of 90 cm (36 in) wide plasticized floral-printed cotton fabric. 5 m (5½ yd) of 24 mm (1 in)-wide blue bias binding. Matching sewing thread.

**Cutting out:** Cut out the apron and the Style 1 pocket once each, without seam allowance. Cut out the tiebands as specified above. Tape or weight the pattern pieces in place when cutting them out, to avoid making permanent pin holes in the plasticized fabric.

**Sewing:** To avoid making holes, pin or baste only within the apron seam allowances. If the coated side of the fabric sticks beneath the machine foot, stitch through sheets of tissue paper.
*Bind all apron edges as follows:* open out one folded edge of the binding. Pin binding to fabric with right sides together and binding foldline 1 cm (⅜ in) from edge of fabric. Stitch along binding foldline. Fold binding over to the wrong side of fabric, so that its remaining folded edge slightly overlaps the seamline. Baste in place. On the right side, stitch just above the lower edge of the binding, taking care to catch in all layers.
*Pocket:* bind the pocket edges in the same way, mitring at top corners.

Stitch the pocket on to apron front, centred, stitching along the binding seam (see photo). Stitch a dividing line down the pocket middle, to make two separate compartments.
*Tiebands:* fold each tieband in half lengthwise, with right sides together. Stitch each tieband together, leaving one short end open. Turn each tieband to right side; press. Stitch the appropriate tiebands on to the apron front or back with two rows of stitching at the positions indicated (see diagram).

**STYLE 2**
(Velveteen apron)

**Size:** 9/10 (height: 134–140 cm [53–55 in])

**Materials:** 1.4 m (1⅝ yd) of 90 cm (36 in)-wide navy blue velveteen. 5 m (5½ yd) of 24 mm (1 in)-wide red bias binding. Matching sewing thread.

**Cutting out/sewing:** Make up like Style 1, but without the pocket.

**STYLE 3**
(Striped apron with self-fabric binding)

**Size:** 5/6 (height: 110–116 cm [42–46 in])

**Materials:** 2 m (2¼ yd) of 90 cm (36 in)-wide striped cotton fabric. Matching sewing thread.

**Cutting out:** Cut out the apron without seam allowance and the tiebands as specified in the General Instructions. Cut out the Style 3 pocket once on the bias, with 15 mm (⅝ in) seam allowance all round. From the remaining fabric, cut out 4 cm (1½ in)-wide bias strips. Seam these together on the straight of grain to make a continuous strip of bias binding.

**Sewing:** *Bind all apron edges as follows:* pin binding to apron with right side of binding to wrong side of fabric and with raw edges even. Stitch a seam 15 mm (⅝ in) from fabric edges. Turn binding to right side, fold under a 1 cm (⅜ in) seam allowance and stitch close to the folded edge, through all fabric layers.
*Pocket:* turn under the top

edge twice and stitch a narrow hem. Press under the remaining seam allowances and edgestitch the pocket on to apron front, centred, as shown (see photo on page 91). Stitch a dividing line down pocket middle.
*Tiebands:* make up and attach tiebands same as for Style 1.

**STYLE 4**
(Blue apron with two patch pockets)

**Size:** 7/8 (height: 122–128 cm [48–51 in])

**Materials:** 1.4 m (1⅝ yd) of 90 cm (36 in)-wide blue floral printed cotton fabric. 5 m (5½ yd) of 12 mm (½ in)-wide blue bias binding. Matching sewing thread.

**Cutting out:** Cut out the apron with 1 cm (⅜ in) seam allowance. Cut out two Style 4 patch pockets, adding 1 cm (⅜ in) seam allowance all round each. Cut out the tiebands as specified in the General Instructions.

**Sewing:** *Apply a bias facing to apron edges as follows:* open out one folded edge of the binding. Pin binding to apron with right sides facing and raw edges even. Stitch along binding foldline. Fold binding over so that its full width lies flat on the wrong side of the apron; press. Sew down the remaining folded edge of the binding by hand.
*Pockets:* finish the top edge of each pocket, then press under all seam allowances. Edgestitch each pocket on to apron front as shown (see photo on page 90).
*Tiebands:* make up and attach tiebands same as for Style 1.

**STYLE 5**
(Red flowered apron)

**Size:** 5/6 (height: 110–116 cm [42–46 in])

**Materials:** 1.3 m (1½ yd) of 90 cm (36 in)-wide floral-printed cotton batiste. 5 m (5½ yd) of 12 mm (½ in)-wide red bias binding. Matching sewing thread.

**Cutting out/sewing:** As Style 4, but without the pockets.

# 37
## Baby Doll

**Size:** Height: approx. 30 cm (12 in)

**Enlarging the pattern:**
Reduced size pattern pieces for the doll's body and clothes are shown in grid form. Each box of the grid measures 2 cm (¾ in) square. To enlarge the pattern pieces, draw grid to scale on paper. Copy each line into exactly the same position in the corresponding box of the full-size grid.

**Materials:** *For the body:* 0.2 m (¼ yd) of flesh-coloured jersey *or* 0.2 m (¼ yd) of white jersey and a pair of mesh tights (pantyhose) (see instructions). Synthetic filling (stuffing), as needed. Brown and red embroidery thread (for eyes and mouth). Matching sewing thread.
*For the clothes:* For dress, cap and self-fabric bias binding; 1 m (1⅛ yd) of 90 cm (36 in)-wide pink and white striped cotton fabric. For panties and mock petticoat: 0.4 m (½ yd) of 90 cm (36 in)-wide white batiste.
*Lace trim for dress, cap and shoes:* 1.8 m (2 yd) of 2 cm (¾ in)-wide cotton broderie anglaise (eyelet lace), with slots for threading binding.
*For panties and mock petticoat:* 1.1 m (1¼ yd) of 2 cm (¾ in)-wide cotton lace edging. 0.2 m (¼ yd) of elastic cord. Matching sewing thread (for all clothes).

**HOW TO MAKE THE DOLL**

**Body:** *Cutting out:* if you are unable to obtain flesh-coloured jersey, you can tint the white jersey with the aid of tights. To do so, cut the head and body out twice roughly and the arm four times from both white jersey and stocking mesh. Baste the corresponding pieces of mesh and jersey together, with the mesh on top. Then trim the pattern pieces to exact size. Treat the basted layers as one, for sewing purposes. (If using flesh-coloured jersey, cut pattern pieces to exact size immediately.) A 5 mm (¼ in) seam allowance is included on all body pieces.

*Sewing:* with right sides facing, stitch the two body pieces together, leaving armholes (lines C–D) and neck (line A–B) open. Turn body right side out. With right sides facing, stitch each arm together leaving the top edge (line C–D) open. Turn arms right side out. With right sides facing, stitch the two head pieces together leaving neck edge (line A–B) open. Turn head right side out. Pad each piece individually with synthetic filling. Embroider the facial features as shown, using stem stitch for the eyes and satin stitch for the mouth. Turn under the seam allowances on head and arms, then stitch each piece on to the body by hand, matching lettered points.

**Clothing:** *Cutting out:* add a 1 cm (⅜ in) seam allowance unless otherwise specified. Panties: cut out twice in batiste. Mock petticoat: cut out twice in batiste, marking the position of the two tucks on each piece. Striped fabric: shoes: cut out shoe pattern twice. Sleeve: cut out twice on the bias, adding 2 cm (¾ in) hem allowance, elsewhere 1 cm (⅜ in). Skirt: cut out twice with 5 cm (2 in) hem allowance, elsewhere 1 cm (⅜ in). Yoke: cut out a 10 × 30 cm (4 × 12 in) piece of fabric for the yoke front. Stitch small, evenly spaced, outward-facing tucks 4 mm (³⁄₁₆ in) in depth on either side of the centre section (see photo on page 92). Position the yoke pattern piece on top of this and cut out. Repeat for yoke back. (Remember to follow correct pattern outlines for yoke front and back necklines.) Cap: cut out the side section once with 2 cm (¾ in) seam allowance at front edge, elsewhere 1 cm (⅜ in). Cut out the back section once. Self-fabric bias binding: from the remaining fabric, cut out 24 mm (1 in)-wide bias strips. Seam the short ends on the straight grain to make a continuous length. Fold the bias strip in half lengthwise, then fold the long raw edges under to meet in the centre (finished width: 8 mm [⁵⁄₁₆ in]). Stitch binding strip together, close

*Continued overleaf*

to folded edges. Thread the bias binding through the lace trim, then cut trim into pieces as follows: cap: 24 cm (9½ in), skirt: 72 cm (28½ in), sleeves: 10 cm (4 in) each. Cut a 104 cm (41 in) strip of binding for the yoke, but do not thread it through trim yet.

*Sewing:* clean-finish all raw edges. Panties: stitch side seams, with right sides together. Turn to right side. Stitch lace edging on to lower edge. Sew front to back at point N only, to make separate leg openings. Make a narrow casing and insert elastic

through the waist. Put panties on doll. Mock petticoat: stitch side seams, with right sides together. Turn to right side. Stitch lace on to hem edge. Stitch the two tucks as marked, matching each X to an O; press tucks downwards. (NOTE: this border piece

creates a petticoat effect when stitched to the hem edge of skirt.) Shoes: with right sides together, stitch the front and back seams of each shoe, matching L–L and K–K. Then stitch the cross seams on each shoe bottom, matching points M. Turn to right side. Gather

the top edge of each shoe to fit the width of each leg. Put the shoes on and sew to doll along each gathered edge. Conceal each top edge with a piece of bias binding-threaded lace trim. Sleeves: with right sides facing, stitch each sleeve seam. Turn sleeve right side

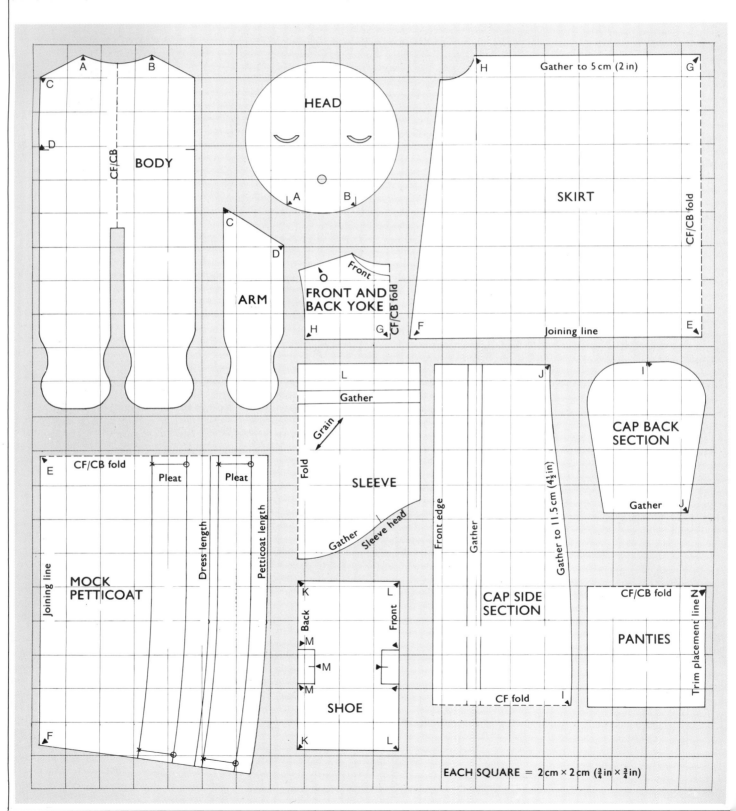

EACH SQUARE = 2 cm × 2 cm (¾ in × ¾ in)

out. Press under hem
allowance and stitch.
Gather bottom of each
sleeve 15 mm ($\frac{5}{8}$ in) above
hem edge, as shown, to fit
the width of each arm.
Conceal the gathering
stitches with binding-
threaded lace trim. Gather
each sleeve head (sleeve
cap) as indicated. Skirt:
stitch side seams with right
sides together. With right
sides together, seam skirt to
mock petticoat along
joining line F–E; press seam
open. Now press under the
remaining 4 cm ($1\frac{1}{2}$ in) of
the skirt hem allowance
and stitch along the skirt/
petticoat joining line. A
tuck has been formed at
the skirt hem edge; fold
down the mock petticoat.
On the right side, stitch on
the binding-threaded lace
trim over the skirt hem
stitching line. Gather the
top edges of the front and
back skirt to the indicated
width. With right sides
together, stitch yoke front
to skirt front and yoke back
to skirt back, matching
points H–G. With right
sides together, stitch one
shoulder seam. Stitch the
other shoulder seam from
the armhole edge to point
O only (the opening at neck
edge is necessary so the
doll's head can pass
through). Set in the sleeves,
with right sides together.
Turn dress right side out.
Stitch the lace trim on all
round the yoke placement
seam (including armhole
edges), mitring at corners.
Then thread through the
bias binding, starting and
finishing at centre front.
Tie the extending lengths of
binding into a bow; knot
the ends (see photo on page
92). Put dress on the doll
and sew up shoulder seam
by hand. Cap: press under
the seam allowance at the
front edge of the side
section. Gather side section
of cap as marked, both
parallel to front edge and
along the back edge. With
right sides together, stitch
side section to cap back,
matching points I and J.
Sew on the binding-
threaded trimming to
conceal the gathering
stitches near the front edge.
Press under the seam
allowance on the bottom
edge of cap. Put the cap on
the doll and draw it up
round the face. Sew the cap
along neck edge, by hand.

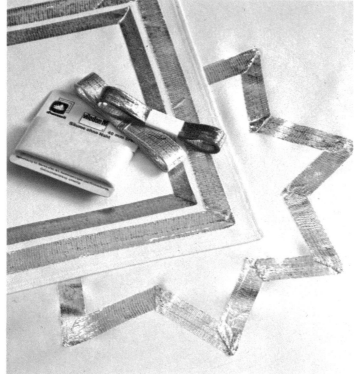

# 38

## Star-shaped Tablecloth and Matching Place Mats

### TABLECLOTH

**Size:** approx. 140 cm
(55 in) in diameter

**Materials:** 1.4 m ($1\frac{5}{8}$ yd) of
150 cm (58–60 in)-wide or
2.8 m ($3\frac{1}{8}$ yd) of 115 cm
(44–45 in)-wide white
satin. 6.5 m ($7\frac{1}{8}$ yd) of
15 mm ($\frac{5}{8}$ in)-wide silver
metallic woven ribbon.
6.5 m ($7\frac{1}{8}$ in) of 15 mm
($\frac{5}{8}$ in)-wide iron-on adhesive
(fusible) web. White sewing
thread (for edgestitching
the tablecloth). Iron.
Tailor's chalk or pencil.
Approx. 1 m (1 yd) string.
One drawing-pin
(thumbtack). Tracing paper
(optional).

**Cutting out:** First, cut a
140 × 140 cm (55 × 55 in)
square from the satin. If
you are unable to obtain
the wider width satin, it
will be necessary to join
lengths of fabric to make
up the tablecloth
dimensions. To do so, stitch
together a full-width centre
panel, flanked by narrow
fabric strips on either side.
This way, the seams are
positioned inconspicuously
on the tablecloth overhang.
Draw the star-shaped
tablecloth pattern directly
on to the wrong side of the
fabric using a string-and-
pencil compass: mark the
centre point of the fabric
square with tailor's chalk
or a pencil. Pin a drawing-
pin to the centre point,
placing a thick piece of
card underneath, to hold it.
Tie the piece of string to a
pencil or a piece of tailor's
chalk; secure it with tape.
Starting from the pencil
end, measure the string so
that it is exactly the length
of the radius of the circle
you wish to draw. Tie the
string to the drawing-pin at
that point. The string must
be able to swing freely.
Using this method, draw
four concentric circles as
follows (see diagram). First,
draw the tablecloth
circumference (radius:
70 cm [$27\frac{1}{2}$ in]). Next, draw
a circle with a 53 cm
($20\frac{1}{2}$ in) radius. Draw
another circle with a radius

*Continued overleaf*

of 18 cm (6½ in), then draw the inner circle with a radius of 13 cm (4½ in). The two outer circles are guidelines for drawing the star-shaped tablecloth edge. The two inner circles are guidelines for drawing the centre star. If you wish to play it safe, draw the centre star on tracing paper, then transfer the markings on to the right side of the tablecloth. Otherwise, it will be necessary to transfer the guidelines for the centre star from the wrong side of the satin on to the right side, by another method. To draw the star shapes, divide the circle into quarters, then divide each quarter in four again. Draw in the zigzag points of the star within the outer and inner rings, as shown (see diagram).

**Making up:** Cut out the star-shaped tablecloth outline and edgestitch all round; press. Cut 16 angled strips each from adhesive web and ribbon, to fit along the edge of the star. *Bonding:* place a strip of ribbon neatly on top of a strip of web. Make sure that none of the web is visible, as it melts when exposed to heat. You may wish to trim the width of

the web to prevent this. Now press the carefully positioned strips with a warm dry iron. Complete the bond using a damp cloth and the dry iron, gently pressing so that the ribbon adheres firmly to the fabric. Repeat for each web/ribbon pair, carefully butting the angled corners to form mitres, until the star-shaped edge is completely trimmed (NOTE: do a test piece first on a fabric scrap, to see if the metallic ribbon frays. If it does, cut the web into individual pieces as instructed, but apply the ribbon in a continuous band, mitring at corners. There will be a small triangle of unbonded ribbon at each point, but this should not affect wear.) *Finishing:* repeat the bonding procedure to make the centre star, applying the ribbon to the satin as marked.

**PLACE MATS**

**Finished size:** 30 × 43 cm (12 × 17 in)

**Materials:** *For each place mat, you need:* one 32 × 45 cm (12¾ × 17¾ in) piece of white linen. 1.5 m (1½ yd) of 1 cm (⅜ in)-wide

gold metallic woven ribbon. 1.5 m (1½ yd) of 15 mm (⅝ in)-wide silver metallic woven ribbon. 3 m (3 yd) of 15 mm (⅝ in)-wide iron-on adhesive (fusible) web. White sewing thread (for place mat hem). Tailor's chalk. Iron.

**Making up:** Cut out a rectangular piece of linen to the measurements given. Turn under a 1 cm (⅜ in)-wide hem all round and stitch; press. Using tailor's chalk on the right side of the place mat, draw placement guidelines all the way round 15 mm (⅝ in) and 4 cm (1½ in) from the edge. Cut out two 27 cm (10¾ in) strips and two 40 cm (15¾ in) strips, each 15 mm (⅝ in) wide, from both the adhesive web and the silver ribbon. Cut out two 22 cm (9 in) strips and two 35 cm (14 in) strips, each 1 cm (⅜ in) wide, from both the adhesive web and the gold ribbon (it will be necessary to trim the width of the web). Position the pair of web/ribbon strips along the place mat guidelines to form an outer silver and an inner gold rectangle (see photo on page 101). Angle the strips at each corner so that they butt to form a mitre. Apply

each pair of web/ribbon strips one at a time, following the bonding procedure described in the tablecloth instructions. If you wish, the ribbons may be applied to the place mat in continuous bands. This alternative method is also described in the tablecloth instructions.

NOTE: An everyday version of our festive tablecloth and place mat set can easily be made up using plain-coloured woven satin ribbon and coordinating fabric. Do not use gift wrap ribbon; it might melt.

# 39

## Indian Chief and Squaw Costumes

**Size:** To fit 6–8-year-old children (height: 116–128 cm [46–51 in])

**SQUAW**

**Tunic (Girl's):** *Materials:* 180 cm (72 in)-wide felt (available at department stores): 0.6 m (¾ yd) of light brown, 0.1 m (⅛ yd) of dark brown. Yellow, red, orange and blue felt rectangles (craft departments). Matching sewing thread. One button. Fabric glue.

**Cutting out:** Enlarge pattern pieces. From the light brown felt, cut out two tunic fronts and one tunic back (on the fold). Add a 1 cm (⅜ in) seam allowance, except to hem (without seam allowance). *Sleeve fringe:* using pinking shears, cut out two strips of dark brown felt, each measuring 7 × 26 cm (2¾ × 10¼ in). Cut fringe to a depth of 5.5 cm (2⅛ in). *Felt strips:* using pinking shears, cut the felt rectangles into 1 cm (⅜ in)-wide strips.

**Sewing:** Glue felt strips to front yoke and sleeves, spacing them 1 cm (⅜ in) apart (see photo on page 94). With right sides together, stitch garment seams, catching in the fringe along the lower sleeve seams. (To do this, sandwich each piece of fringe between seams with fringe facing inwards.) Leave the side and front slits open. Turn tunic right side out. Turn under the seam allowances round the neck opening and sleeve hems and stitch. Glue on felt strips to form hem border (see photo). Sew on a button and loop to the neck edge.

**Headdress:** *Materials:* 0.1 m (⅛ yd) of 180 cm (72 in)-wide light brown felt. *Heavy-weight non-woven interfacing:* one piece, 10 × 60 cm (4 × 24 in). *Narrow braid:* 1.25 m (1½ yd) each of yellow, red and blue. Matching sewing thread. One feather. 10 cm (4 in) of touch and close tape.

**Cutting out:** Cut out one

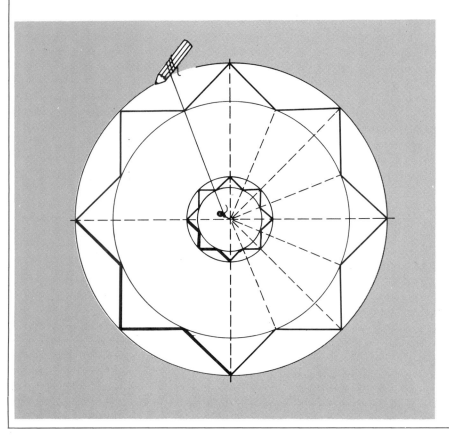

$9 \times 55$ cm ($3\frac{1}{2} \times 21\frac{5}{8}$ in) strip each of felt and interfacing.

**Sewing:** Fold the interfacing in half lengthwise, baste felt around it. Stitch on the braid and the feather (see photo, right). Stitch on the touch and close tape, near the ends of the band.

**Sandals:** *Materials:* 0.1 m ($\frac{1}{8}$ yd) of 180 cm (72 in)-wide light brown felt. One pair of flip-flops (rubber beach thongs). Contact adhesive.

**Cutting out:** Using the pinking shears, cut out the following 1 cm ($\frac{3}{8}$ in)-wide felt strips: four 110 cm ($42\frac{1}{2}$ in), two 15 cm (6 in) and two 50 cm (20 in) long.

**Making up:** Glue the felt strips on to each sandal as shown in photo. The 15 cm (6 in) strip covers the thong, the 50 cm (20 in) strip goes around the sides of the sole. The long strips are for lacing; knot the end of each round the back post at each side of the thong.

**INDIAN CHIEF**

**Tunic (boy's):** *Materials:* 180 cm (72 in)-wide felt: 0.6 m ($\frac{3}{4}$ yd) of light brown, 0.1 m ($\frac{1}{8}$ yd) of yellow. *Narrow braid:* 4.2 m ($4\frac{5}{8}$ yd) each of yellow, red and blue. Matching sewing thread. One button,

**Cutting out:** Enlarge pattern pieces. From the brown felt, cut out two tunic fronts and two backs, adding a 1 cm ($\frac{3}{8}$ in) seam allowance except to neckline and hem (without seam allowance).
*Fringe:* using pinking shears, cut out *four* 5 cm (2 in)-wide strips in *each* of the following lengths: top fringe: 24 cm ($9\frac{1}{2}$ in), middle fringe: 44 cm ($17\frac{1}{4}$ in), hem fringe: 29 cm ($11\frac{3}{8}$ in). Cut fringe to a depth of 4 cm ($1\frac{1}{2}$ in), with regular scissors. Cut out one pinked yellow strip measuring $1 \times 34$ cm ($\frac{3}{8} \times 13\frac{1}{4}$ in), for the neck edge.

**Sewing:** On each of the two front and two back pieces, stitch on the braids 3 mm ($\frac{1}{8}$ in) apart with the appropriate piece of fringe on the placement lines below (see photo on page 94 and diagram). Stitch on the braid above the sleeve hems. Stitch seams, with right sides together, leaving back slit open and taking care not to catch in the fringe. Press seams open. Turn tunic right side out. Stitch on the felt at the neck. Turn under sleeve hems and stitch. Sew on the button and a loop to the back neck.

**Trousers:** *Materials:* 180 cm (72 in)-wide felt: 0.55 m ($\frac{5}{8}$ yd) of light brown, 0.1 m ($\frac{1}{8}$ yd) of dark brown. Yellow, red and orange felt

rectangles. Waist length + 2 cm ($\frac{3}{4}$ in) of 2.5 cm (1 in)-wide elastic. Matching sewing thread. Fabric glue.

**Cutting out:** Enlarge the front/back piece and cut it out twice from light brown felt, adding 1 cm ($\frac{3}{8}$ in) seam allowance all round.
*Fringe:* using pinking shears, cut two strips of dark brown felt, each measuring $7 \times 62$ cm ($2\frac{3}{4} \times 24\frac{3}{8}$ in). Cut fringe to a depth of 5 cm (2 in), using regular scissors.
*Felt strips:* using pinking shears, cut the coloured felt rectangles into 1 cm ($\frac{3}{8}$ in)-wide strips.

**Sewing:** Glue on coloured strips above trouser hems (see photo). With right

sides together, stitch the inside leg seam and then the crutch (crotch) seam, leaving front slit open. Turn right side out. Turn up trouser hems and stitch. Turn under the waistline casing and stitch close to edge. Thread elastic through the casing and stitch short ends together. Position the fringe along the placement line on each trouser leg; stitch in place (see photo, diagram).

**Headdress:** *Materials:* 0.1 m ($\frac{1}{8}$ yd) of 180 cm (72 in)-wide light brown felt. Yellow, red and orange felt rectangles. Heavy-weight non-woven interfacing: one piece, $10 \times 60$ cm

($4 \times 24$ in). Thirteen feathers. 10 cm (4 in) touch and close tape. Matching sewing thread.

**Cutting out:** Cut out one $9 \times 55$ cm ($3\frac{1}{2} \times 21\frac{5}{8}$ in) strip each of felt and interfacing. Using pinking shears, cut out 1 cm ($\frac{1}{8}$ in)-wide strips from the coloured felt rectangles.

**Sewing:** Fold the interfacing in half lengthwise; baste felt around it. Sew on the feathers, 4 cm ($1\frac{1}{2}$ in) apart. Stitch on the felt strips over the feathers, spacing them evenly apart (see photo). Stitch on the touch and close tape, near the ends of the band.

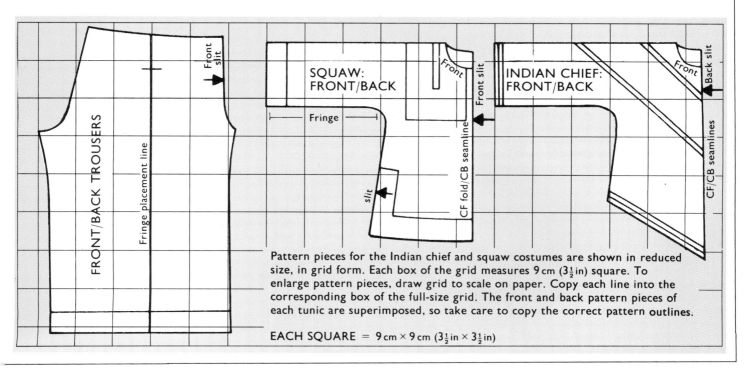

FRONT/BACK TROUSERS — Fringe placement line — Front slit

SQUAW: FRONT/BACK — Fringe — slit — Front slit — CF fold/CB seamline — Front

INDIAN CHIEF: FRONT/BACK — Back slit — Front — CF/CB seamlines

Pattern pieces for the Indian chief and squaw costumes are shown in reduced size, in grid form. Each box of the grid measures 9 cm ($3\frac{1}{2}$ in) square. To enlarge pattern pieces, draw grid to scale on paper. Copy each line into the corresponding box of the full-size grid. The front and back pattern pieces of each tunic are superimposed, so take care to copy the correct pattern outlines.

**EACH SQUARE = 9 cm × 9 cm ($3\frac{1}{2}$ in × $3\frac{1}{2}$ in)**

# 40

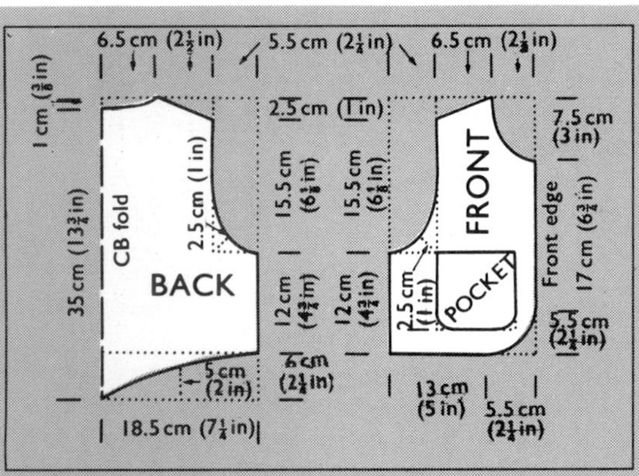
6.5 cm (2½ in)
5.5 cm (2¼ in)
6.5 cm (2½ in)
1 cm (⅜ in)
2.5 cm (1 in)
7.5 cm (3 in)
35 cm (13¾ in)
CB fold
2.5 cm (1 in)
BACK
15.5 cm (6⅛ in)
15.5 cm (6⅛ in)
FRONT
Front edge
17 cm (6¾ in)
12 cm (4¾ in)
12 cm (4¾ in)
2.5 cm (1 in)
POCKET
5.5 cm (2¼ in)
5 cm (2 in)
6 cm (2¼ in)
13 cm (5 in)
5.5 cm (2¼ in)
18.5 cm (7¼ in)

The pattern for the pirate's bolero is shown in reduced size. Enlarge the measurements given (in centimetres or inches) to full size. The dotted lines are guidelines.

## Clown and Pirate Costumes

**Size:** Made-to-measure

CLOWN

**Materials:** One pair of Dad's old pyjama (pajama) trousers. 0.2 m (¼ yd) of 180 cm (72 in)-wide red felt. 0.4 m (½ yd) of 90 cm (36 in)-wide heavy-weight iron-on interfacing. Two yellow felt rectangles. 1.6 m (1¾ yd) of 15 mm (⅝ in)-wide braid. 1 cm (⅜ in)-wide elastic (for waistband and ankle casings, bow tie). Colourful fabric scraps. Eight buttons. Embroidery thread. Matching sewing thread. Fabric glue.

**Making up:** *Trousers:* cut the length of the pyjama trousers down to kid size, leaving plenty of room for elastic casings at the waist and ankles. (The finished trousers should be baggy, for a comical effect.) Over the knees, sew on funny-shaped patches using large hand stitches and embroidery thread. Add patch pockets at hip level (see photo on page 95). Cut the patches and the pockets from fabric scraps, using pinking shears. Fold under the waist and ankle casings and stitch; insert elastic to fit and secure the ends together.
*Braces (suspenders):* make the braces out of felt which has been reinforced with heavy-weight iron-on interfacing on the back. Cut out each brace strap 4 cm (1½ in) wide. Each strap must be wide enough to reach from front waist to back waist, criss-crossing at the back. Stitch a piece of braid down the centre of each strap. From reinforced felt, cut out eight double-button tabs in the shape shown (see photo), for the front and back ends of each strap. Sandwich a pair of tabs over each brace end and blanket-stitch it in place by hand (see photo). The back button tabs must be attached to each strap at a slant, because of the angle caused by the criss-cross. Cover the eight buttons with felt (glue it on). Attach the braces on to the trousers, sewing them in place through the buttons. Fasten the straps with a safety pin where they cross.
*Bow tie:* cut out a 10 × 25 cm (4 × 10 in) strip from reinforced red felt and a 4 × 12 cm (1½ × 4¾ in) strip from reinforced yellow felt. Overcast the short ends of the red strip together, forming a loop. Wrap the small yellow strip tightly round the middle of the loop and sew it in place. Use a holepunch to cut out dots from yellow felt. Glue these on to the bow tie (see photo). For fastening, sew on an elastic loop.
*Finishing touches:* buy the hat and nose and apply make-up as shown, to complete the costume.

PIRATE

**Materials:** One pair of old jeans. Colourful fabric scraps (for patches). Fabric remnants (for scarf and sash; dimensions below). Red embroidery thread. For bolero: 0.35 m (½ yd) of 180 cm (72 in)-wide blue felt.

**Making up:** *Trousers:* cut the patches out using pinking shears and sew them on by hand, with embroidery thread (see photo). Fringe one leg and roll the other one up (see photo on page 95).
*Sash:* cut a strip of fabric measuring 30 × 100 cm (12 × 39.5 in).
*Scarf:* cut a strip measuring 12 × 90 cm (5 × 36 in).
*Bolero:* enlarge pattern pieces. Cut out the front twice and the back and pocket once each, without seam allowance. Overcast the bolero fronts to the back at the shoulders and side seams, using embroidery thread and decorative hand stitching (see photo). Sew on the pocket as shown.
*Finishing touches:* the eye patch can be purchased inexpensively at the chemist's (drugstore). The bolero looks best with a nautical-style striped T-shirt. If you wish to make a swag bag (for stashing booty) to go with the outfit, cut out a 36 cm (14 in)-diameter felt circle. Draw through a piece of elastic 2 cm (¾ in) from the edge.

# 41

## Child's Fleecy Jacket

**Size:** To fit a 4-year-old child (height: 104 cm [41 in])
Finished length of jacket back, collar to hem: 39.5 cm (15½ in)

**Materials:** 0.75 m (⅞ yd) of 140–160 cm (54–62 in)-wide man-made fleece. 3 m (3⅜ yd) of 12 mm (½ in)-wide knitted fold-over braid in a contrasting colour. Three large covered hooks and eyes (for fur). Matching sewing thread.

**Enlarging the pattern:** The reduced size jacket pattern is shown in grid form. Each box of the grid measures 3.2 cm (1¼ in) square. To enlarge the pattern pieces, draw grid to scale on paper. Copy each line into exactly the same position in the corresponding box of the full-size grid.
IMPORTANT: since children vary greatly in size, it is advisable to test the pattern for fit before making it up. Enlarge the pattern on to tissue paper, pin it together, then try it on your child. Make any necessary adjustments.

**Cutting out:** Enlarge the pattern pieces as directed. For easy cutting, cut the pattern pieces from a single layer of fleece. Cut out all pieces along the lengthwise grain, with the pile running downwards. Cut out one full jacket back and two jacket fronts. (Remember to reverse the jacket front and back pieces to get a right and a left side of each.) Cut out one full stand-up collar. Cut out the sleeve and the patch pocket twice each. Add a 15 mm (⅝ in) seam allowance to the side, shoulder, armhole, sleeve head (sleeve cap) and sleeve seams. Cut out all edges which are to be bound without seam allowance (see photo on page 96). Elsewhere, add 1 cm (⅜ in) seam allowance.

**Sewing:** Stitch in the direction of the pile and hold fabric taut while stitching. Baste seams together before stitching, as fleece tends to pull when sewn. With right sides together, stitch the side and shoulder seams, then clean-finish the seam allowances together with machine zigzag. With right sides together and points **a** matching, stitch the stand-up collar to the neck edge. Clean-finish the seam allowances together and press upwards towards the collar.
*Sleeves:* with right sides together, stitch and clean-finish each sleeve seam. Set in the sleeves, with right sides together. The grain at the top of the sleeve head should match that of the shoulder seam exactly, as should the grain at the sleeve and side seams underneath. Now clean-finish the armhole seam allowances together.
*Bind the jacket edges:* open out the folded braid. With wrong side of braid to right side of jacket, pin the braid in place so that the raw edge of the jacket meets the centre fold of the braid. Fold the braid over to the wrong side and slipstitch the remaining edge to the seamline. Turn the braid under at each corner and sew the short ends together by hand. Before you bind the bottom edge of each sleeve, join the braid to form a ring.
*Patch pockets:* bind the top edge of each pocket. Baste under the seam allowances of each pocket, then sew a pocket on to each jacket front by hand, at the indicated position (see diagram).
*Finishing:* sew the hooks and eyes on to the jacket front, placing each hook approx. 2–3 mm ($\frac{1}{16}$–⅛ in) from one edge and the eye correspondingly on the other edge. Sew the first hook and eye on at the top edge of the jacket front (just below point **a**), the two others at the positions marked (X's on the diagram).

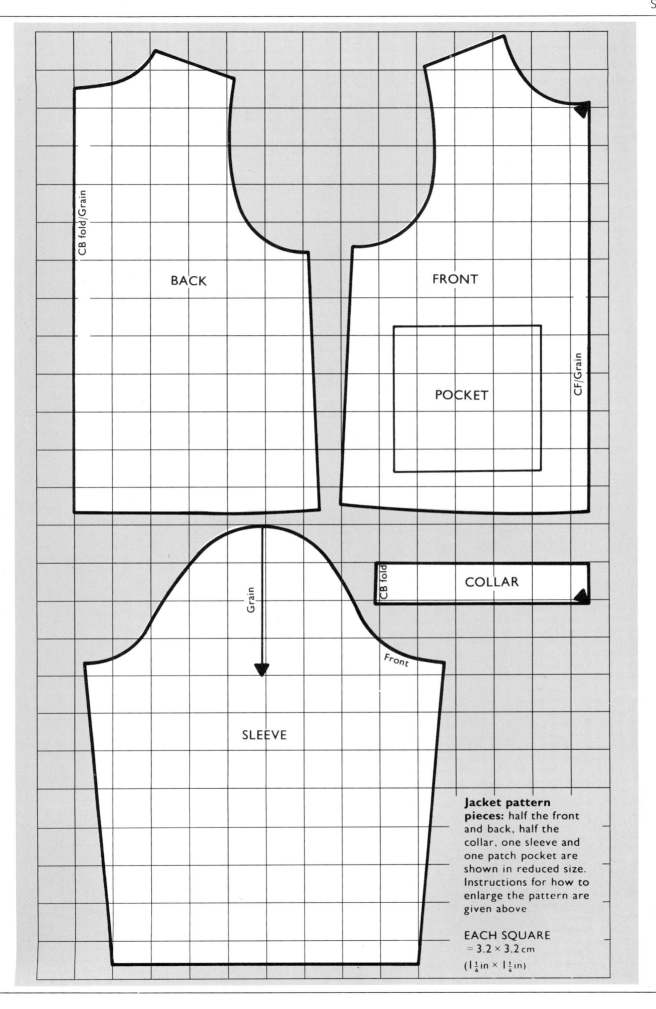

BACK

FRONT

CB fold/Grain

POCKET

CF/Grain

CB fold

COLLAR

Grain

Front

SLEEVE

**Jacket pattern pieces:** half the front and back, half the collar, one sleeve and one patch pocket are shown in reduced size. Instructions for how to enlarge the pattern are given above.

EACH SQUARE
= 3.2 × 3.2 cm
(1¼in × 1¼in)

# 42

## Windcheater (Windbreaker)

**Size:** To fit a six to seven year-old child (height: 116–122 cm [46–48 in]). Finished length of jacket: 52 cm (20½ in).

**Materials:** 1.6 m (1¾ yd) of 90 cm (36 in)-wide sailcloth or lightweight denim. 3.3 m (3⅝ yd) of 24 mm (1 in)-wide contrasting bias binding. One 16 cm (6 in) zip. 0.4 m (½ yd) of 3 cm (1 in)-wide elastic. One button. Matching sewing thread.

**Cutting out:** Enlarge pattern as directed. Cut out two jacket fronts (centre seam simplifies sewing of slit), one back, one hood, two sleeves, one flap and one pocket. Cut out two sleeve gussets on the cross (bias).
*Seam allowances:* refer to photo. Cut all edges which are to be bound without seam allowance. Add 4 cm (1½ in) to sleeve hem; add 2 cm (¾ in) to sleeve seam, side seam and front seam; remaining seams have a 1 cm (⅜ in) allowance.

**Sewing:** Clean-finish all raw edges apart from those which are to be bound. With right sides together, stitch the centre front seam up to the slit mark (an arrow); press open. With right sides together, stitch shoulder seams; press open. With right sides together, stitch centre section of side seams (between arrows), leaving slit at lower edge and armhole opening at top; press open.
*Hood:* stitch centre top seam, with right sides together; press open. Match points **c**, then stitch the cross seam. To stitch pleats on lower edge, match **x** to **o**, folding pleats towards hood back; stitch pleats along hem allowance. With right sides together, pin hood on to jacket neckline, matching points **d** and easing in any fullness; stitch. Bind the hood and

the slit, turning under raw ends of binding at point of slit. (For how to apply binding, see Mother Goose Waistcoat, page 21.)
Next, bind jacket bottom, starting at the point of each side slit and mitring at the corners. (Fold under raw ends at slits, as for hood.) Position, then insert the zip underneath the front slit. Bind all round pocket, mitring at corners. Bind only the side and bottom edges of the pocket flap, mitring at corners and leaving the sides free of binding at the top seam allowance. Pin pocket on to jacket front as shown; stitch in place along side and bottom edges. Make a vertical machine buttonhole above the point of the flap. Press under the flap seam allowance. Pin flap to jacket front 1 cm (⅜ in) above the pocket. Stitch top of flap to jacket, close to the edge.
*Sleeves:* with right sides together, stitch each sleeve top on to jacket, matching points **a** and **b** and not stitching beyond seam allowance. Press seam towards sleeve and topstitch close to seam, through seam allowances. With right sides together, stitch each underarm seam as far as gusset; press open. Press under the seam allowance of the diamond-shaped gusset. With right sides together, pin, then baste the gusset in place, matching points **b** and all seams; stitch in place. Press gusset seams towards centre of gusset and baste them down. To strengthen gusset, topstitch just inside gusset seams, through all thicknesses. To make casing for elastic, turn sleeve cuffs under 1 cm (⅜ in), then again 3.5 cm (1¼ in). Stitch casing along inside edge, leaving an opening for elastic. Cut elastic 2 cm (¾ in) larger than child's wrist. Thread elastic through the casing. Stitch elastic ends together, overlapping them slightly. Stitch the opening shut.

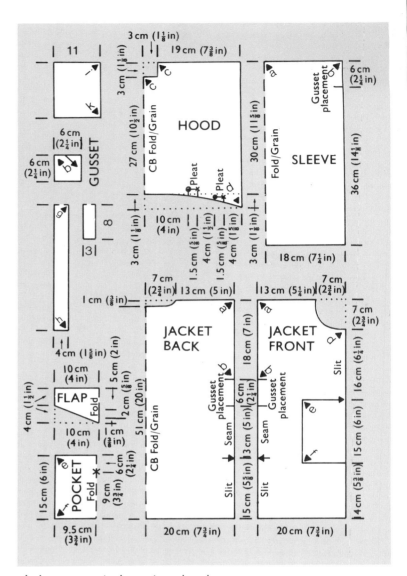

Jacket pattern is shown in reduced size. Enlarge the measurements given (in centimetres or inches) to full size. The dotted lines are guidelines.
**Important:** since children vary greatly in size, it is advisable to test the pattern for fit before making it up. Enlarge the pattern pieces on tissue paper, pin-baste together, then make any necessary alterations. Or make the pattern up in muslin first.

# 43

## Colourful Satchels for Kids

Carrying things incorrectly can do a lot of damage. The way to lift things properly is to spread the weight across the shoulders. A satchel with shoulder straps is the ideal solution for schoolchildren who are laden with heavy books.

Our rucksacks are popular with parents and youngsters alike. Children like them because they don't get in the way while walking and adults are pleased because they promote good posture. These rucksacks are handy for recreational use, too. Make one for your next country walk or picnic.

The natural-ground striped rucksack is made of sturdy cotton. Its jute straps are fastened with snap hooks. Eyelets have been punched in along the top and the bag is then fastened with thick cord ties.

The red rucksack with plaid trim is completely wind- and water-resistant because it's made out of nylon. The flap and pocket are secured with snap fasteners.

Instructions for the rucksacks are on page 114.

## 45

## Sweet Summer Sundresses with Embroidered Detail

You don't have to be an expert needlewoman to make the designs on these pages. They are worked quickly using astonishingly simple techniques which look more complicated than they really are. Your daughter will wear these dresses proudly.

The cross-stitched bodice, straps and pockets on the gingham sundresses create the illusion of smocking but are embroidered in a fraction of the time. The all-over cross-stitched patterns are worked across the checked gingham before each dress is made up. There are two different cross-stitch designs to choose from.

The cute toddler's smock-dress features a yoke made from an embroidered place mat. Cut a neck opening in the mat, gather the dress fabric to fit: abracadabra! – a delightful summer dress in no time.

Instructions for the dresses are on pages 115 and 116.

## All-weather Jackets for Men and Women

Both these styles, which are made from water- and wind-resistant fabrics, were created so that you could go for walks even in inclement weather. Make the jackets roomy enough so that you can wear them with a sweater. His jacket is made from water-repellent poplin; hers is made from nylon ciré. These materials protect against wind and moisture, but they don't provide warmth, so it's important to wear the right clothes underneath.

Instructions for these jackets are on pages 116 to 119.

## Ethnic Styles with Colourful Trims

Every year the fashion designers show us folkloristic garments. They're perennial favourites because the traditional cuts, colours and patterns are exceedingly tasteful and timeless. East European styles are particularly popular; hence our selection of a Russian and a Hungarian-style design.

The special attraction of the waistcoat comes from the contrast of the vivid braiding and rickrack against the black flannel.

The dress is cut wide like a smock and the cuffs and belt give it its particular shape. The tones of the fabric and the embroidered trim were matched very carefully. The bright red binding around the edges adds a colourful note.

Sewing these garments should present no problems even to beginners.

Instructions for the dress and waistcoat are on pages 119, 120 and 121.

**49**

# 43

## Children's Rucksacks (Knapsacks)

**Size:** approx. 30 × 35 cm (12 × 14 in)

**Materials**

*Nylon rucksack:* 0.7 m ($\frac{7}{8}$ yd) of 115 cm (44–45 in)-wide nylon. 2.8 m ($3\frac{1}{8}$ yd) of 5 cm (2 in)-wide plaid nylon webbing (or synthetic woven ribbon). 1.2 m ($1\frac{3}{8}$ yd) of 3 mm ($\frac{1}{8}$ in)-wide nylon cord. Matching sewing thread. Eighteen eyelets and insertion tool. Ten medium-sized snap fasteners and insertion tool. Two 6 cm ($2\frac{1}{4}$ in)-long snap hooks. Four D-rings. Foam rubber for the straps: two strips, each 4 × 50 cm ($1\frac{1}{2}$ × 20 in). Pieces of heavy-weight non-woven sew-in interfacing (to reinforce fabric surrounding snap fasteners and eyelets).
*Canvas rucksack:* 0.7 m ($\frac{3}{4}$ yd) of 150 cm (58–60 in)-wide striped canvas. 2.8 m ($3\frac{1}{8}$ yd) of 6 cm ($2\frac{1}{4}$ in)-wide jute webbing. 3.7 m ($4\frac{1}{8}$ yd) of 3 mm ($\frac{1}{8}$ in)-wide cotton cord. Matching sewing thread. Thirty-two eyelets and insertion tool. Two 6 cm ($2\frac{1}{4}$ in)-long snap hooks. Four D-rings. Foam rubber for the straps: two strips, each 4 × 50 cm ($1\frac{1}{2}$ × 20 in). Pieces of heavy-weight iron-on interfacing (for eyelets and snap fasteners). Size 110 (18) sewing machine needle (canvas-weight).

**Cutting out** (both styles): Enlarge pattern pieces. Cut out the back section once, adding 2 cm ($\frac{3}{4}$ in) seam allowance except round the flap, which is without seam allowance. Cut out the bag front and the patch pocket once each, adding 5 cm (2 in) to each top edge, 2 cm ($\frac{3}{4}$ in) elsewhere. Cut out the pocket flap twice from fabric and once from interfacing, adding 1 cm ($\frac{3}{8}$ in) seam allowance.
*Straps:* cut out two strips of nylon or jute webbing, each 1 m ($1\frac{1}{8}$ yd) in length. From nylon webbing or canvas, cut out one 5 × 14 cm (2 × $5\frac{1}{2}$ in) strip and two 5 × 18 cm (2 × 7 in) strips.

**Sewing** (both styles): Attach interfacing (sew-in

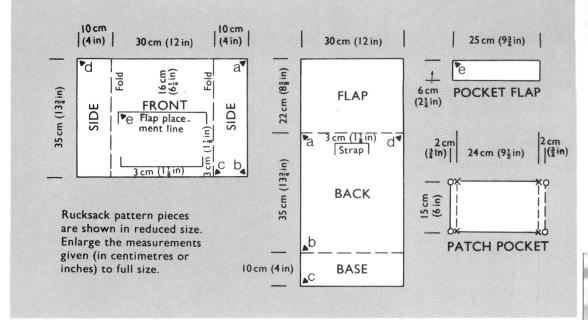

Rucksack pattern pieces are shown in reduced size. Enlarge the measurements given (in centimetres or inches) to full size.

for nylon, iron-on for canvas) to the seam allowance on the top edge of the bag front. Clean-finish the raw edge. Turn under the seam allowance and stitch down. Do the same with the patch pocket. Cut out two strips of interfacing, each measuring 4 × 14 cm ($1\frac{1}{2}$ × $5\frac{1}{2}$ in). Attach these (baste them on to nylon, iron them on to canvas) down the wrong side of the bag front, positioning them 3 cm ($1\frac{1}{8}$ in) below the top edge and bending each piece round the fold on each side. Punch in eyelets 15 mm ($\frac{5}{8}$ in) below the top edge: four on each of the sides and ten along the front.
*Pocket flap:* with right sides together, stitch front to back leaving top edge open. Turn right side out; topstitch round the seams. Clean-finish the raw edges together.

**Nylon rucksack:** *Patch pocket:* punch the top part of a snap fastener into each side of the flap (see photo on page 107). Punch in two snap fastener sockets, one above the other, in the corresponding position on either side of the pocket. (This way, pocket can be adjusted.)

**Canvas rucksack:** Punch in four eyelets, in a vertical line, into each side section of bag front. Position them 2 cm ($\frac{3}{4}$ in) before fold and 2 cm ($\frac{3}{4}$ in) apart. The first one is 5 cm (2 in) down.
*Patch pocket:* punch in two

pairs of eyelets, 5 cm (2 in) below the top edge, 2 cm ($\frac{3}{4}$ in) before the pleat and 3 cm ($1\frac{1}{8}$ in) away from each other. Edgestitch the front folds of the pleats.
*Pocket flap:* punch an eyelet into each side of the flap, 2 cm ($\frac{3}{4}$ in) from each side and 1 cm ($\frac{3}{8}$ in) above the bottom edge.

**Both styles:** *Patch pocket:* turn under the seam allowance on the bottom edge of the pocket. Turn under the side seam allowance and edgestitch them on to the bag front at the position marked, with wrong side of pocket to right side of bag. Fold the side pleats, matching each X to an O. Edgestitch the bottom edge of the pocket on to the bag front, stitching over the pleats.
*Pocket flap:* pin pocket flap to bag front 1 cm ($\frac{3}{8}$ in) above the pocket, with right sides together and point e matching (flap points upwards). Stitch along the flap placement line, then fold flap down and topstitch through all layers along the top edge. Stitch bag front to back: start at point **a** at the top of one side. Stitch together with right sides facing until corner **b**. Tie the thread securely. Clip into the seam allowance of the back section, to the last stitch at point **b**. Join base seams **b–c**, then clip into the seam allowance at point **c**. Stitch across the front of the base, then join the remaining side of the bag together in the same way. Trim seam

allowances. Turn bag right side out. Pinch seams together. Pinch the seam allowances in between. Edgestitch the seams together on the right side of the fabric, forming a narrow ridge (see photo).

**Canvas rucksack:** *Bind the flap edges:* cut a strip of webbing to fit round the flap. Press the strip in half lengthwise, fold it over the raw edge and stitch in place, mitring corners and turning the ends under.

**Nylon rucksack:** *Bind the flap edges:* cut a strip of plaid webbing to fit round the flap. Press the strip under 1 cm ($\frac{3}{8}$ in) along one long edge. Pin webbing to flap with the 1 cm ($\frac{3}{8}$ in) seam allowance on wrong side of flap and raw edge of flap along webbing fold. Also, turn under the short ends of the webbing. Stitch webbing to flap along edges. Fold the remaining 4 cm ($1\frac{1}{2}$ in) of webbing on to the right side of the flap and edgestitch it in place, mitring the corners. Now punch in the top part of three snap fasteners on each side of the flap, inserting the first one 15 mm ($\frac{5}{8}$ in) from the edge and spacing them 5 cm (2 in) apart (see photo). Punch in two corresponding snap fastener sockets on either side of the front section, placing each one 3 cm ($1\frac{1}{8}$ in) from the top edge.

**Both styles:** *Straps:* fold each strap piece in half

crosswise. Baste a piece of foam rubber on to one half of each strap piece. Slide a snap hook threaded on a D-ring to the middle fold of each strip. Fold each strap piece in half over the bar of the D-ring and stitch together along both edges, with the foam rubber to the inside. Baste each strap on to the back section as illustrated, with the raw ends facing downwards. Turn under the raw edges on the 14 cm ($5\frac{1}{2}$ in) strip and stitch the strip crosswise over the strap ends. Turn under the raw edges on the two 18 cm (7 in) strips. Fold each strip in half crosswise over the bar of a D-ring, stitch the long edges together. Fold under the bottom of each strip and stitch it to the base of the bag (see photo).

**Canvas rucksack:** *Cut the cotton cord as follows:* cut two flap fastening pieces, each 50 cm (20 in) long. Sew them by hand under the flap corners, along half their length. Cut two pieces, each 12 cm (5 in), to be threaded vertically through the eyelets on the sides of the front section, forming loops. These will be used for tying the flap fastening pieces. Cut two 70 cm ($27\frac{1}{2}$ in) pieces to be threaded in and out along the top edge, from the side to the middle.
*For the patch pocket, you need:* two 45 cm (18 in) pieces which are fastened to the flap eyelets and two 5 cm (2 in) lengths. these are threaded

crosswise through the eyelets directly beneath to form loops. The flap fastening cords are tied with these. Fasten each cord with a large knot on the inside of the bag. Knot the free end to prevent ravelling.

**Nylon rucksack:** Cut the piece of nylon cord in half. Thread each piece in and out through the eyelets on the top edge of the bag, from the side to the middle. Knot the ends of the cord.

# 44

## Cross-stitched Gingham Sundresses

**Sizes:** *To fit a 4-year-old child (height: 104 cm [41 in]):*
Finished length, bodice to hem: 36 cm (14⅛ in)
Finished bodice circumference: 52 cm (20 in)
*To fit a 6-year-old child (height: 116 cm [46 in]):*
Finished length, bodice to hem: 41 cm (16 in)
Finished bodice circumference: 56 (22 in)

**Materials**
*Dress:* 115 cm (44–45 in)-wide blue gingham fabric: size 4: 1 m (1⅛ yd), size 6: 1.1 m (1¼ yd). One 18 cm (7 in) zip. Matching sewing thread.
*Embroidery:* Stranded embroidery cotton (floss): size 4: 7 skeins of blue, 4 skeins of red; size 6: 3 skeins of white, 3 skeins of blue, 2 skeins of red. One crewel needle.

**Preparation:** Pre-shrink the fabric before you begin. Enlarge the pattern pieces and lay them out on the fabric (remember to leave space for seam allowances). Transfer the outlines of the pattern pieces to be embroidered (bodice front and back, straps and two pockets) on to the gingham using basting stitch. Do not embroider the seam allowances. Do not cut the pattern pieces out until embroidery is complete.

**Embroidery:** Work both patterns with four to six strands of thread, depending on the size of the gingham check. It may help to use a round embroidery frame (hoop) to hold fabric taut.
*Pattern 1 (size 4):* first embroider the blue grid. Work the first row from left to right. Bring the thread out at the lower right-hand corner of the first square, take it up to the upper left-hand corner and pass it under a few threads of fabric. Bring the thread down to the lower left-hand corner of the next square; pass it under a few threads. Repeat this zigzag pattern across the row. Work the next row from left to right, reversing the pattern (see photo 1). Continue this two-row sequence to make a diamond grid.
At the points where the stitches meet along each row of squares, embroider a red cross parallel to the grain of the fabric. In the middle of each diamond-shaped box, embroider a French knot using blue thread (see photo 2).
*Pattern 2 (size 6):* embroider one double cross-stitch in blue on each

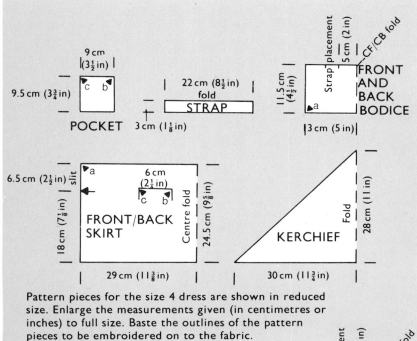

Pattern pieces for the size 4 dress are shown in reduced size. Enlarge the measurements given (in centimetres or inches) to full size. Baste the outlines of the pattern pieces to be embroidered on to the fabric.

**POCKET** 9 cm (3½ in), 9.5 cm (3¾ in), c b

**STRAP** 22 cm (8½ in) fold, 3 cm (1⅛ in)

**FRONT AND BACK BODICE** Strap placement, 5 cm (2 in), CF/CB fold, 11.5 cm (4½ in), 3 cm (5 in), a

**FRONT/BACK SKIRT** 6.5 cm (2½ in) slit, a, 6 cm (2¼ in), c b, 18 cm (7⅛ in), 24.5 cm (9⅝ in), Centre fold, 29 cm (11⅜ in)

**KERCHIEF** Fold, 28 cm (11 in), 30 cm (11¾ in)

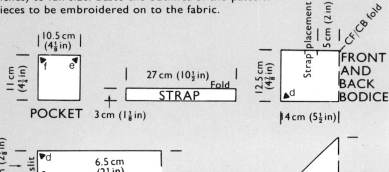

**POCKET** 10.5 cm (4⅛ in), 11 cm (4¼ in), f e

**STRAP** 27 cm (10½ in) Fold, 3 cm (1⅛ in)

**FRONT AND BACK BODICE** Strap placement, 5 cm (2 in), CF/CB fold, 12.5 cm (4⅞ in), 4 cm (5½ in), d

**FRONT/BACK SKIRT** 5.5 cm (2⅛ in) slit, d, 6.5 cm (2½ in), f e, 23 cm (9⅛ in), 28.5 cm (11¼ in), Centre fold, 31 cm (12⅛ in)

**KERCHIEF** Fold, 32 cm (12½ in), 34 cm (13¼ in)

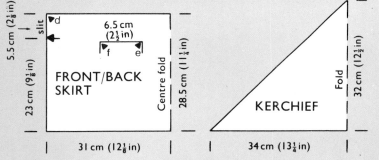

Pattern pieces for the size 6 dress.

*Continued overleaf*

of the white squares and one double cross-stitch in white on each of the blue squares (see photo 3 on previous page). Embroider a red French knot between each double cross-stitch.

**Cutting out:** Cut out the bodice twice on the fold with 1 cm ($\frac{3}{8}$ in) seam allowance at the waist, 2 cm ($\frac{1}{4}$ in) elsewhere. Cut out the strap twice on a lengthwise fold, adding 1 cm ($\frac{3}{8}$ in) seam allowance all round. Cut out the skirt twice on the fold, adding 1 cm ($\frac{3}{8}$ in) seam allowance to the waist edge, 2 cm ($\frac{1}{4}$ in) to the side seams and 5 cm (2 in) at the hem. Cut out the pocket four times, adding 1 cm ($\frac{3}{8}$ in) seam allowance all round (only pocket fronts are embroidered). Cut out the kerchief once on the fold, adding 1 cm ($\frac{3}{8}$ in) seam allowance all round.

**Sewing:** Clean-finish all raw edges on skirt and bodice. With right sides together, stitch the right side seam of bodice. Press under the seam allowance on the left-hand side of bodice, then the seam allowance on the top edge. Fold straps in half lengthwise, with right sides together. Stitch each strap together leaving one end open. Turn to right side, tuck in seam allowances on short end; slipstitch shut. Stitch each strap under top edge of bodice front and back as illustrated. With right sides facing, stitch right side seam of skirt; stitch the left side seam as far as the slit mark. Press under the hem allowance and sew. With right sides together, stitch each embroidered pocket on to a plain pocket, leaving an opening for turning. Turn to right side, slipstitch opening shut and stitch each pocket on to skirt as shown. Gather the skirt top to fit the width of the bodice. With right sides together, stitch skirt to lower edge of bodice, distributing the gathers evenly. Insert the zip into the side opening, using a lapped application.
**Kerchief:** turn under the seam allowance twice and stitch.

# 45

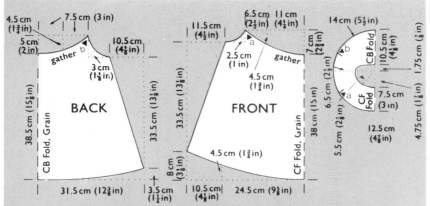

Pattern for the girl's dress is shown in reduced size. Enlarge the measurements given (in centimetres or inches) to full size. The dotted lines are guidelines. For yoke, use a compass to draw a semicircle (radius: 12.25 cm [4$\frac{3}{4}$ in]) on a folded piece of tracing paper. Transfer the diagram measurements on to the tracing. Turn the tracing over, copy the mirror image, open out for full yoke pattern. Copy the markings on to the place mat.

## Summer Dress With Place Mat Yoke

**Size:** To fit a two-year-old child (height: 104 cm [41 in])

**Materials:** One round embroidered place mat (diameter: 24 cm [9$\frac{1}{2}$ in]) or a rectangular place mat with smallest dimension greater than 24 cm (9$\frac{1}{2}$ in). 1 m (1$\frac{1}{8}$ yd) of 90 cm (36 in)-wide light blue cotton fabric. 1.5 m (1$\frac{1}{2}$ yd) of 12 mm ($\frac{1}{2}$ in)-wide light blue bias binding (or 2.5 m [2$\frac{1}{2}$ yd] of binding, including outer mat edge). Three buttons. Matching sewing thread.

**Cutting out:** Enlarge pattern pieces as directed. The whole place mat is inset as the dress yoke. Cut neck opening in place mat centre, without seam allowance. If you cannot

find a circular mat, cut a circle (12.25 cm [4$\frac{3}{4}$ in]radius) from a rectangular place mat or a piece of quilted fabric. *Dress front and back:* cut out armholes without seam allowance; hem allowance is 4 cm (1$\frac{1}{2}$ in); elsewhere add 1 cm ($\frac{3}{8}$ in) seam allowance. *Cut out the following bias strips:* one 35 cm (13$\frac{3}{4}$ in) long for neck edge, one 35 cm (13$\frac{3}{4}$ in) long for back slit, one 15 cm (6 in) long for centre back loops, two each 18 cm (7 in) long for armholes. If outer edge of yoke is unbound, cut an 80 cm (31$\frac{1}{2}$ in) binding strip for it.

**Sewing:** Stitch the side seams and press them open. Bind armhole and neck edges (and outer edge of yoke, if necessary). (For how to apply binding, see instructions for Mother Goose Waistcoat, page 21.) Gather the front to

25 cm (9$\frac{3}{4}$ in) and the back to 28 cm (11 in). (To gather: run parallel rows of machine basting 6 and 12 mm [$\frac{1}{4}$ and $\frac{1}{2}$ in] from fabric edge, then carefully draw up the threads.) Pin and baste the gathered front and back to the yoke, between the markings on the diagram. Stitch dress to yoke, seaming just above top of yoke binding. Make a 15 cm (6 in) slit in centre back, cutting across yoke and into dress fabric. *Make three button loops:* fold binding strip in half lengthwise; stitch close to binding edges. Cut into three equal pieces. Pin button loops to right side of centre back slit, spacing them evenly apart with loops facing away from slit. Bind the slit (open the slit out to do this), catching in the three loops. Press loops towards slit, stitch them down close to the base end. Sew on buttons. Turn up and sew hem.

# 46

## Man's All-weather Jacket

**Size:** One size fits 38–42

**Materials:** 1.6 m (1$\frac{3}{4}$ yd) of 150 cm (58–60 in)-wide water-repellent poplin or gaberdine (oilcloth or lightweight PVC are also suitable). Fourteen 20 mm ($\frac{3}{4}$ in)-diameter eyelets and insertion tool. 3.7 m (4$\frac{1}{8}$ yd) of cotton cord. Matching sewing thread.

**Cutting out:** Enlarge the jacket pattern, drawing a separate pattern piece for the front neckline facing. Cut the pattern pieces out following the pattern layout. Cut out the front, back and collar once each on the fold. Cut out the sleeve twice on the fold. Cut out the gusset twice and the pocket once. *Seam allowances:* add 2 cm ($\frac{3}{4}$ in) to the side seams and hem of front and back. Add 5 cm (2 in) to top edge of pocket, elsewhere add 1 cm ($\frac{3}{8}$ in).

**Sewing:** *Front slit:* clean-finish edges of facing. Baste facing on to jacket front, with right sides together. Stitch 5 mm ($\frac{1}{4}$ in) away from marked slit. Stop 5 cm (2 in) from bottom point. Change to small stitches for 5 cm (2 in) on either side of the point. Taper the stitching to the bottom and take one or two stitches across the point. Slash the opening to the stitching. Press the facing to the inside.
*Pocket:* turn under the 5 cm (2 in) pocket top seam allowance, then topstitch pocket along upper edge and 4 cm (1$\frac{1}{2}$ in) below. Press under the remaining seam allowances, then edgestitch pocket on to jacket front as shown. Next, stitch front to back at shoulder seams and along the side seams between slit mark and gusset, with right sides together.
*Collar:* with right sides together, stitch short sides of collar. With right sides together, stitch the under section of the collar on to the neck edges of the front and back. Stitch upper collar on to the facing as far as the shoulder seams. Press under the remaining collar seam allowance;

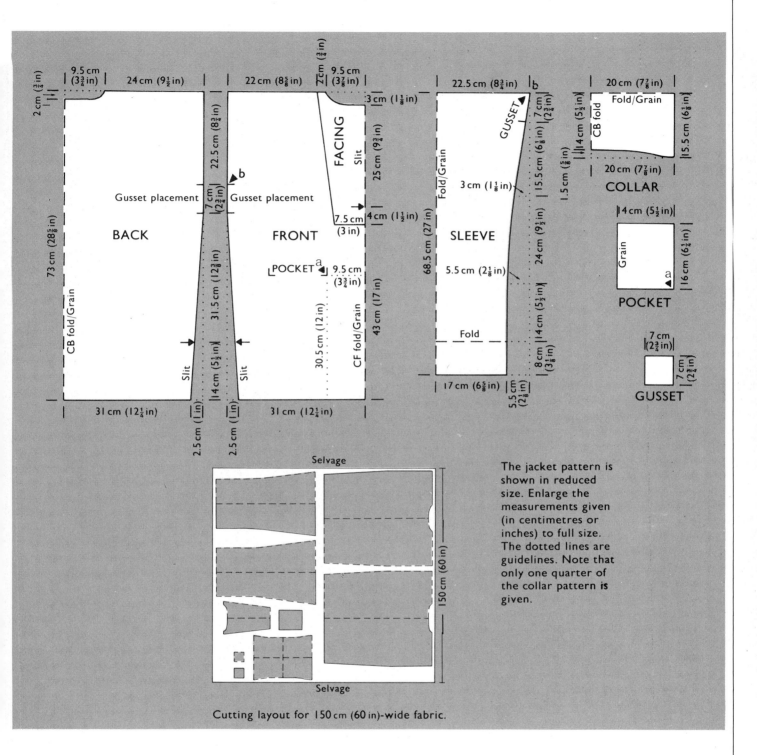

**BACK**

9.5 cm (3¾ in) | 24 cm (9½ in)

2 cm (¾ in)

73 cm (28⅝ in)

CB fold/Grain

22.5 cm (8¾ in)

7 cm (2¾ in)

Gusset placement

31.5 cm (12⅜ in)

Slit

14 cm (5½ in)

31 cm (12¼ in)

2.5 cm (1 in)

**FRONT**

22 cm (8⅝ in)

7 cm (2¾ in)

Gusset placement

30.5 cm (12 in)

CF fold/Grain

2.5 cm (1 in)

31 cm (12¼ in)

POCKET a | 9.5 cm (3¾ in)

Slit

**FACING**

9.5 cm (3¾ in)

3 cm (1⅛ in)

25 cm (9¾ in)

Slit

7.5 cm (3 in) | 4 cm (1½ in)

43 cm (17 in)

**SLEEVE**

22.5 cm (8¾ in) | b

GUSSET

7 cm (2¾ in)

15.5 cm (6⅛ in)

68.5 cm (27 in)

Fold/Grain

3 cm (1⅛ in)

5.5 cm (2⅛ in)

24 cm (9½ in)

14 cm (5½ in)

8 cm (3⅛ in)

Fold

17 cm (6⅝ in) | 5.5 cm (2⅛ in)

1.5 cm (⅝ in)

4 cm (1½ in)

CB fold

**COLLAR**

20 cm (7⅞ in)

Fold/Grain

15.5 cm (6⅛ in)

20 cm (7⅞ in)

**POCKET**

14 cm (5½ in)

Grain

16 cm (6¼ in)

a

**GUSSET**

7 cm (2¾ in)

7 cm (2¾ in)

Selvage

150 cm (60 in)

Selvage

Cutting layout for 150 cm (60 in)-wide fabric.

The jacket pattern is shown in reduced size. Enlarge the measurements given (in centimetres or inches) to full size. The dotted lines are guidelines. Note that only one quarter of the collar pattern is given.

slipstitch it to the back neck edge. Topstitch all round the collar and the neckline slit the width of the machine foot. Slipstitch the bottom edge of the neckline facing to the jacket. Press under and stitch the hem, then topstitch all round hem and side slits the width of the machine foot.
*Sleeves:* with right sides together, stitch the sleeve seams as far as the start of the gusset. Turn under each sleeve along the fold

line and stitch the hem. Turn up the sleeve cuffs. With right sides together, stitch on each sleeve as far as the gusset (with points **b** matching), but not beyond the seam allowance. With right sides together, set in each gusset.
*Punch in three eyelets on both sides of the front slit:* insert the top ones 3 cm (1⅛ in) below the neck edge and 3 cm (1⅛ in) to either side of the slit. Insert two more eyelets on either side, each spaced 9.5 cm (3¾ in)

below the previous eyelet. Next, punch in two eyelets on both sides of each side slit. Insert the lower eyelets 4 cm (1½ in) above the hem edge and 3 cm (1⅛ in) from the slit edge. Insert the upper eyelets 7.5 cm (3 in) above these. Lace a 2.1 m (2⅜ yd) cord through the neckline eyelets and an 80 cm (32 in) cord through each set of side slit eyelets. Knot the ends of the cord.

# 47

## Woman's All-weather Jacket

**Size:** One size fits 12–16 (10–14 U.S.)

**Materials:** 1.7 m (1⅞ yd) of 150 cm (58–60 in)-wide nylon ciré or water-repellent gaberdine. Separating zips in a contrasting colour: one 65 cm (26 in) zip, two 18 cm (7 in) and three 12 cm (5 in) zips. Elastic thread (for shirring). 2 m (2¼ yd) of nylon cord (same colour as zip tape). Matching polyester thread.

**Cutting out:** Enlarge pattern pieces, drawing a separate pattern piece for the front facing. Check sleeve and jacket pattern length to see if length is correct, before cutting out. (Remember: if you alter the jacket length, change the zip length accordingly.) Do not use pins when cutting out the pattern pieces; they will make permanent holes in the nylon ciré. Instead, weight or tape pattern pieces in place. Referring to pattern layout, cut out the following pieces: cut out the front and back twice each, adding 3 cm (1⅛ in) at the hem, 2 cm (¾ in) at the sleeve hems and 1 cm (⅜ in) elsewhere. Cut out the front facing twice, adding 5 mm (¼ in) seam allowance to the neck edge, elsewhere 1 cm (⅜ in). Cut out the hood once on the fold, adding 5 mm (¼ in) seam allowance at the neck, 2 cm (¾ in) at the front edge and 1 cm (⅜ in) elsewhere. Cut out the small pocket and pocket top three times each with 1 cm (⅜ in) seam allowance all round. Cut out the large pocket and pocket top twice each with 1 cm (⅜ in) seam allowance all round.

**Sewing:** To avoid making holes, pin or baste only within the seam allowances. Nylon ciré may slip under the machine foot. If this happens, stitch through strips of tissue paper placed under fabric, between fabric and machine feed. Afterwards, the tissue paper tears away easily.

*Jacket assembly:* insert and stitch the front zip: pin wrong side of zip on to right side of the front facing strips, turning under the neck edge seam allowances of the facing strips as you do so. The raw edge of the facing strips should meet in the middle of the zip. Stitch zip on to facing 1 cm (⅜ in) to either side of the zip middle. Turn back and baste down the facing seam allowances to either side of the zip, then turn the remaining facing seam allowances on to the wrong side of the fabric. Turn under the seam allowances at the front edges of the jacket. Centre the zip between the two jacket fronts so that the folded edges of the jacket fronts lie on top of the previous zip stitching lines; baste zip in place. Edgestitch both sides of the zip from neck to hem edge.

*Pockets:* turn under the seam allowance on the interior edges (between pocket top and main section) where the zip is to be inserted. Centre the zip (of appropriate size) underneath so that 2 cm (¾ in) of the zip tape is visible; baste in place. Stitch zip close to the edges. Turn under the outer pocket edges, then edgestitch the breast and hip pockets on to jacket at the positions marked, matching the lettered points. With right sides together, stitch the centre back seam, the shoulder seams and the undersleeve/side seams. Turn right side out. Edgestitch the sleeve pocket in place. Turn under the hem allowance and stitch it close to the edge.

*Shirring:* wind elastic thread on to the bobbin and thread the top of the machine with polyester. (For tips on shirring, see maternity blouse instructions, page 80.) Stitch on the right side of the fabric. For the waist shirring, stitch six rows spaced 1 cm (⅜ in) apart, in the area marked. Turn under each sleeve hem allowance twice (1 cm [⅜ in] each time); baste in place. Shirr each cuff within the area marked, stitching five rows spaced 1 cm (⅜ in) apart and catching in the hem allowance as you do so.

*Hood:* with right sides together, stitch the centre back seam of the hood, then the cross seam,

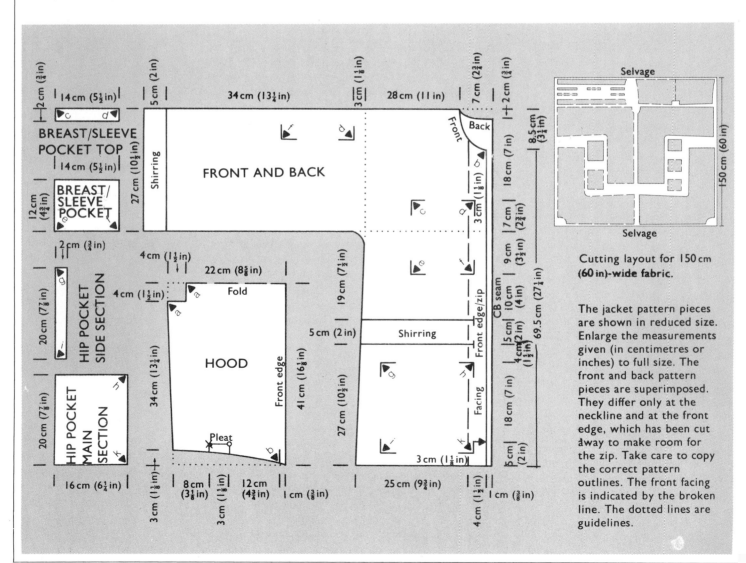

Cutting layout for 150 cm (60 in)-wide fabric.

The jacket pattern pieces are shown in reduced size. Enlarge the measurements given (in centimetres or inches) to full size. The front and back pattern pieces are superimposed. They differ only at the neckline and at the front edge, which has been cut away to make room for the zip. Take care to copy the correct pattern outlines. The front facing is indicated by the broken line. The dotted lines are guidelines.

matching points **a**. To form bottom pleats, match each X to an O, then stitch along the neckline seam allowance. With right sides together, stitch hood on to neck edge, matching points **b** and with a pleat falling at each shoulder seam. Turn under the neck edge seam allowance and stitch a narrow seam. Turn under the front edge of the hood twice and stitch 1 cm (⅜ in) from the edge, forming a casing. Thread the cord through the casing and knot the ends.

# 48
## Hungarian-style Waistcoat (Vest)

**Size:** Medium: to fit 12–14 (10–12 u.s.)

**Materials:** 0.65 m (¾ yd) of 150 cm (58–60 in)-wide black flannel or similar woollen fabric. 1.45 m (1¼ yd) of 5 cm (2 in)-wide embroidered trim. 2.65 m (3 yd) of narrow green rickrack. 4.65 m (5⅛ yd) of narrow red rickrack. Matching sewing thread.

**Cutting out:** Enlarge the waistcoat pattern making separate pattern pieces for the front, the back and the front, back and armhole facings. Cut out the pattern pieces from a double layer of fabric, following the cutting layout. Cut out the back and the back facing once on the fold. Cut out two waistcoat fronts (a right and a left side), two front facings and two front and two back armhole facings. Add 2 cm (¾ in) seam allowance to the waistcoat shoulder and side seams, add a 4 cm (1½ in) hem allowance and a 1 cm (⅜ in) seam allowance elsewhere. Add a 1 cm (⅜ in) seam allowance to all facings. Mark the position of the centre back dart on the wrong side of the fabric.

**Sewing:** With right sides together, stitch the shoulder and side seams. Clean-finish the seam allowances. With right sides together, stitch the back dart. Slit it and press it open, clean-finishing the edges. With right sides together, stitch back facing to each front facing at the shoulder seams and seam each pair of front and back armhole facings at shoulder and side seams, forming a ring. Clean-finish the outer edges of the facings. With right sides together and the raw edges even, stitch the front/back and armhole facings on to the waistcoat, matching shoulder and/or side seams. Turn up and stitch the hem.
*Trimming:* baste a piece of embroidered trim down the centre back, starting from the neck edge down to 11 cm (4¼ in) above the hem edge. Before basting, turn under the top and bottom ends of the trim 5 mm (¼ in) and overcast the edges if they tend to fray. Stitch along both edges of the trim. On either side of the trim, stitch a row of green rickrack 1 cm (⅜ in) away and a row of red rickrack 2.5 cm (1 in) away. Continue each band of red rickrack 1 cm (⅜ in) from the edge of the back neckline, the front neckline and the front edge. Stop 11 cm (4¼ in) from the hem edge. Arrange the rickrack so that an outer point turns each of the two corners.

Stitch a row of red rickrack round each armhole 1 cm (⅜ in) from the edge. Stitch the embroidered trim along the bottom of the waistcoat, 3.5 cm (1–1¼ in) above the hem edge. On either side of the trim, stitch a row of green rickrack 1 cm (⅜ in) away and a row of red rickrack 2.5 cm (1 in) away. The top row of red rickrack conceals the ends of the previously applied trimming. Narrowly turn under rickrack ends at waistcoat front. Apply the embroidered trim in the same way as before.

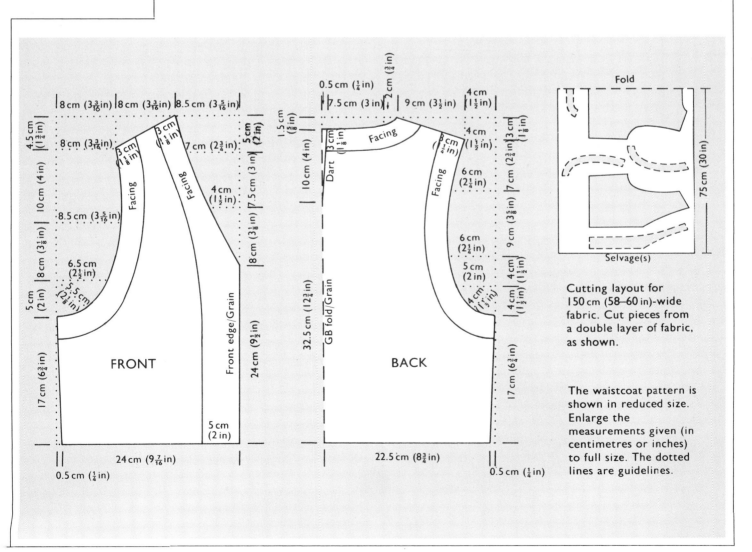

Cutting layout for 150 cm (58–60 in)-wide fabric. Cut pieces from a double layer of fabric, as shown.

The waistcoat pattern is shown in reduced size. Enlarge the measurements given (in centimetres or inches) to full size. The dotted lines are guidelines.

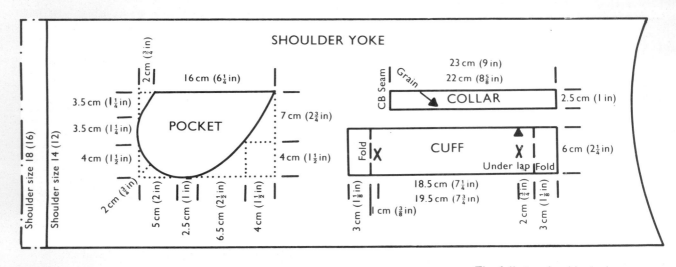

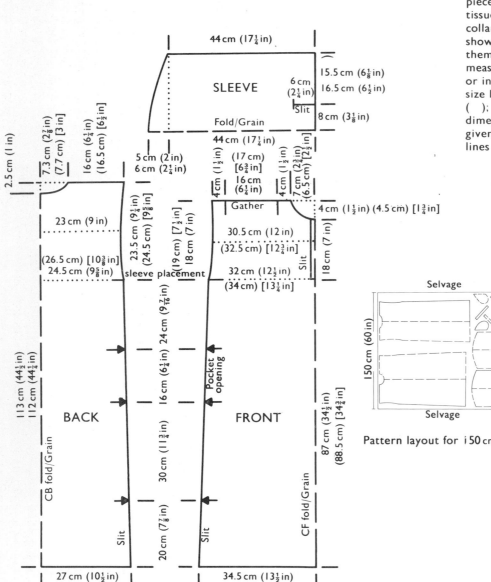

The full size shoulder/yoke pattern piece is given above; trace it on to tissue paper. The pocket, stand-up collar and cuff pattern pieces are shown in reduced size. Enlarge them according to the measurements given (in centimetres or inches). Metric dimensions for size large are given in parentheses ( ); Imperial/U.S. standard dimensions for size 18 (16) are given in brackets [ ]. The dotted lines are guidelines.

Pattern pieces for the sleeve, dress front and back are shown here in reduced size. Enlarge the measurements given (in centimetres or inches) to full size. Dimensions for size large are in parentheses ( ) or brackets [ ]. The dotted lines are guidelines.

Pattern layout for 150 cm (60 in)-wide fabric (both sizes).

# 49

## Russian-inspired Dress

**Sizes:** *Medium:* to fit 12–14 (10–12 U.S.) or *Large:* to fit 16–18 (14–16 U.S.)

**Materials:** 1.8 m (2 yds) of 150 cm (58–60 in)-wide or 3 m (3⅜ yd) of 90 cm (36 in)-wide poplin. Embroidered trim, 6 cm (2¼ in) wide: size medium: 1.7 m (1⅞ yd), size large: 1.8 m (2 yd). Contrasting bias binding, 24 mm (1 in) wide: size medium: 1.9 m (2⅛ yd), size large: 2 m (2¼ yd). 0.1 m (⅛ yd) of iron-on interfacing (for collar, cuffs). One wooden toggle button. 25 cm (10 in) of elastic cord (for belt fastening). Two large snap fasteners. Matching sewing thread.

**Cutting out:** Enlarge the pattern pieces for the dress front and back, sleeve, cuff, collar and pocket, in the appropriate size. Trace the full size collar pattern on to tissue paper. Referring to pattern layout (for 150 cm [60 in]-wide fabric), cut out the following: cut out front and back once each with 1 cm (⅜ in) seam allowance on shoulder and sleeve placement seams, 2 cm (¾ in) at side seams and hem. Cut sleeve out twice, adding 1 cm (⅜ in) seam allowance all round. Cut out the stand-up collar four times from fabric (on the bias) and twice from iron-on interfacing, adding 1 cm (⅜ in) seam allowance along neck edge, none elsewhere. Iron interfacing on to two of the fabric collars. Cut out the in-seam pocket four times with 1 cm (⅜ in) seam allowance all round. If using 90 cm (36 in)-wide poplin, disregard the given pattern layout and cut out main pattern pieces (dress front, back, sleeves) end-to-end on the fold. Then cut other pieces from remaining fabric. Cut a 14 cm (5½ in) strip of bias binding for each sleeve placket. Cut out the shoulder yoke and the cuff twice each from embroidered trim (seam allowance included). Cut the cuff out twice in interfacing and iron a piece on to the wrong side of each trim cuff. Cut a strip of embroidered trim to waist length *minus* 4 cm (1½ in), for the belt.

**Sewing:** *Clean-finish the following raw edges:* side and shoulder yoke seams on dress front and back, sleeve and cuff placement seams, the straight edge of the in-seam pockets and the short ends of cuffs.

*Pockets:* with right sides together and straight edges even, stitch each pocket piece between the pocket opening markings on the dress front and back. Press pocket and side seam allowances outwards. With right sides together, stitch front to back at side seams, starting from below armhole opening and continuing round the pocket curve as far as the bottom slit. Press pockets towards the front and clip the pocket back seam allowance diagonally into the corners. Clean-finish the pocket seam allowances together. Next, press hem allowance under twice and stitch. Press under the seam allowances on the side slits and stitch. On the dress front, gather the shoulder yoke placement seam within the area marked to 8 cm (3⅛ in) for size medium or 9 cm (3½ in) for size large. Edgestitch each shoulder yoke (embroidered trim) between front and back of the dress, with wrong side of trim to right side of dress. With right sides together, stitch the centre back seams of the fabric and interfaced stand-up collar pieces. On the dress front, measure and mark 1 cm (⅜ in) to either side of the neckline slit; slash along the middle and then clip diagonally into the corners.

*Collar:* pin the stand-up collar without interfacing on to the neck edge, with right sides together and raw edges even. Pin the interfaced collar on to the neck edge, right side to wrong (the dress fabric is sandwiched in between). Stitch the collar on in one seam, press upwards and baste together along the sides and top edge. Bind all round the edges of the neckline and collar: press the binding in half lengthwise to fit over the raw edges of the fabric. Baste binding in place through all layers, leaving 15 mm (⅝ in) extending at the starting and finishing points at the slit bottom. Turn under the ends of the binding, enclosing the fabric triangle at slit bottom (to do so, cut middle of triangle down to the base). Edgestitch the binding in place, taking care to catch in all layers.

*Bound sleeve plackets:* cut along the marked slit line at the cuff edge of each sleeve (on the left side of the right sleeve and the right side of the left sleeve). Press each 14 cm (5½ in) binding strip in half lengthwise. Spread each slit apart and baste the bias binding over the raw edges with wrong side of binding to right side of fabric and with a 5 mm (¼ in) seam allowance at cuff edge tapering off as narrowly as possible at the point of the slit. Edgestitch the binding in place, taking care to catch in all layers. From the right side of the fabric, press the placket underlap towards the nearest sleeve seam. To prevent the placket from rolling outwards, topstitch diagonally across the binding fold at the top of the slit. Next, stitch the sleeve seams with right sides facing.

*Cuffs:* gather each sleeve hem to 19.5 cm (7¾ in) for size medium or to 20.5 cm (8 in) for size large. Edgestitch the embroidered trim cuff on, with wrong side of cuff to right side of fabric, wrapping the folds around the seam allowance on the wrong side as you do so. Sew a snap fastener on to each cuff. Next, set in the sleeves, with wrong sides together; trim seam allowances down to 5 mm (¼ in).

*Bind the armhole seams:* for each sleeve, cut a strip of binding to armhole circumference + 3 cm (1⅛ in); press binding in half lengthwise. Fit the binding over the raw edges of each armhole, leaving 15 mm (⅝ in) extending at the starting and finishing points at the side seam. Baste binding in place, then edgestitch it round each armhole, taking care to catch in all layers.

*Belt:* clean-finish the raw edges of the short ends; press each end under 3 cm (1⅛ in) and sew down. Cut two 12 cm (5 in) pieces of elastic cord. Knot each piece into a loop, passing the left-hand one through the hole in the toggle. On the wrong side of the belt, sew each loop on to the middle of the corresponding short end.

# SEWING COURSE

*A Basic Guide to Sewing Techniques*

## Stitch Glossary

1) *Basting:* a temporary stitch used during garment construction. The thread runs alternately above and below the fabric. Work from right to left. Basting is used to hold two layers of fabric together during garment fittings and to secure seams while sewing.

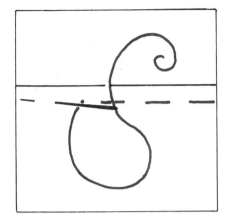
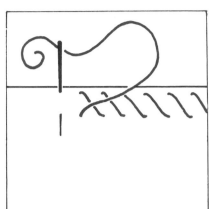

2) *Diagonal tacking:* a wide covering stitch used to hold fabric layers together. Use it on seams which lie along the edge (e.g. collar), to prevent slipping during pressing or topstitching. Insert the needle at a right angle to the edge and make short, straight stitches. Diagonal stitches result. You can work this stitch in various directions.

3) *Backstitch:* a permanent stitch used for repairing seams. Work it from right to left. Bring the needle out, then insert it horizontally into the hole made by the previous stitch. Carry the thread on the back the distance of two stitches, then bring the needle out again. On the right side, backstitch resembles machine stitching. On the wrong side, the stitches overlap.

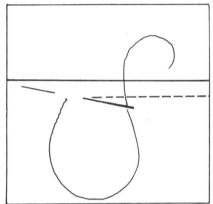
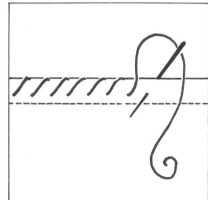

4a) *Overcasting (a):* to clean-finish raw edges which fray easily when machine zigzag is impractical. Working from right to left, take slanted stitches over the edge. Space the stitches closely and uniformly. Do not pull the thread too tight. The raw edges to be clean-finished should be as straight as possible and neat.

4b) *Overcasting (b):* as a joining stitch. This gives you a flat seam when fabrics are stitched edge-to-edge. Use it on fabrics which do not fray (leather, fur, felt).

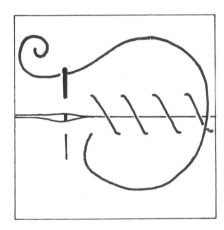
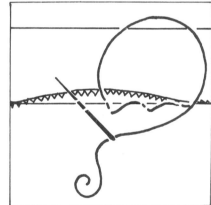

5) *Blindstitch:* this produces a hem which is invisible on both sides of the garment. Work from right to left. With the needle pick up one or two threads of the top layer and at the same time insert the needle into the turned up hem edge. The stitches are slightly diagonal. Keep the thread fairly loose. Use it to hold facings in place.

6) *Herringbone stitch (catchstitch):* holds two layers of fabric loosely in place. Work from left to right. With each backstitch catch a few threads from the hem and the upper fabric layer alternately, forming small crosses. Use herringbone stitch to hem stretchy fabrics and to secure interfacing or facings on to the wrong side of fabric.

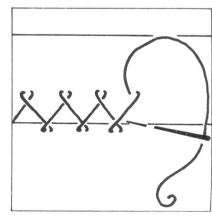

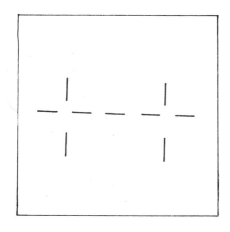

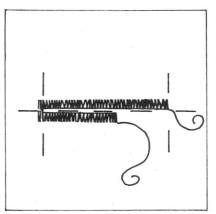

## Machine buttonholes

1) A machine-made buttonhole is worked into the finished garment. Transfer buttonhole markings from pattern on to the wrong side of the fabric. Sew a basting thread along the lines.

2) Stitch using closely spaced zigzag stitches. Keep the stitch length as short as possible, the stitch width approx. 2 mm ($\frac{1}{8}$ in). For the bar, set the machine to double the stitch width i.e. 4 mm ($\frac{1}{4}$ in), and make a few stitches backwards and forwards. Leave the needle in the fabric and pivot the garment round in the machine. Re-set the width to approx. 2 mm ($\frac{1}{8}$ in) and finish sewing the buttonhole.

3) Fasten the thread on the wrong side. Cut open the middle of the buttonhole using seam ripper, single-edged razor blade or very sharp scissors. On machines which make buttonholes automatically, follow the manufacturer's instructions.

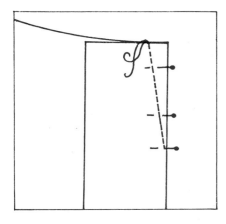

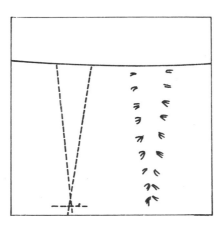

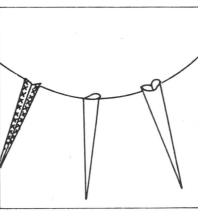

## Simple dart

1) Darts have to be made very carefully in the fabric so that they come out evenly. You can transfer the pattern markings using tailor's tacks or a tracing wheel and dressmaker's carbon paper in a colour which contrasts with the fabric. Mark a small cross at the point of the dart.

2) Fold the dart exactly along the middle and mark this with pins stuck crosswise into the fabric.
Important note: *Tack* the dart from the point to the fabric edge; *stitch* it from the wide part to the point.

3) *Three ways of pressing a dart (left to right):* with heavy fabrics or curved darts, slash them open along the fold, clean-finish and press them apart. When using thin fabric, press the dart to one side towards the middle of the garment or iron it flat so that the stitching line lies along the middle of the dart.

## Eyelets – punched in

1) Mark the point where you are going to punch in the eyelet. Make a hole with a riveting tool or, depending on the fabric, cut out a small triangle (on the fold) with a pair of scissors. Eyelets often come packaged in kit form, with an insertion tool. In this case, follow the manufacturer's instructions.

2) On the right side of the fabric use your hand to press the eyelet into the hole you have pre-punched or cut.

3) Rivet the eyelet on the wrong side of the fabric: place the eyelet-threaded fabric on a firm, protected surface. Position the tool horizontally on top; hit hard and straight on.

4) Use eyelets when you want a laced fastening. The contrasting colour of the cord will look very attractive.

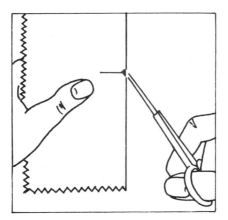
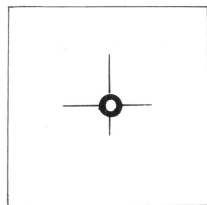
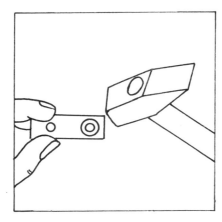
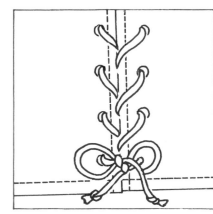

## Zip: centred application

1) Machine-stitch the seam to the point where the zip is to start. Hand- or machine-baste the remainder of the seam where the zip is to go. Press the whole seam open. Then press underneath the seam allowance to remove pressure marks.

2) Place the teeth of the open zip along the closed seam. Make sure that the wrong side of the zip faces upwards. Pin down firmly and baste using diagonal tacking stitches. Make sure when tacking that the fabric and the zip lie absolutely flat; take great care when tacking.

3) When you have basted both sides of the zip, stitch it in place on the *right side* of the fabric. The zip foot attachment on the machine will be a help here. Stitch along one side of the zip taking care to catch in the tape. Stop when you are near the bottom of the zip. Pivot the machine needle in the fabric, stitch across the base, pivot the needle again and stitch back up the other side.

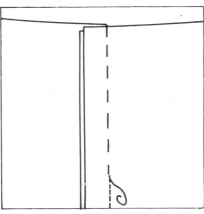
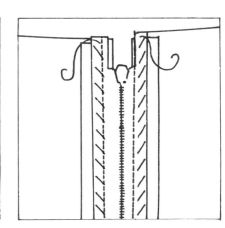
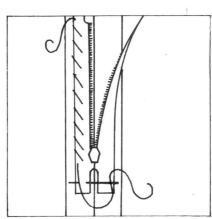

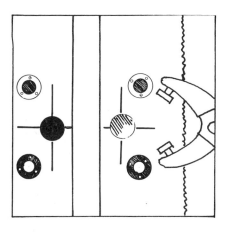
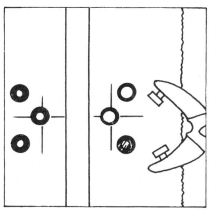

## Punching in snap fasteners

1) Mark the point where you are going to punch in the fastener with a cross. *Underlap:* place stud above, ring with prongs below. *Overlap:* cap above, ring with prongs in tool. Press tool together. The cross should be in the centre.

2) *Alternative method:* snap fastener with open ring visible on overlap. *Underlap:* spring above, insert ring below. *Overlap:* pronged ring above, place stud in tool.

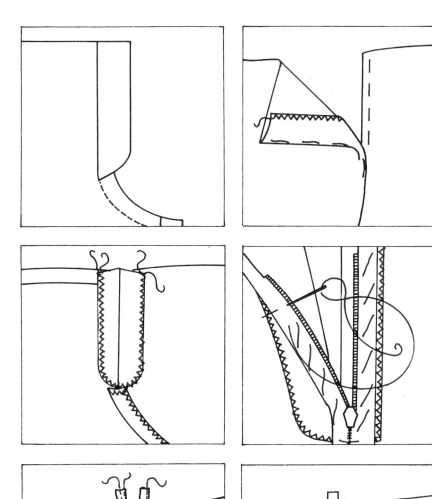

## Zips on trousers

1) Cut out both trouser sections together. Cut a slit overlap on both. This acts as the seam allowance for finishing off the slit. First of all, stitch the crutch (crotch) seam as far as the start of the zip and secure the end using machine backstitches. Here, we show women's trousers which lap right over left.

2) Do not stitch on the zip as a continuation of the seam. Instead, mark the centre front line (the continuation of the seam) on both pieces with basting stitches. On the left trouser piece, extend 5 mm ($\frac{1}{4}$ in) of the seam allowance beyond the basted line. Press this fold under, first clipping 5 mm ($\frac{1}{4}$ in) crosswise into the seam allowance at the bottom of the zip opening. On the right trouser piece press the flap under along the marked centre front line.

3) Clean-finish the edges of the flap using zigzag stitching, remembering to stitch the crosswise cut as well.

4) Baste the zip in with diagonal tacking stitches. On the left-hand side (underlap) the fold runs close to the zip teeth. The right hand side (overlap) should fully conceal the closed zip. If you are more used to doing this, it is sufficient to just pin it.

5) Stitch the zip on by machine. Stitch the left hand side of the zip close to the teeth, using a one-sided zip foot. Stitch along the edge of the zip. Make sure that the other half of the zip is positioned so that the overlap edge lies exactly along the original seamline of the underlap (zip closed).

6) After you have finished sewing, remove tacking stitches. Press the finished zip carefully on the right side.

## Flat-fell seam

This seam is fully reversible. Stitch both layers of fabric together with a simple seam, wrong sides facing. The seam allowances then lie on the right side. Press the seam towards garment back. Trim 5 mm ($\frac{1}{4}$ in) off the lower seam. Fold the top seam over this, turning the raw edge under. Stitch through all layers, close to the fold.

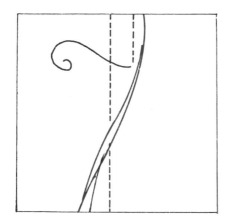

## Binding using bias binding or bias tape

1) *Binding a straight edge:* pin the binding to the edge, right sides together, and stitch. The distance from the edge to the stitching line is the finished width of the binding. The binding is then folded up and over the edge of the fabric and stitched along the seamline, catching in all layers.

2) *Binding a curved edge:* press the bias binding into shape before sewing. To do this, stretch one long side and ease in the opposite long side. Bias strips made from very stiff fabric are easier to press into shape when damp.

3) Here you can see a curved edge being bound. After the bias binding has been pressed into shape, it is stitched on along the stretched edge, right sides together. Stitch the edge you have folded on to the wrong side to the seamline using small handstitches.

4) *Binding a collar corner:* baste together top and bottom collar pieces wrong sides facing using diagonal stitches. Stitch together along outside edges taking a narrow seam. Stitch the bias binding to the bottom collar piece as far as the corner. Fasten off the end of the thread and take the needle out of the fabric. Fold the binding at a right angle to the stitched edge and insert needle on the other side at the last stitch. Fasten off the thread and stitch to the next corner.

5) Fold the full width of the binding on to the right side of the fabric. The binding is then laid round the corner. The mitre will form automatically in the corner on the right side and can be sewn down by hand. Baste binding in place, then stitch down close to inside edge.

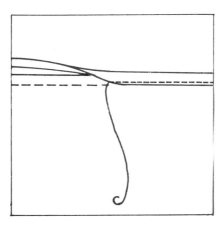

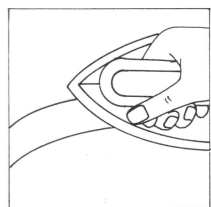

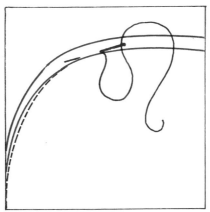

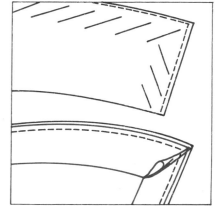

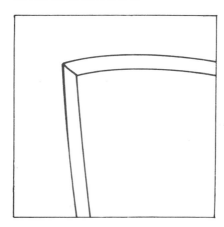

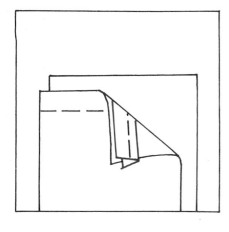

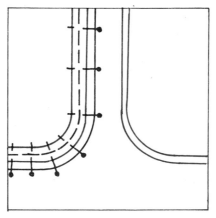

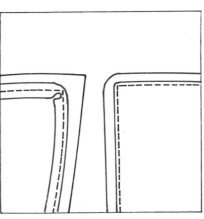

## Piping

1) Piping is a narrow bias strip, either folded flat or cord-filled, which is *inserted into a seam* as a decorative trim. To sew piping along a straight seam, baste the folded bias strip or purchased piping on to the right side of one piece of fabric, with seamlines matching and raw edges facing outwards. (The finished width extends below the seamline.) Baste the other piece of fabric over the piping with right sides together; stitch along seamline through all layers. If piping is filled, use a zip foot.

2) *Piping a curved edge:* shape the folded bias strip or purchased cord-filled piping round the curve (stretch the raw edges, ease in the fold). Baste it on to the right side of the fabric, with seamlines matching and raw edges facing outwards. Baste the garment facing or other piece of fabric over the piping, with right sides together; stitch along the seamline, through all layers. When it is turned right side out, the piping projects from the edge.

3) *Piping a corner:* baste the folded bias strip or purchased piping on to right side of fabric, with seamlines matching and raw edges outwards. (If piping a collar, baste piping on to undercollar.) A small pleat forms at the corner. Baste garment facing or other piece of fabric over piping, with right sides facing. Stitch through all layers, pivoting machine needle at corner and taking care not to catch in the pleat. Turn piped edge to right side, then edgestitch through all thicknesses.

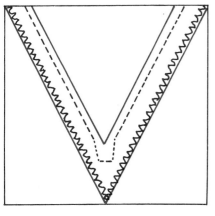

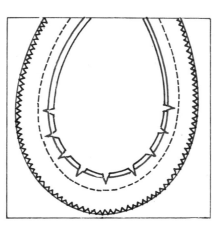

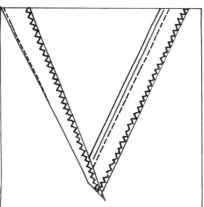

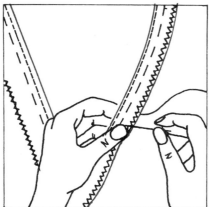

## Facing a neckline

1) *Stitching a facing on to a V-cut neckline:* if the garment is unlined, clean-finish the outer edges of the facing. The facing is then stitched on, right sides together, along the seamline. Just above the V point, on either side, stitch the facing on using small stitches. Sew one or two stitches across the point of the V. Clip into the seam allowance at the point.

2) *On armholes:* stitch the facing on right sides together here as well. Clip into the seam allowances repeatedly along the curved edge.

3) Press the seam allowances towards the facing. To prevent the facing from rolling outwards, understitch the facing through all thicknesses. Now turn the facing inside. Baste through the edge, pushing the seam 2 mm (⅛ in) below the fold so that it cannot be seen on the right side. Press the edge.

4) With unlined garments, stitch the free edge of the facing on by hand to make an invisible seam. With lined garments it is sufficient to tack the facing on to the shoulders and side seams.

## Skirt waistband

1) On the wrong side of the waistband strip, press iron-on interfacing on to the lengthwise half of the waistband which is to be stitched on to the skirt. Clean-finish the long edge of the waistband on the interfaced half.

2) Pin the waistband on to the waist edge of the skirt with right sides together. Fix the band at four points by sticking pins vertically into the seam edge. Match the pattern markings. Ease top edge of skirt to fit waistband. Baste the waistband, then stitch along the seamline. If there is an end tab, make sure it extends the proper distance.

3) To ensure that the seam is flat on the right side, press the seam allowances apart. The waistband should be behind the seam allowance. Press both seam allowances straight up. For heavy fabrics, grade and clip the seam allowances.

4) Stitch the short ends together with right sides facing. Trim diagonally across the corners. Do not stitch the short ends too close to the waistband; leave room for the seam allowances when the band is turned.

5) On the wrong side of the waistband, turn under the seam allowance on the free edge. Pin or baste the waistband in place through all layers with the folded edge on the back slightly overlapping the seamline. Stitch the waistband along the seamline, catching in all layers.

6) Place the waistband overlap over the underlap and sew on a skirt hook and bar using strong thread. Hooks and bars, which are specially designed for waistbands, are available in haberdashery (notions) departments. They are easy to sew on and do not show.

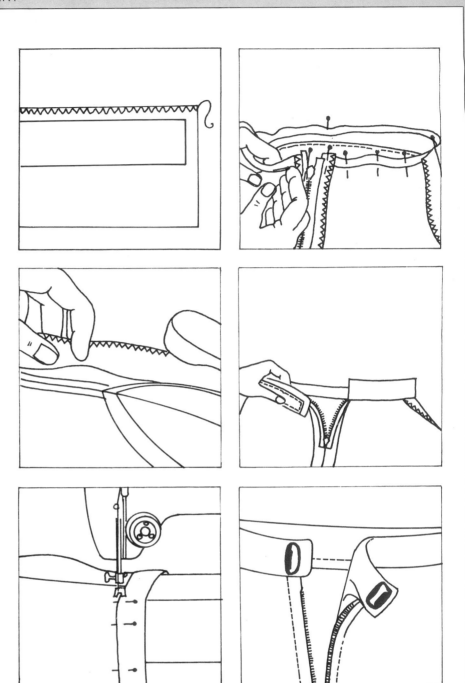

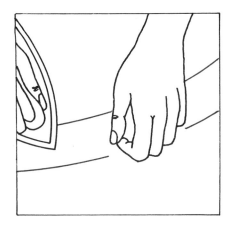
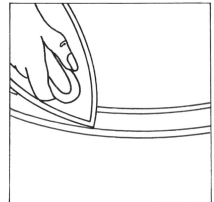
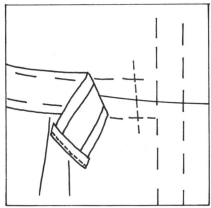
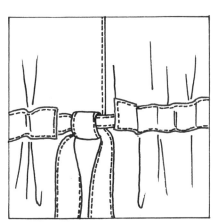

## Waistband casing

1) Before you sew on the strip you will have to shape it to the contours of the waist. Stretch the bias binding on one long side (pull it lengthwise a little) and ease in the other long side. Bias binding made from very stiff material can be pressed into shape more easily when damp.

2) Now mark the finished width and length of the strip using basting thread. Then press under the seam allowances all round. Stitch down the seam allowances on both short ends of the strip.

3) Mark the garment at equal distances along both sides of the waist seam to indicate the placement line for the casing. Then baste the strip on firmly, wrong side to right, with the stretched side towards skirt. Now stitch the strip on along both long sides, keeping close to the edge. Sew the tieband together and topstitch.

4) Thread the tieband through the channel between the fabric and the casing strip; draw it up to fit. The picture shows the finished casing on the garment.

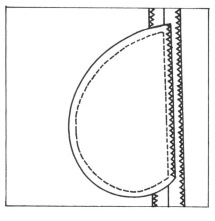
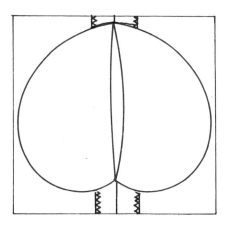
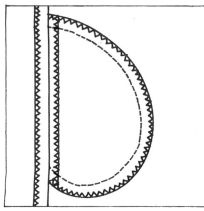
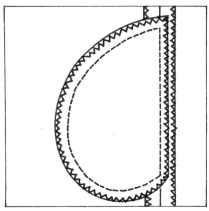

## In-seam pocket

1) Pin one pocket pouch to the garment, right side to wrong, and with the rounded edge at the bottom, along the slit line of the back piece. Stitch the pocket pouch along the slit line only; do not stitch into the seam allowances. Tie the thread ends securely.

2) Stitch the other pocket pouch along the slit line of the front section. This is the top pocket piece. Edgestitch this pocket piece just inside the placement seam on the seam allowance. This prevents the pocket from rolling outwards.

3) Stitch both pocket pouches together, right sides facing, round the curved edges. Here again you must sew exactly to the end of the slit and fasten the thread securely with a few backstitches. Finally clean-finish the seam allowances of the pocket pouches together. Press the pocket towards the front of the garment.

4) This is the finished in-seam pocket. In this method the pocket has been inserted as a separate unit. It is also possible to attach an in-seam pocket in a single operation while stitching the side seam (see maternity blouse, page 80).

## Simple rolled collar

1) Cut out the upper collar and the undercollar along the indicated grain adding 1 cm (⅜ in) seam allowance. To stiffen the collar, cut out a piece of iron-on interfacing for the undercollar. Make sure that the interfacing fibres run in the same direction as the collar grain. Trim interfacing, then iron it on to the undercollar. Transfer pattern markings with dressmaker's carbon paper.

2) Mark the roll line on the upper collar with a line of basting. Pin both collar pieces together with right sides facing and raw edges even. Distribute the excess fullness of the upper collar evenly in the corners.

3) With upper collar on top, stitch the collar pieces together along the sides and outer edge. Adjust the machine to a small stitch length on either side of each corner. Take one or two stitches diagonally across each corner. (This leaves room for the seam allowances when the corner is turned.) Trim seam allowances to 5 mm (¼ in); clip diagonally across corners, almost to the stitching line.

4) After turning, baste the edge of the collar carefully using diagonal hand stitches. On the upper collar side, roll the seam out with your hand and push it back so that it lies just under the edge. The seam should not be visible on the upper collar. Press the edge on the under collar side.

5) Baste upper and under collar pieces together along the roll line using diagonal tacking. Shape the collar around your hand as you do this so that it rolls easily. Steam-press the collar on a tailor's ham, if you have one, to set the shape.

6) Arrange the collar the way it is to appear on your garment. If you have carried out the instructions correctly, it should fall properly on its own. It shouldn't bulge, pull or stretch. Both halves should be identical in appearance and size.

7) Baste both neck edges together as they fall, following the undercollar seamline. Pin the collar on to the garment neckline, starting at the centre and working out towards the shoulder seams. Insert pins crosswise, matching pattern markings.

8) Finish the neck edge with a facing. Join the shoulder seams on the front and back facing. Pin the facing, right sides together, on to the neck edge, sandwiching the collar between garment and facing. Stitch all layers together in one seam. Trim the seam allowances down to 5 mm (¼ in).

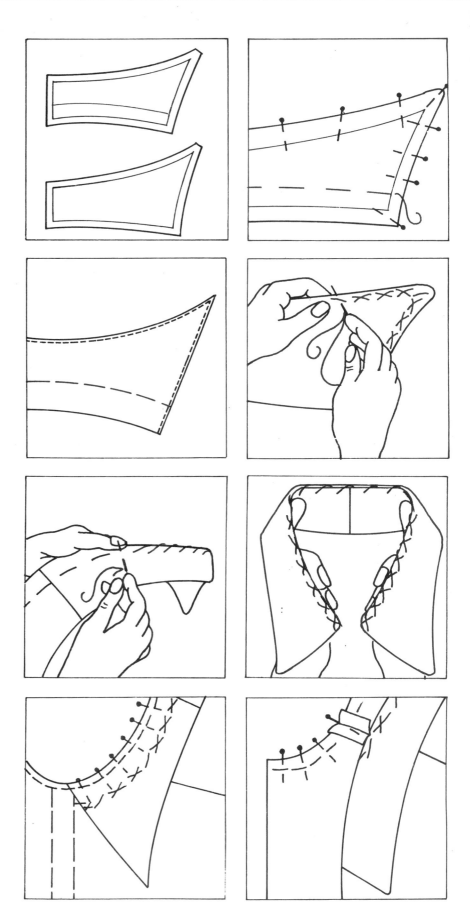

# EMBROIDERY

From simple cross-stitch to intricate openwork, from jobs you can complete quickly to those which demand a greater investment of time – you will find *many* attractive designs on the following pages,

featuring virtually all the important techniques used in embroidery. We have chosen tasteful, stylish motifs which can be embroidered on all different types of garments and materials, not just the ones we suggest.

Let your imagination run free. Embroidering only the corner of a handkerchief is enough to make it a unique and special gift; and stitchery can transform a simple blouse into a real work of art.

The course section at the end of this part is very comprehensive. It explains and illustrates all the major embroidery stitches step-by-step, so that you can first learn and then later use it as a handy

reference when doing future projects.

Take your time, as your grandmothers used to do, and you will discover the rewards and pleasures that embroidery can bring.

## The ABC's of Embroidery: Cross-stitched Alphabets

Here's a fitting beginning to our embroidery section: two cross-stitched alphabets, all in capital letters. The photo serves as your stitching guide; simply count the number of stitches per letter. Use these multipurpose letters to monogram clothing such as sweaters, blouses and scarves or on household items such as bed linen and kitchen textiles. You will doubtless also find a home for the decorative motifs embroidered in grey, which are scattered throughout the alphabets. Designs like these are always fashionable and add a distinctive touch to a garment. You can use all these letters and designs to make embroidered greetings to commemorate birthdays, anniversaries . . . any special occasion or celebration. Then again, you may just wish to use them for a small embroidery sampler.

Instructions for the cross-stitched alphabets are on page 144.

# 2

## A Graceful Herbaceous Border to Embroider in Counted Cross-stitch

We used this delicate flowery border to decorate a white tablecloth. You can, however, stitch this attractive design on a host of other articles. The embroidery is worked on coarse cotton fabric which shows the fragile-looking stitchery to advantage. The leaves and petals are cross-stitched, the slender stems worked in backstitch. The subtle gradations of colour make this a rich, multi-hued piece; this variety adds interest to the actual needlework process. This photo doubles as your embroidery pattern. The flowers are shown in full size to enable you to identify the proper colour and stitch sequence.

It is not necessary to work the entire border as a repeating design. The floral motifs can be used on their own or in random patterns to decorate household linens or items of clothing, such as a nightdress or blouse.

Instructions for the floral border are on page 144.

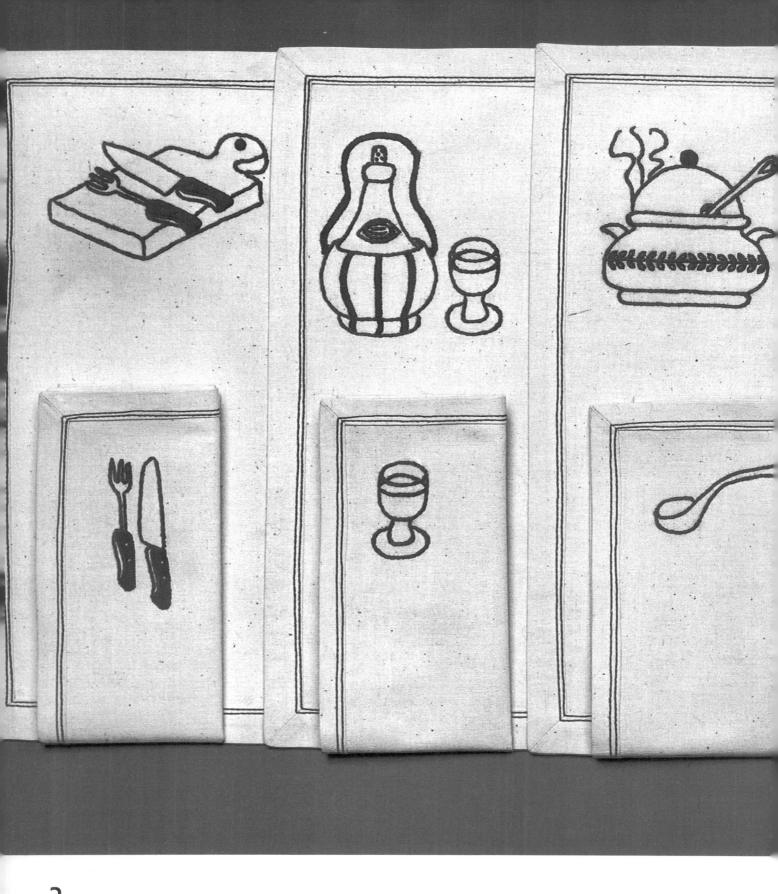

# 3

**Table Linen to Enhance Your Mealtimes**

When you eat a meal, you appreciate its visual appeal as much as you savour its taste. These coordinated place mats and serviettes (napkins), decorated with food-related designs, are enough to whet your appetite. You can embroider these attractive, out-of-the-ordinary motifs on lots of other kitchen textiles. Have a look round and you're bound to find something suitable.

Each member of the family will want to select a favourite design to identify his

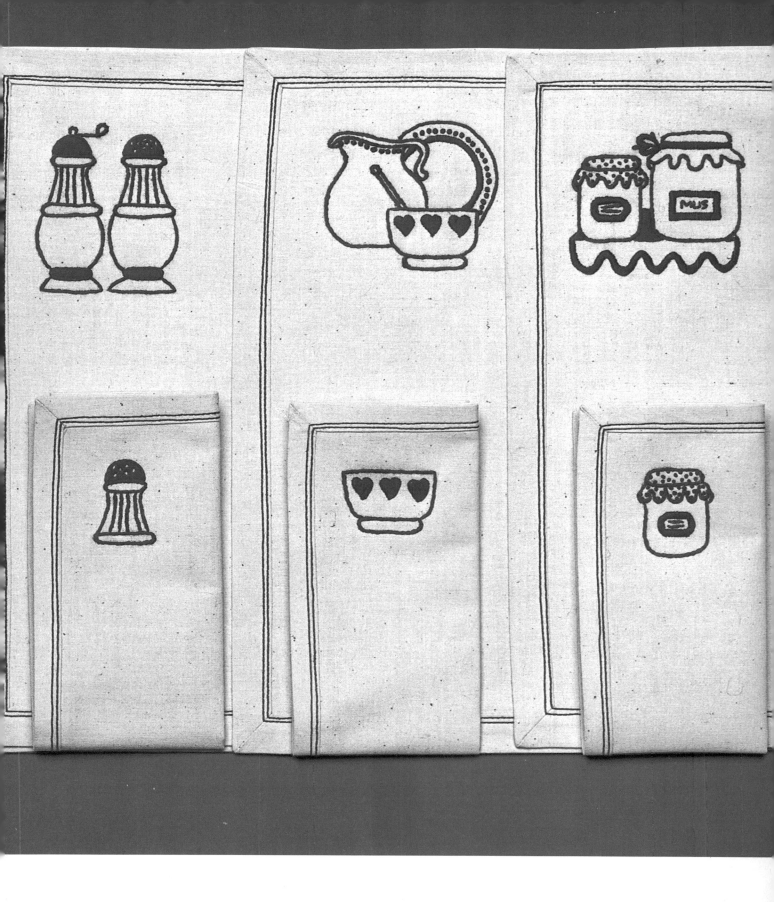

or her seat at the dinner table. Or, you may wish to make up these table linens as a house-warming gift for a special friend.

The motifs are embroidered in two tones of red, a subtle, offbeat combination which comes as a pleasant surprise. Good news for inexperienced stitchers: the designs are worked mostly in stem- and satin stitches, two of the principal embroidery stitches. If you are unfamiliar with them, you can check them up in the course section.

Instructions for the place mats and matching serviettes are on pages 144, 145 and 146.

# 4

## Kid's Art as Inspiration: Designed by Children, Stitched with Love

There are no instructions for this winsome picture. It is meant to stimulate your ideas about what you can do using the simple technique of cross-stitch. The individual squares measure 15 × 15 cm (6 × 6 in).

They were designed by children and embroidered by young and old alike. The younger the child, the coarser the material should be. For this type of work, use an evenweave fabric or one with a surface patterned with squares, such as gingham.

A picture like ours is an ideal group project. Divide the fabric into squares using running stitch, then let each child embroider his or her own design in the allotted space. Our embroidery is multi-directional, so it is most appropriate for use as a table

covering. For a wall hanging, all the motifs should face the same way.

You may wish to copy this picture using the photo as a *guide*; better still, ask your child to draw some original artwork on graph paper. To embroider each design, count out the squares on the graph paper, then work the stitches in the corresponding positions on the fabric.

It is the naïve quality of children's artwork that we find so appealing. That's why it translates so successfully into the basic needle-art of cross-stitch. The work of amateur artists can often have a similar simplicity and vivacity, so why not pick up paper and pencil and create your own design?

It isn't necessary to undertake a large-scale project like ours. A single motif, embroidered and framed, is already a unique keepsake which will surely give someone a great deal of pleasure.

# 5
## Kaleidoscopic Tablecloth: Medallions Embroidered on Handkerchief Squares

This dainty tablecloth consists of embroidered squares, each measuring 14 × 14 cm (5½ × 5½ in), which are then joined together with lace trim. Its charm lies in the variety which is achieved through using the very simplest of stitches in kaleidoscopic patterns. Even a novice needleworker is familiar with straight stitch, cross-stitch, stem stitch, lazy daisy and French knots. These form pretty multi-coloured symmetrical medallions which look much more complicated than they are. Each square is completely different. The more experienced embroiderer might wish to develop similar designs using more sophisticated stitches.

There are several advantages to working square by square. First of all, you can make up the tablecloth to fit any size of table. For those with little time or patience to spare, this project produces immediate results. You can work a whole medallion at each sitting and this tablecloth is an ideal mother/daughter endeavour.

Instructions for the tablecloth are on page 147.

# 6

## A Triangular Shawl for Incurable Romantics

You'll want this shawl for Sunday best – or a night on the town. It's made out of lightweight woollen fabric which is deliciously soft and drapes exquisitely. The pastel coloration of the embroidered flower clusters complements the delicacy of the fabric. The lacy crocheted border and shimmery fringing complete the romantic look.

This is a fascinating project because making it up involves sewing, embroidery, crochet and fringing. You'll never be bored! The flower clusters are worked in satin stitch. After embroidering, you sew a luxurious hand-rolled hem, a prized technique which is used for top-quality scarves and wraps. Blanket stitching is then worked over this, as a base for the crocheted border. The crocheting is quite simple and should present no problem, even for novices. The fringe is made from embroidery cotton, which gives it an attractive lustre. It's knotted using lark's head knots, one of the principal macramé knots.

A shawl like this is a real treasure and should be cared for accordingly. Wash it by hand in a mild detergent especially for woollens. When it's dry, hold the shawl with fringe downwards and shake it out to undo any tangles. If the shawl is a bit creased, iron it on the wrong side. You should always press embroidered articles on the wrong side so the stitching won't be flattened. If the shawl is going to be stored for any length of time, wrap it up in acid-free tissue paper or in a clean old pillowcase.

Instructions and full-size embroidery motifs for the shawl are on page 147.

# 1
## Cross-Stitched Alphabets

**Instructions**

The letters are embroidered on a piece of fabric with a natural grid (an evenweave fabric or one which has an even surface pattern, for example, gingham), using stranded embroidery cotton (floss). Select a needle compatible with your fabric. Use a tapestry needle for coarse evenweave fabric (the blunt tip slips between the threads) or a sharp-pointed crewel or chenille needle to pierce a tightly woven fabric. Work each stitch over two fabric threads, both vertically and horizontally. Stitch placement is easily determined by referring to the photograph. In the top alphabet, each letter is embroidered in one colour; each letter of the bottom alphabet is worked in two different but related colours. You can either work each stitch individually or embroider adjacent cross-stitches in rows; both methods are explained in the Embroidery Course (page 223). Whichever method you choose, always make sure that the top threads lie on all the crosses lie in the same direction. It may help to use a round embroidery frame (hoop) to hold the fabric taut. If your fabric does not have a natural grid, embroider over a single-thread canvas and pull the threads out afterwards (see Embroidery Course, page 235). The size of the letters can be varied by changing the thickness of the thread (increasing or decreasing the number of strands) and/or the size of each stitch (the number of fabric threads that the stitch covers). These instructions also apply to the decorative designs which are spaced throughout the alphabets.

# 2
## Tablecloth with Floral Border

**Size:** $132 \times 132$ ($52 \times 52$ in)

**Stitches:** Cross-stitch, backstitch.

**Materials:** *Embroidery thread:* Anchor Stranded Cotton (Anchor Bates/U.S.) in the following colours and quantities: three skeins each of grass green no. 244, light grey-green no. 875, medium grey-green no. 876, light parrot green no. 255, dark parrot green no. 257, emerald green no. 228 and light grass green no. 242; two skeins each of mist green no. 861, light forest green no. 214, dark parrot green no. 258, olive no. 843, delphinium blue no. 121, light cornflower blue no. 145, parma violet no. 110, dark parma violet no. 112, old rose pink no. 74, flame red no. 335, nasturtium orange no. 329, canary yellow no. 288 and lemon yellow no. 290; one skein each of dark grey-green no. 879, medium cornflower blue no. 146, dark cornflower blue no. 147, violet no. 97, jade green no. 185, deep old rose pink no. 75, dark red no. 44, amber gold no. 308 and corn yellow no. 305. Crewel needle. Coloured basting thread. *For tablecloth, you need:* 1.4 m ($1\frac{5}{8}$ yd) of 140 cm (54 in)-wide or 3 m ($3\frac{3}{8}$) of 90 cm (36 in)-wide evenweave linen. Matching sewing thread.

**Cutting out/preparation:** Cut the tablecloth $140 \times 140$ cm ($54 \times 54$ in) and along the grain. If it is necessary to join lengths of fabric to make up the tablecloth dimensions, stitch together a full-width centre panel flanked by narrower fabric strips on either side. As an alternative, you may wish to work the embroidery on a store-bought linen tablecloth. Using coloured thread, baste a stitching guideline to indicate the lower edge of the border 9 cm ($3\frac{1}{2}$ in) above the raw edge (5 cm [2 in] above hem on purchased tablecloth) and along the grain.

**Embroidery:** Work cross-stitch over two fabric threads, both vertically and horizontally. Use four strands of thread throughout. The stems are worked in backstitch. Embroider the border using the photograph to determine stitch and colour placement. Use the natural grid of the fabric for counting. Use the pansy shown on the top left to begin the flowery border and the yellow flower next to it to end the border repeat. The pansy on the top right is the corner motif. It is advisable to work out the spacing of the individual border motifs on tracing paper before you start. The border pattern can easily be adjusted to fit different-sized tablecloths. The flowers can be embroidered with bigger gaps between them or you may wish to swap their positions around within the border. You may wish to eliminate one of the motifs within the pattern repeat or to use a particular flower more than once. The corner pansy is ideal for use on matching serviettes (napkins).

# 3
## Kitchen Motif Place Mats and Matching Serviettes

**Finished sizes:** *Place mat:* $35 \times 50$ cm ($13\frac{3}{4} \times 19\frac{3}{4}$ in) *Serviette:* $35 \times 35$ cm ($13\frac{3}{4} \times 13\frac{3}{4}$ in)

**Materials:** *For two place mats and two serviettes, you need:* one skein each of light red and dark red stranded embroidery cotton (floss). One crewel needle. 1 m ($1\frac{1}{8}$ yd) of 90 cm (36 in)-wide natural-coloured cotton fabric. Matching sewing thread. Red buttonhole thread (to match embroidery cotton).

**Cutting out:** Cut out each place mat to measure $41 \times 56$ cm ($16 \times 22$ in); this includes a 3 cm ($1\frac{1}{8}$ in) hem allowance all round. Cut out each serviette to measure $39 \times 39$ cm ($15\frac{1}{4} \times 15\frac{1}{4}$ in); this includes a 2 cm ($\frac{3}{4}$ in) hem allowance all round.

**Embroidery:** Full-size patterns for all the motifs are given on the right and overleaf. For the mat, trace a large motif on to the upper left-hand corner, 6.5 cm ($2\frac{1}{2}$ in) in from the raw edges, as shown. For the serviette, trace the corresponding small motif on to the upper left-hand corner, 4.5 cm ($1\frac{3}{4}$ in) in from the raw edges, as shown. Embroider the mats referring to the photo on pages 136–7 and using four strands of floss throughout. Work outlines in stem stitch, smaller areas in satin stitch; for dots work French knots and work the vine pattern on the soup tureen in lazy daisy stitch. The outlines are embroidered in light red. Work the following in dark red: the knob and vine pattern on the soup tureen, the handle and middle stripes on the wine bottle, the second ring on the glass, the handles on the cutlery, the dots and hearts on the crockery, the middle lines on the salt and pepper pots; the bow, the labels and the edge of each cover on the preserve jars.

*Continued on page 146*

**Sewing:** *Place mats:* run parallel basting threads all round each mat, 1 cm ($\frac{3}{8}$ in) and 3 cm ($1\frac{1}{8}$ in) from the raw edges. Press the hem allowance on to the wrong side along the 3 cm ($1\frac{1}{8}$ in) guideline. Mitre the corners, leaving the last 1 cm ($\frac{3}{8}$ in) of each seam unstitched. Press corner seams open. Turn the whole hem on to the right side, then press under 1 cm ($\frac{3}{8}$ in) all round. Stitch the hem down, working two parallel rows of Holbein stitch in buttonhole thread, close to the folded inner edges. *Serviettes:* run parallel basting threads all round each serviette, 5 mm ($\frac{1}{4}$ in) and 2 cm ($\frac{3}{4}$ in) from the raw edges. Press the hem allowance on to the wrong side along the 2 cm ($\frac{3}{4}$ in) guideline. Mitre the corners, leaving the last 5 mm ($\frac{1}{4}$ in) of each seam unstitched. Press seams open. Turn hem on to the right side, then press under 5 mm ($\frac{1}{4}$ in) all round. Finish same as for place mats.

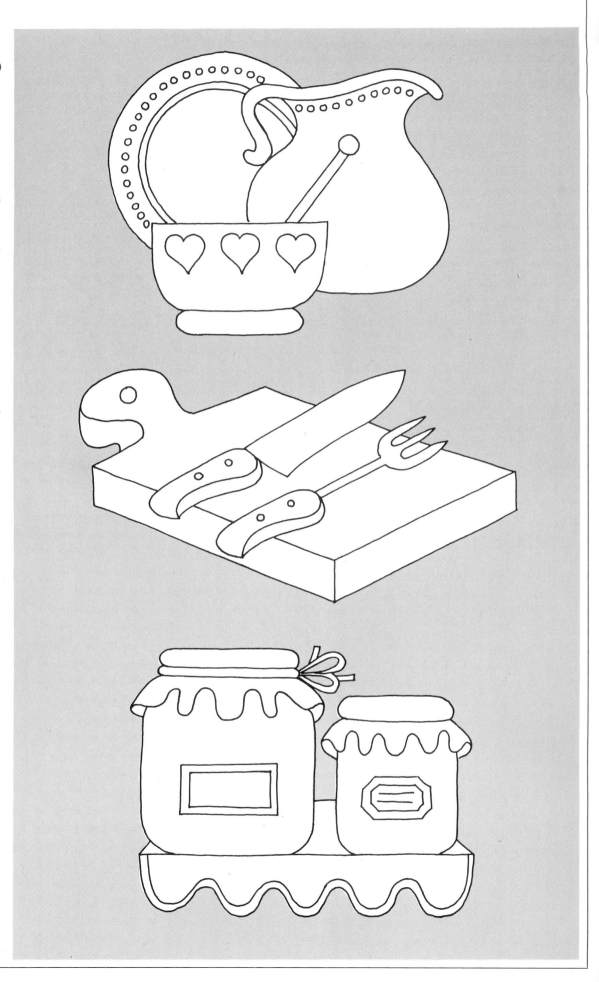

# 5

## Tablecloth with Medallion Motif Squares

**Size:** 132 × 132 cm (52 × 52 in)

**Stitches:** Straight, back-, lazy daisy, stem, French knots and cross-stitch.

**Materials:** Remnants of stranded embroidery cotton (floss) in various colours. One crewel needle. 1.9 m (2⅛ yd) of 115 cm (44–45 in)-wide medium-weave linen. 25 m (27½ yd) of 2.5 cm (1 in)-wide cotton lace trim. 5.5 m (6 yd) of 15 mm (⅝ in)-wide cotton lace edging (for border). Matching sewing thread. Coloured basting thread.

**Cutting out/preparation:** Mark sixty-four squares on the linen, each measuring 17 × 17 cm (6¾ × 6¾ in), including a 15 mm (⅝ in) seam allowance all round (finished width of each square: 14 × 14 cm [5½ × 5½ in]). It is best to cut the squares out in blocks of four, to produce pieces of fabric large enough to insert in a round embroidery frame (hoop). The individual squares can be cut apart when the embroidery is completed. Make circular templates from card (cardboard), all with different diameters. To determine the centre point of each square, fold it into quarters. All of the medallion designs are based on circular stitch formations. Select an embroidery design from the photo on pages 140–1, then pick out templates in the sizes necessary to achieve it. Centre the templates, one by one, on the fabric square and baste guidelines round each (the centre of each template exactly coincides with the centre of the square). Concentric circles will be formed. Next, use the basting thread to divide each circle into four or eight equal sections, as necessary to give the correct spacing for that particular embroidery motif. Each dividing line passes through the centre point of the square.

**Embroidery:** Use three strands of thread throughout. Referring to the photo, work individual lines, stars, zigzags or bows in straight stitch or backstitch, work the flowers in lazy daisy stitch; work outlines in stem stitch, small dots in French knots and crosses in cross-stitch. Remove basting when stitching is complete. NOTE: if you wish, you can use the examples given to develop similar motifs using more complicated stitches.

**Sewing:** Press under the seam allowances on all the squares. Arrange the squares in eight rows of eight, placing the various designs in a pleasing order. First join the squares side-to-side to form each row, using short lengths of trim. Cut out fifty-six linking strips, each 17 cm (6¾ in) long. Baste the edges of each trim strip between two fabric squares, with 15 mm (⅝ in) seam allowance extending at both top and bottom. Stitch the trim to the fabric, close to the edges, using closely spaced machine zigzag. Next, cut out seven 132 cm (52 in) strips of trim and stitch these between the lengthwise rows in the same way, turning under the seam allowances on the linking strips. Stitch the lace edging on all around the tablecloth. Trim off the seam allowances on the wrong side of the tablecloth.

# 6

## Triangular Shawl

**Size:** Top width: 110 cm (43½ in)
*Height* (from the centre top edge to point): 52 cm (20½ in), without fringe

**Embroidery stitches:** *Satin stitch.*

**Materials:** *Embroidery thread:* Anchor Stranded Cotton (Anchor Bates/U.S.), in the following colours and quantities: twenty-five skeins of white no. 2 (two skeins for embroidery, twenty-three for fringe); one skein each of light grey no. 397, grey no. 398, light lilac no. 96, lilac no. 98, light cobalt blue no. 128 and cobalt blue no. 130. Crewel needle. Round embroidery frame (hoop). *For the shawl:* 0.8 m (⅞ yd) of 140 cm (54 in)-wide lightweight off-white woollen fabric. Matching sewing thread (for hand-rolled hem). *Crochet:* 1 50 g (1¾ oz) ball of Coats Mercer crochet cotton No. 20. Steel crochet hook no. 1.25 mm (size 8/U.S.).
Details of abbreviations and American equivalents are on page 236.

**Cutting out/preparation:** Cut out a triangular piece of fabric with the top width of 111 cm (43⅞ in) placed across the width of the fabric and with sides of 77 cm (30¼ in) each. The full-size embroidery motifs are transferred on to the shawl by the pricking and pounce method (see Embroidery Course, page 235). Copy the embroidery motif on to tracing paper, then prick holes along the design lines. Pounce the six motifs on to the shawl, positioning them as follows: place one motif 6 cm (2¼ in) above the bottom point, two more further up, each 8 cm (3⅛ in) above the first motif and 4 cm (1½ in) from the edge of the shawl. For the remaining three motifs: place one 29 cm (11⅜ in) straight up, above the point; place the remaining two, one to each side of that one and 4 cm (1½ in) from the edge of the shawl. Work a hand-rolled hem at this stage, to prevent fraying. To do so, with the fabric facing towards you and using the thumb and forefinger (index finger) on both hands, roll the narrowest possible hem, concealing the raw edge of the fabric. As you roll the hem, secure it with tiny hemming stitches.

**Embroidery:** Embroider in satin stitch using two strands thread throughout. Stitch the leaves and centres of all the flowers in white. Within each motif, embroider one flower each in grey, blue and lilac. On each flower, work the inner petal ring in a darker shade, the outer ring in a lighter shade of that particular colour.

**Finishing:** Work blanket stitch along both short sides of the shawl. Space the stitches 4 mm (³⁄₁₆ in) apart. There must be an odd number of blanket stitch loops along each edge. *Crochet border:* mark the 2 centre lps at the point of the triangle.
*1st row:* with right side facing attach crochet cotton to first lp at left corner (1 dc [1 sc], 4 ch, 1 dc[1 sc]) into same place as join, * 4 ch, miss (skip) next lp, 1 dc (1 sc) into next lp;
repeat from * to 1 lp before marked lps, 4 ch, 1 dc (1 sc) into first marked lp, 4 ch, 1 dc (1 sc) into 2nd marked lp, ** 4 ch, miss (skip) next lp, 1 dc (1 sc) into next lp; repeat from ** to end, 2 ch, 1 tr (1 dc) into same place as last dc (sc), turn.
*2nd row:* * 4 ch, 1 dc (1 sc) into next 4 ch lp; repeat from * to within last 1p, end with 2 ch, 1 tr (1 dc) into last lp, turn. Repeat last row once more. Fasten off.
*Fringe:* cut across one end of each skein of embroidery cotton to halve it. This cuts the skein into 30 cm (12 in) lengths. Divide the lengths of embroidery cotton into groups of three whole strands each. Fold each fringe group in half, forming a loop. Insert the loop of a fringe group into each loop of the crocheted border (fringe loop points towards back of crocheted loop). Slip the ends of the fringe through the fringe loop and tighten it round the crocheted loop, forming a lark's head knot.

# 7

## The Look of Weaving: Couched Cushion Covers in Vivid Geometric Designs

The cushions on this page are brightening up an old sofa. The modern clear-cut geometric designs fit in well with the atmosphere of nostalgia, and that's exactly the point we wish to demonstrate. The combination of strong colours and bold patterns can be compatible with most styles. If one of the colours in the cushion covers harmonizes with that of the couch, an attractive composition results. Our cushions are embroidered in various couching stitches, all of which are explained on page 228 of the Embroidery Course. This technique gives the cushions a 'hand-woven' appearance. This personal touch pleasantly complements the streamlined designs.

In the couching technique, yarns are secured to the fabric surface by means of regularly spaced overstitches. Once you've had a bit of practice, you should have no difficulty in developing your own variations to use for original designs.

The cushions are worked with Persian yarn, which contributes to the highly desirable hand-woven effect. Each skein of yarn consists of three strands of wool. This enables you to choose the necessary number of strands to suit your base fabric. The couching will look right only if it covers the cushion surface completely. Experiment on a fabric scrap before you begin the actual embroidery. Embroidered in thick pure wool, the work looks particularly lavish and appealing.

Instructions and pattern diagrams for the couched cushion covers are on pages 158 and 159.

**8**

**Rustic or Refined: Counted Thread Table Linen Designs for Any Occasion**

The colourful tablecloth pictured above has a wide border embroidered in cross-stitch using a folkloristic design.

The stitchery is worked in tapestry wool for an unexpected and interesting textural effect. You could also

use this pattern for a table runner or adapt it for kitchen curtains or dining room cushions.

The elegant white runner on this page has been worked in the Hardanger technique using grey pearl cotton. This style of openwork embroidery comes from Norway. It is explained in detail on page 229 of the Embroidery Course.

You must be very precise to work the regular repeating pattern, but the embroidery itself is quite simple. The border on the green tablecloth has a similar geometric pattern, featuring diamonds and triangular shapes.

Instructions and grid patterns are on pages 159 and 160.

# 10

## White on White – Always Right

You can never have too many cushions. They always add a touch of comfort and visual appeal to armchairs, sofas or bedding.

These sophisticated beauties will make a we come addition to any room. We've made them up all in white in order to focus attention on the subtleties of their textured surface patterns. The four different but related patterns flatter each other, producing an attractive and tasteful grouping.

The cushions are embroidered in satin stitch on canvas, using Persian yarn to create a cloth-like appearance. As a final touch, the cushions are trimmed with twisted cord which you make yourself from strands of Persian yarn. Our instructions tell you how.

When the white is no longer quite white, remove the cord and open one of the side seams. Remove the cushion pad (pillow form) and wash the cover by hand in lukewarm, almost cold, water using a mild washing powder or a liquid cleanser especially for woollens.

If you find white a rather cold and impersonal colour and still feel, despite our photo, that this aesthetic elegance is not quite to your liking, choose another colour to make the cushions in. Made up in delicate pastel shades, the cushions will work well together. If you think that plain (solid) colours are a trifle boring, you might wish to divide each pattern up into its various geometric components and then work the shapes or stripes in different colours. The possibilities are endless and success is guaranteed.

Do remember the other colours in the room when exercising your colour judgement. A pile of colourful cushions looks good only if the colours harmonize with all the other colours surrounding it. A different nuance is acceptable, but there should be no glaring contrasts. Cushions should be as easy on the eyes as they are comfortable to lean against. You will have no difficulty in finding suitable matching colours because Persian yarns are available in a wide range of shades.

Instructions and pattern grids for these cushions are on page 161.

## 11
### Seafaring Vessels in Counted Cross-Stitch

We've captured the seaworthy appearance of two ships of yesteryear in this pair of cross-stitched pictures. To conjure up ocean images, the designs are embroidered in the crisp combination of maritime blue and white; you can almost feel the sea breeze. The sailing ship, above, is a cutter. Below, you have a paddle-steamer.

Stitching these pictures is a refreshing change of pace. Unlike most traditional cross-stitched designs, the background is stitched and the motifs are left plain. The shapes that you see are created by the blank spaces.

Meticulously embroidered and framed, these ships will delight landlubber and sailor alike.

Instructions and embroidery diagrams for the ships are on page 162.

## 12, 13, 14
### Winning Ways with Red on White: Simple Projects with Classic Appeal

At the top, the gently rolling hills of our country landscape border adorn an unusual window treatment — a stationary fabric blind. The cheerful repeat design would be equally at home worked on conventional curtains. We personalized the cross-stitched drawstring bag with initials. Our instructions include patterns for upper and lower case letters from A to Z, so that you can do the same. The embroidery on the vintage damask cloth and serviette echoes the elaborate patterns woven into them. This sort of embellishment is an appreciation of the unexcelled workmanship of times gone by.

Instructions for the border, bag and damask embroidery are on pages 163, 164 and 165.

# 15

**Country-Style Checks to Sew, Embroider and Crochet**

The friendly charm of our table covering will enhance many a cosy hour. Breakfast, tea or just a leisurely chat round this informally clad table will be a real pleasure for all concerned.

If you have acquired a modest level of skill in the various techniques involved, making the cloth should present no problems. With the aid of the Embroidery Course section and our detailed instructions, beginners, too, will be able to work this rewarding project successfully.

The tablecloth consists of 36 squares of coarsely woven embroidery fabric. The key to a perfect tablecloth lies in the accuracy of your cutting. The checks of the individual squares must all run straight along the grain and match up properly. Take the time to cut precisely and your care will be rewarded.

On 18 of the 36 squares, we've embroidered stylized flower designs, using satin stitch, French knots and stem stitch. You can copy the flowers from our photo or make up your own simple motifs. After the embroidery is completed, the squares are joined together using interlinked blanket stitch. This stitch is described on page 225 of the Embroidery Course. To create a unified appearance, the linking stitches are worked using the same blue crochet cotton as for the tablecloth edging.

The generous crocheted border gives this tablecloth its final touch. The crocheting is worked over the cloth's outer row of blanket stitching. The pattern for the zigzag border is given in easy-to-read chart form.

We made the tablecloth up in blue and white checks with red embroidered accents, but you might wish to reverse the combination and make it up in red and white checks with blue flowers. Colour choice is a matter of personal taste, but you should take the colour scheme of your home decor into consideration. The colours of a tablecloth should harmonize with your tableware as well as with the kitchen or dining room surroundings. A table looks particularly attractive and thoughtfully set when all the colours (of the serviettes, egg cosies, etc.) match. Why not make up some checked serviettes to match or coordinate with the tablecloth?

Instructions for the country-style tablecloth are on page 165.

# 7

## Four Couched Cushion Covers in Geometric Designs

**Size:** *Rectangular cushion:* 48 × 56 cm (19 × 22 in) *Square cushion:* 40 × 40 cm (16 × 16 in)

**Stitches:** Basic couching stitch, couching with slanting overstitches, Bokhara couching.

**Materials:** *Embroidery yarn:* Paterna Persian Yarn in the colours and quantities specified in the colour key next to each pattern diagram. (Each skein has three strands of wool, 7.4 m [8 yd] long). Tapestry needle. Round embroidery frame (hoop).
*To make all four cushion fronts, you need:* 1.1 m (1¼ yd) of 115 cm (44–45 in)-wide evenweave cotton or linen. For all four cushion backs: 1.1 m (1¼ yd) of 115 cm (44–45 in)-wide cotton or linen fabric in a colour to match the embroidery. *You also need:* matching sewing thread. Cushion pad (pillow form) for each cushion, either store-bought or home-made.

**Diagrams:** Reduced-size pattern diagrams for all four cushions are given at right. They are all shown at a scale of 1:8. That is, 1 cm (1 in) in the drawing represents 8 cm (8 in) in full size. To find out what a design dimension is at any given point, measure it (in centimetres or inches) and multiply by eight. To enlarge each design to full size, measure each design line, then reproduce it in full size in the correct position within the design. First draw the outlines, then mark in the horizontal and vertical interior lines. Finally, draw the diagonal lines.

**Cutting out:** Cut out a piece of evenweave fabric for each cushion front, adding a 2.5 cm (1 in) seam allowance all round to the dimensions given above. Cut out a corresponding piece of fabric for each cushion back. Transfer the appropriate enlarged design on to each cushion front.

**Embroidery:** Before you begin, read about couching on page 000 of the Embroidery Course. To work the couching on each cushion front, use as many strands of Persian yarn as are necessary to cover the fabric surface completely. Embroider each colour area individually. When changing colour vertically, insert the needle with the laid·yarn in the new colour at the same thread intersection as was used for taking the needle out with the laid yarn in the previous colour. To work a diagonal colour area, follow the contours of the marked diagonal line as closely as possible. Stitch the adjacent laid yarns in steps, with each successive yarn along the diagonal line two – three thread intersections above or below (depending on stitching direction) the previous one. The laid yarns along the diagonal edge of the neighbouring colour area should emerge at the same stepped thread intersections. The following instructions refer to the cushion covers in the order in which they are shown at right:
*Design 1:* embroidery direction: work from one short side to the other.
*Design 2:* embroidery direction: work diagonal areas from outer edge to straight centre area, then centre area from one short side to the other.
*Design 3:* embroidery direction: work from one long side to the other.
*Design 4:* embroidery direction: work centre square horizontally; work all other design areas vertically.

**Stitch key:**
*Design 1:* embroider in couching with diagonal overstitches (see Embroidery Course, page 228, frame 4).
*Design 2:* embroider in couching with the overstitches forming 'V's (Embroidery Course, page 228, frames 5 and 6).
*Design 3:* embroider in Bokhara couching (Embroidery Course, page 228, frame 7).
*Design 4:* embroider in basic couching, keeping the stitches small (Embroidery Course, page 228, frames 1–3).

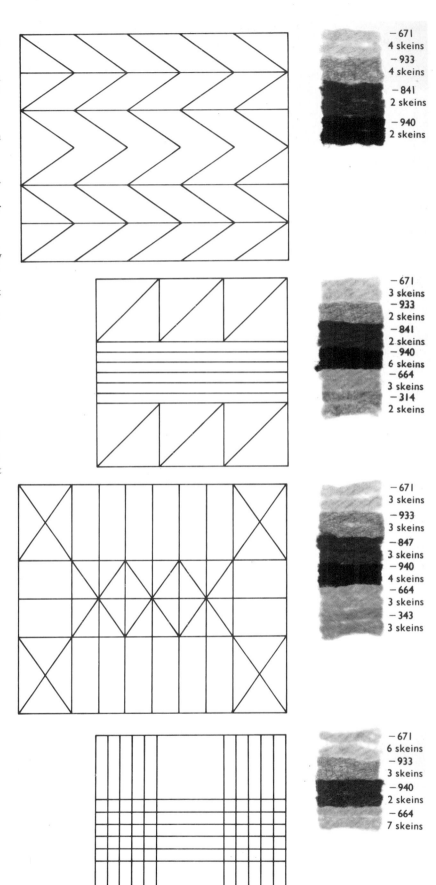

–671 4 skeins
–933 4 skeins
–841 2 skeins
–940 2 skeins

–671 3 skeins
–933 2 skeins
–841 2 skeins
–940 6 skeins
–664 3 skeins
–314 2 skeins

–671 3 skeins
–933 3 skeins
–847 3 skeins
–940 4 skeins
–664 3 skeins
–343 3 skeins

–671 6 skeins
–933 3 skeins
–940 2 skeins
–664 7 skeins

# 8

**Finishing:** To remove *wrinkles and distortions,* stretch (block) each completed cushion front, right side up, on a wooden board, placing the pins close to the embroidered area. Cover the embroidery with a wet cloth and leave to dry. When dry, assemble each cushion cover: stitch each cushion front on to the corresponding cushion back, with right sides together and leaving one side open for turning. Turn right side out. Insert the appropriate cushion pad and slipstitch the opening shut.

## Rustic Tablecloth

**Size:** 136 × 136 cm (52 × 52 in)

**Stitches:** Cross-stitch.

**Materials:** For embroidery: Anchor Tapisserie (Tapestry) Wool (Anchor Bates/u.s.) or another good-quality tapestry wool: thirty-four skeins of cream no. 0386, six skeins of cardinal red no. 0701. Size 18 tapestry needle. Round embroidery frame (hoop). For tablecloth: 1.4 m (1⅝ yd) of 140 cm (54 in)-wide or 2.8 m (3⅛ yd) of 90 cm (36 in)-wide green evenweave fabric with 27 threads per 5 cm (2 in). Matching sewing thread. Coloured basting thread.

**Stitch gauge:** 18 cross-stitches (54 fabric threads) = 10 cm (4 in).

**Stitch diagram:** The pattern grid for the tablecloth border is given below. Each red or white cross represents one cross-stitch worked over three horizontal and three vertical fabric threads in that colour. Each green

square represents three threads (both directions) of the background fabric. The border is divided into the following sections: the corner, the pattern continuation, the pattern repeat and the pattern complement. All of these sections are clearly labelled so you can count the stitches in each.

**Cutting out/preparation:** Cut the tablecloth 140 × 140 cm (54 × 54 in) and along the grain. If it is necessary to join lengths of fabric to make up the tablecloth dimensions, stitch together a full-width centre panel flanked by narrow fabric strips on either side. Clean-finish the raw edges. Using coloured basting thread, sew a guideline all round the tablecloth to indicate the lower edge of the embroidered border, 10 cm (3 in) above the edge.

**Embroidery:** *Border motif:* start the embroidery with a corner worked within the basted guidelines. Then work the pattern continuation, the pattern repeat six times and the pattern complement. Next, work both the pattern

continuation and the corner in reverse. This completes the first side of the border = 217 cross-stitches, measuring approx. 120 cm (48 in). When you turn the tablecloth to embroider the next side, you will find that the corner section has already been stitched. Because of this, you must pick up the pattern sequence beginning with the pattern continuation, then complete the side in the usual way. This is the case for all the remaining sides. To embroider the cross-stitched square in the centre of the tablecloth, count seventy-five fabric threads above the border and work a single row of cross-stitch all round. Work each cross-stitch in cream, over three horizontal and three vertical fabric threads.

**Finishing:** Stitch a narrow hem all round the tablecloth.

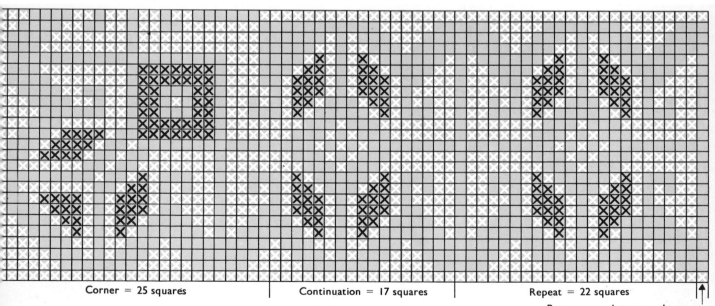

Corner = 25 squares    Continuation = 17 squares    Repeat = 22 squares

Pattern complement = 1 square

**Stitch diagram:** Above is the pattern grid for the tablecloth border. It is divided into these sections: the corner, the pattern continuation, the pattern repeat and the pattern complement. Each red or white cross = 1 cross-stitch in that colour. Plain green squares = background fabric.

# 9

## Hardanger Table Runner

**Size:** 46 × 116 cm (18⅛ × 45¾ in)

**Stitches:** Satin stitch, backstitch.

**Materials:** *Embroidery thread:* Anchor Pearl Cotton No. 5 (Anchor Bates/u.s.): twelve skeins of grey no. 397. Tapestry needle. Sharp embroidery scissors. Pair of tweezers. Round embroidery frame (hoop). For table runner: 0.6 m (⅝ yd) of 140 cm (54 in)-wide white evenweave cotton or linen fabric with 9 threads per cm [22 per in] or 1.2 m (1⅜ yd) of 115 cm (44–45 in)-wide fabric (enough for two runners). Coloured basting thread.

**Instructions:** Before you begin, read about Hardanger embroidery on page 229 of the Embroidery Course. *Preparation:* cut a 52 × 122 cm (20⅜ × 48 in) piece of fabric along the grain; clean-finish the edges. *Motif placement:* use the photo as a reference for positioning the various stitch formations. The counting grid at right shows the exact position of each stitch within the diamond motif. Each kloster block within the diamond motif consists of five satin stitches worked over four fabric threads. Start the first diamond in the middle of the short side, 9 cm (3½ in) from the edge. Be sure to begin with the kloster block at the top edge of the counting grid and always work clockwise round the design. One-quarter of the diamond is shown here, including the corners. The pattern has to be worked in reverse going downwards and to the left for completion. Each background line of the counting grid represents one fabric thread. Work the stitches running diagonally within the diamond in backstitch. The green lines on the diagram represent the fabric threads which are later withdrawn to work the openwork in the middle of the diamond. Work seven diamonds down the centre of the runner with four fabric threads between each. *Thread withdrawal:* **Do not withdraw the threads from the interior of each diamond motif until the** surrounding kloster blocks are completed. To withdraw the threads, cut the four threads at the base of the selected kloster block and the same four threads at the base of the opposite block. Cut only the threads running in the same direction as the satin stitches, not the intersecting threads. Remove the threads with a pair of tweezers. Withdraw all the threads running in one direction, then those going the other way. *Openwork embroidery:* after the indicated threads have been removed, cover the remaining thread bars with needleweaving as described in the Embroidery Course, page 229. *Additional embroidery:* parallel rows of backstitching: when the diamonds are finished, work two parallel rows of backstitching along the long sides. Work the backstitching four fabric threads to either side of the diamonds, with each backstitch four fabric threads long. Space these rows of stitching two rows apart from each other, staggering the stitches in the second row. Work the beginning and end of the second row two stitches longer than the last diamond. Two fabric threads away from the second row of backstitching, work two more rows of backstitching. Stitch the first row the same as the previous row, then stagger the stitches in the second row. *Zigzag border:* embroider the zigzag border according to the grid pattern, eight fabric threads away from the diamonds, to either side. Work the border in satin stitch and backstitch, beginning at the same level as the parallel rows of backstitching. *Backstitch surround:* next, work a single row of backstitch as a border round the edge of the runner. Embroider the backstitching along the short sides four fabric threads away from the outer diamonds and two fabric threads away from the end of the zigzag border. On the long sides, work the row of backstitching 9 cm (3½ in) away from the lowest point of the zigzag border. Work the stitching carefully, so you have neat turnings at the corners. It is best to start in the middle of one of the short sides. *Hem:* two fabric threads outside the backstitched border, withdraw one fabric thread all round. To do so, cut the thread in the middle of each side, then work it out towards each corner. Trim the thread close to each corner, turn under the ends and sew them down. Trim off 1 cm (⅜ in) all round from the 3 cm (1⅛ in) hem allowance; cut along the grain. Turn under and baste down the hem (two 2 cm [¾ in] turnings), mitring the corners. Sew the hem with hemstitch, always encircling four fabric threads at a time.

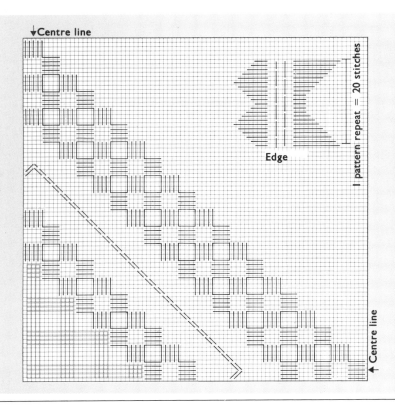

**↓Centre line**

1 pattern repeat = 20 stitches

Edge

Centre line

**Stitch counting grid:** Shown here is one-quarter of the diamond motif including the corners and, in the upper right-hand corner, one repeat of the zigzag border. Each background line on the grid represents one fabric thread. The heavy lines represent the embroidery stitches. The green lines indicate those fabric threads which are to be withdrawn from the central openwork area of the motif.

# 10

## White Textured Cushions

**Size:** Approx. 38–39.5 cm square (15–15½ in square)

**Stitches:** Satin stitch on canvas.

**Materials:** Zweigart white cotton interlock canvas (article no. 604/56) with 14 holes per 2.5 cm (1 in), 100 cm (40 in) wide: 0.5 m (⅝ yd) is enough for two cushion fronts. Size 18 tapestry needle. Straight-sided embroidery frame (optional).
*Embroidery thread:* Paterna Persian Yarn, white/cream no. 261, in the following quantities: thirteen skeins each for cushions 1 and 4, ten skeins for cushion 2 and nine skeins for cushion 3. For each cushion, you need two additional skeins for the twisted cord trim. You also need: cushion backing: 1 m (1⅛ yd) of 115 cm (44–45 in)-wide cotton fabric (enough for all four cushions). Synthetic filling (stuffing) as required *or* cushion pads (pillow forms) in the appropriate sizes. Matching sewing thread.

**Stitch Diagrams:** Below are pattern grids for each of the four cushions. The background lines on each diagram represent the canvas threads. Each heavy line represents a satin stitch worked over the indicated number of canvas threads.

**Cutting out/Preparation:** For each cushion, cut out a piece of canvas measuring 50 × 50 cm (19¾ × 19¾ in). If you wish, mount the canvas in the embroidery frame as described on page 233 of the Embroidery Course.

**Embroidery:** The cushions are worked in satin stitch using two strands of Persian yarn throughout. Satin stitch on canvas is explained on pages 224–5 of the Embroidery Course. Begin embroidering approx. 6 cm (2¼ in) from the edge of the canvas. Work the central pattern area first, then stitch the border all round. Embroider each cushion as follows:
*Cushion 1:* Embroider the

'Start' section, then embroider the pattern repeat eight and a half times across the width (total width = 207 canvas holes). To complete the pattern, work continuous diagonal stripes until a height of 207 canvas holes is reached. Then work the border all round.
*Cushion 2:* Work the pattern repeat eight and a half times across the width (total width = 205 canvas holes). To embroider the cushion vertically, work the 'Start' section, then work the vertical repeat sixteen and a half times until the pattern reaches 205 canvas holes in height. Then work the border all round.

*Cushion 3:* Work the pattern repeat 11 times across the width (total width = 198 canvas holes). To create the zigzag effect, * work one half pattern repeat vertically, add the middle stitch, then finish off the pattern repeat in the reverse direction. Repeat from * seven more times until the pattern reaches 200 canvas holes in height. Then work the border all round.
*Cushion 4:* Work the pattern repeat five times across the width, then work a partial sixth repeat, stopping just before the last vertical pattern bar (total width = 211 canvas holes). Embroider the

repeat vertically eight and a half times, until the pattern reaches 205 canvas holes in height. Then work the border all round.

**Finishing:** Stretch (block) each cushion, if necessary. Trim off excess canvas to 3 cm (1⅛ in) all round. Cut out a cushion back to fit each cushion. With right sides together, stitch around three sides of each cushion, leaving the fourth side open. Turn right side out. Pad the cushion with synthetic filling or insert cushion pad. Slipstitch the opening shut. To make twisted cord trim: for each cushion, cut six strands of Persian yarn, each 5 m

(5½ yd) long. Twist the strands together until they begin to kink, then fold them in half. Knot the raw ends and insert a pencil through the loop end. Grasp the knotted end and continue twisting until a cord is formed. Sew the cord round each cushion as shown.

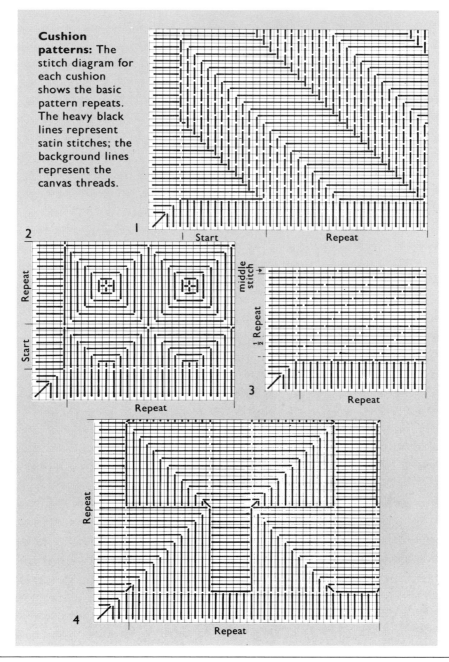

**Cushion patterns:** The stitch diagram for each cushion shows the basic pattern repeats. The heavy black lines represent satin stitches; the background lines represent the canvas threads.

# 11

## Ships in Counted Cross-stitch

**Size:** Each picture measures 17.5 × 21 cm (6⅞ × 8¼ in)

**Stitches:** Cross-stitch.

**Materials:** *Blue stranded embroidery cotton (floss):* six skeins for the sailing ship, seven skeins for the steamship. Tapestry needle. *For each picture, you need:* 0.3 m (⅜ yd) of 90 cm (36 in)-wide evenweave embroidery fabric (thread count: 10 threads per cm [25 per in]).

**Stitch gauge:** 50 cross-stitches (100 fabric threads) = 10 cm (4 in).

**Cutting out/preparation:** For each picture, cut out a rectangle of fabric measuring 27.5 × 31 cm (10⅞ × 12¼ in); this includes a 5 cm (2 in) allowance all round.

**Stitch diagrams:** Each picture measures 87 cross-stitches down and 105 across. Each blue square on the diagram represents one cross-stitch worked over two fabric threads both vertically and horizontally. Each blank square represents two fabric threads (both directions) of unembroidered fabric.

**Embroidery:** Cross-stitch over two fabric threads, vertically and horizontally. Use three strands of thread throughout. Start approximately 5 cm (2 in) from the edge of the fabric.

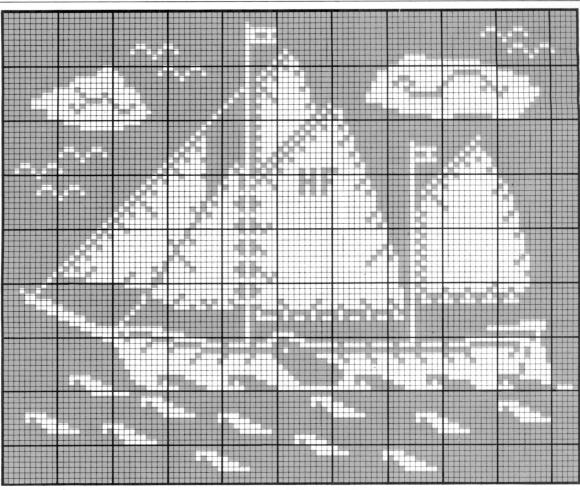

# 12

## Window Blind (Shade) with Country Landscape Border

**Sizes:** *Pattern repeat:* 16.5 cm (6½ in)
*Blind:* finished height: 42 cm (16½ in); finished width: as necessary, to fit windows up to 132 cm (52 in) wide

**Stitches:** Satin stitch, running stitch, French knots.

**Materials:** Four skeins of red coton à broder. One crewel needle. 0.65 m (¾ yd) of 140 cm (54 in)-wide finely woven linen. Matching sewing thread. One curtain rail (rod), to fit window dimensions. NOTE: We worked this border pattern on a stationary fabric blind (window shade), a partial window treatment similar in length to café curtains. The blind, which is hung from a curtain rail, is a straight expanse of fabric particularly suitable for providing privacy or blocking undesirable views. If you wish, you can embroider the same design on conventional window-length gathered curtains.

**Cutting out/preparation:** Cut out a piece of fabric for the blind, measuring 64 cm (25¼ in) by the window width + 4 cm (1½ in). (The width of the blind runs from selvage to selvage.) These measurements include an 11 cm (4⅜ in) hem allowance at blind top and bottom and a 2 cm (¾ in) hem allowance at each side. Press under the bottom edge of the fabric 1 cm (⅜ in), then press it under again 5 cm (2 in); stitch the hem close to the folded edge. The border pattern is given in full size grid form. Each square of the grid measures 16 × 16 mm (⅝ × ⅝ in) and each pattern repeat measures 16.5 cm (6½ in) from side to side. The broken lines on the grid indicate the starting and finishing points of the pattern repeat. Trace the border pattern above the top edge of the hem, on the right side of the fabric using dressmaker's carbon. Leave approximately 10 cm (4 in) unembroidered at each side of the blind. It is advisable to work out the positioning of the pattern repeats on tracing paper beforehand, to make sure that the end pattern repeats do not fall awkwardly (e.g. in the middle of a tree).

**Embroidery:** Use the photo as a reference. Embroider most of the design in satin stitch, slanting each stitch over three fabric threads. The tree trunks are worked straight across in satin stitch, also over three threads. Embroider those heart-shaped flowers shown as blank outlines on the pattern diagrams in running stitch. Make French knots for all dots.

**Finishing:** Turn under a double hem at each side and stitch. Stitch a wide casing at the top, as necessary to fit your curtain rail.

# 13

## Cross-stitched Drawstring Bag

**Finished size:** 30 × 40 cm (12 × 16 in)

**Stitches:** Cross-stitch.

**Materials:** One skein of red pearl cotton No. 3. One crewel needle. 0.5 m (⅝ yd) of 90 cm (36 in)-wide medium-weight evenweave cotton or linen fabric. Matching sewing thread. Coloured basting thread. One chenille needle.

**Cutting out:** Cut out a piece of fabric measuring 66 × 50 cm (26 × 20 in); press it in half widthwise to form the bag front and back. These measurements include a 3 cm (1 in) seam allowance at the one side seam, 2 cm (¾ in) at the bag bottom and an 8 cm (3¼ in) hem allowance at the top.

**Embroidery:** Pattern diagrams are given for the motif on the bag front and for an entire cross-stitched alphabet in both upper and lower case letters. Each square on both grids represents two vertical and two horizontal fabric threads; each 'X' represents one cross-stitch worked over two vertical and two horizontal threads. Mark the lengthwise centre of the bag front with basting. This guideline will run through the middle tulip-sprigged stem of the motif. Work the design as shown, substituting the appropriate initials from those given in the cross-stitched alphabets. Embroider the top parallel line of the cross-stitched border 9 cm (3½ in) below the top raw edge of the bag front. NOTE: the size of each cross-stitch depends upon the fineness or coarseness of the fabric weave. To increase the size of each cross-stitch, work it over a greater number of threads.

**Sewing:** With right sides together, stitch the bag side and bottom seams. Turn bag right side out. Press under the top edge of the bag 1 cm (½ in), then press it under again 3.5 cm (1⅜ in). Sew the hem close to the bottom folded edge. To make the drawstring, thread a chenille needle with several lengths of pearl cotton which have been twisted together. Work running stitch all round the bag, 9 cm (3½ in) below the top edge. Knot the ends of the drawstring.

*Patterns overleaf*

Grid is shown in full size.
Each square = 16 cm × 16 cm (⅝ in × ⅝ in)

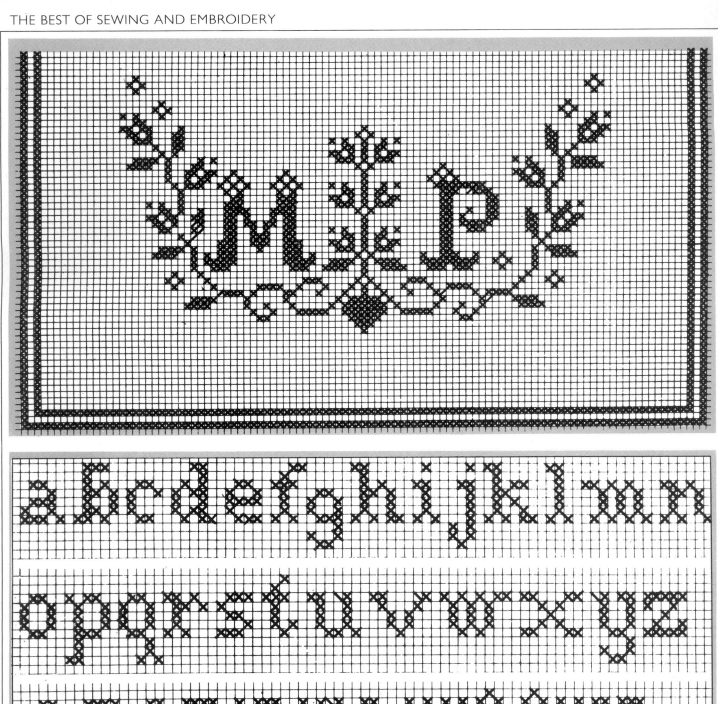

# 14
## Embroidered Damask Cloths

**Stitches:** Satin stitch, stem stitch.

**Materials:** Damask serviette (napkin) or tablecloth suitable for embroidery (the intricate flower and garland designs on older cloths are ideal). Red coton à broder or stranded embroidery cotton (floss). One crewel needle.

**Instructions:** Our damask cloths are flea market finds; you should be able to find similar good-quality secondhand pieces with little difficulty. Apart from doves and flourishes, our tablecloth had an enormous monogram woven into each corner of the pattern. We imitated one of them using stem and satin stitches. Satin stitch is particularly effective on damask because its 'floats' echo the texture of the pattern areas of the cloth. We copied another corner design, a basket of roses, on the serviette. When you purchase your cloth, pick out likely embroidery motifs. You can either stitch directly over the actual woven motifs, or you can select a favourite motif, trace it and simplify it, then reposition it elsewhere on the cloth. The overlapping patterns are quite pleasing. Your embroidery should be no more than an accent, or you will detract from the beauty of the cloth itself. Follow these damask embroidery tips: work with fine thread, such as coton à broder or two strands of embroidery cotton. Excessively thick thread damages the fabric. Use bright, primary colours; they stand out best on a white background. When embroidering small areas, limit yourself to one type of stitch. On larger areas, you can use several different stitches effectively.

# 15
## Checked Tablecloth

**Size:** Approx. 135 × 135 cm (53 × 53 in)

**Embroidery stitches:** Straight, slanting and encroaching satin stitch; stem stitch, French knots, interlinked blanket stitch.

**Materials:** *Embroidery thread:* Anchor Soft Embroidery (matte embroidery cotton) or coton à broder (Anchor Bates/u.s.): three skeins of white no. 2, ten skeins of red no. 46. Crewel needle. Round embroidery frame (hoop).
*Tablecloth fabric:* 2.8 m (3⅛ yd) of 85 cm (34 in)-wide Zweigart 'Gerda' blue and white checked cotton embroidery fabric (article no. 1535/51) or same quantity of 90 cm (36 in)-wide coarsely woven cotton fabric with checks approx. 5 mm(¼ in) square. Matching sewing thread. We used Twilleys Lyscordet no. 5 cotton (for joining the squares and crochet edging). The amount required will vary according to the size of the tablecloth. Crochet hook No. 3.00 mm (u.s. 2). Basting thread. Details of abbreviations and American equivalents are on page 236.

**Cutting out/Preparation:** Cut out 36 fabric 'squares' as follows: the woven checks are not absolutely square; to compensate for this cut each piece of fabric 39 checks across and 43 down, starting with a white check in the upper left-hand corner (each piece measures approx. 22 × 22.5 cm [8½ × 8¾ in]). When cutting these squares, you will be left with a waste strip of blue and mixed blue and white checks in between. Clean-finish the edges of each square with machine zigzag stitching. Next, turn under and baste down a seam allowance two checks wide all round each square, mitring the corners. The finished size of each square is approx. 20.5 × 21 cm (8 × 8¼ in).

**Embroidery:** In the middle of 18 of the squares, draw various flower motifs of your own design (use the photo as a reference). Embroider each flower using non-stranded embroidery thread (as specified above). Work the filled-in-areas in straight, slanting or encroaching satin stitch (the last-named is described in the instructions for embroidery project 19, page 182), depending upon which is most appropriate for the particular shape. Work the flower centres in white satin stitch, the dots in French knots and the dividing lines in stem stitch.

**Joining the squares:** Arrange the squares in six rows of six, alternating the embroidered with the unembroidered squares. The squares are joined together with interlinked blanket stitch (see page 225 of the Embroidery Course), using the blue crochet cotton as embroidery thread. *Join the squares in the following sequence:* first align two fabric squares, one above the other. In the first check of the top square work four blanket stitches; then work four blanket stitches in the second check of the bottom square. Carry on in this way, working four blanket stitches in alternate checks of the two squares. When you've finished the first pair of squares, proceed to the next pair of vertically aligned squares, slackening the tension as you do so. Continue in this way until you have joined two rows of six squares each (six top/bottom pairs). Then work interlinked blanket stitch between the squares, to join them together from side to side within the double-row strip. Repeat this procedure two more times, until you have a total of three double-row strips with twelve squares in each. Work interlinked blanket stitch to join the double-row strips together lengthwise. Finally, edge the outside of the tablecloth in blanket stitch, working four blanket stitches in every other check and five blanket stitches into each corner.
Mark the centre lp at each corner of the tablecloth. There must be a multiple of 32 blanket stitch loops between each marked stitch.
*Crochet edging 1st rnd:* Attach crochet cotton to 32nd lp before any marked stitch, 4 ch (miss [skip] next 3 lps, 1 tr [1 dc] into next lp, 1 ch) 7 times, miss (skip) next 3 lps, (1 tr [1 dc], 1 ch) twice into marked lp, ** *miss (skip) next 3 lps, 1 tr (1 dc) into next lp, 1 ch; repeat from * to within 1 lp of next marked lp (1 tr [1 dc], 1 ch) twice into marked lp, ** repeat from ** to ** twice more, *** miss (skip) next 3 lps, 1 tr (1 dc) into next lp, 1 ch; repeat from *** ending with miss (skip) last 3 lps, 1 ss (sl st) into 3rd of 4 ch.
Continue to work edging following the chart above.

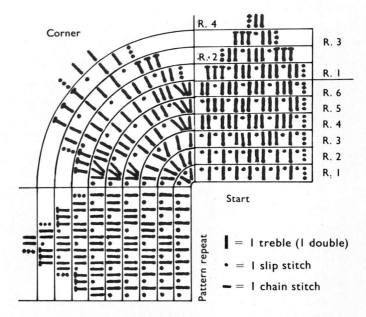

**I** = 1 treble (1 double)
**•** = 1 slip stitch
**—** = 1 chain stitch

The chart above uses symbols to represent crochet stitches. The symbols are identified in the key. The chart is divided into three sections; each one is read from right to left. Begin each row with the 'Start' sequence of stitches, then work the pattern repeat over and over until you reach the corner. Crochet the corner, then go on to the 'Start' sequence of the next row. Work in forward rows until you reach the zigzag edging; then work each triangular point individually, crocheting back and forth.

# 16

## Pretty, Simple Stitchery: Flowers and Birds on a Field of White

You will find full-size trace-off patterns for these attractive designs in the instructions section. Three different stitches are used to embroider these dainty motifs which stand out extremely well on a white background. The use of only one colour draws attention to the graceful, curving design lines.

The motifs are worked in stem and satin stitches and French knots, all of which are familiar to beginners. As you can see from the photos, there are lots of different ways to use our collection of nature-theme motifs. Have a look round your wardrobe and your home and you're bound to think of many other applications.

These demure designs, boldly worked in red, are right for all seasons of the year.

Instructions and full-size patterns for these flower and bird motifs are on pages 176 and 177.

# 17

## Romantic Pillowcases for Sweet Slumber or Pleasant Daydreams

This sort of pillow, slightly larger in size, used to be called a show pillow. Nowadays, these pillows are popular in the smaller dimensions shown here. Such delicate pillowcases are sure to inspire delightful flights of the imagination.

The type of embroidery used, which requires a degree of patience and perseverance, is understandably called white work. Padded satin stitch, used to create the raised circles and petal shapes, is characteristic of this style. The pillowcases with the eyelets are examples of broderie anglaise. In this technique, each motif is cut away and the raw edges of the remaining eyelet hole are covered with overcasting.

We made the pillowcases up in shirting linen. When they get soiled, you can easily launder them in the washing machine.

The exquisite embroidery is shown to best advantage when the pillow cover underneath is in a gentle pastel shade which peeks through the lacy openings. For the cord trim, select a matching pastel.

These pillowcases are so lovely, it is a pity to confine them to the bedroom. Pamper yourself to a living room snooze on them.

Instructions and a full-size embroidery pattern for the pillowcases are on pages 178, 179 and 180.

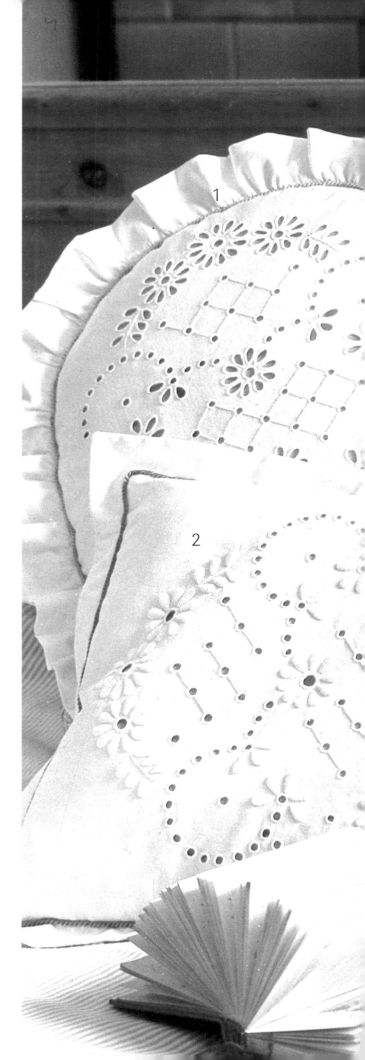

3

# 18
**Luxurious Towel Sets: Splendid Gifts to Make**

These attractive coordinated sets are made from terry towelling (terry cloth) fabric with edges bound in toning bias binding. The striking satin stitch embroidery adds an extra-special touch.

Each grouping in the photo shows a bath, hand and guest towel. To complete each set, we've included instructions for a flannel (face cloth). The embroidery motifs are given in graduated sizes, to correspond with the size of each towel.

3

To work the designs on the textured terry towelling, the motif outlines are traced on to organdie, which is in turn basted on to each towel. The designs are then embroidered in satin stitch and the organdie is completely removed. The amount of work involved is quite reasonable and the exceptional results are their own reward.

Instructions and full-size embroidery patterns for the towel sets are on pages 180, 181 and 182.

**19**

**Summer Fruit on White Linen for Appetizing, Informal Meals**

There's something irresistibly friendly and inviting about the look of hand-worked place mats on a wooden table.

Our charming fruit motif place mats will surely set the mood for a delightful, casual mealtime.

We chose one sort of fruit for each of the place mats, but you can easily mix the motifs to concoct a 'fruit salad' border design of your own.

Encroaching satin stitch has been used to fill in the large single-coloured motifs. These rows of shorter stitches are more practical than long satin stitch floats and they form an attractive textured pattern within the fruit shapes, as you can clearly see on the pear mat. To work it, the first row is embroidered in satin stitch as usual, then the following rows are staggered so that the tops of the new stitches come between the bases of the stitches above. Instructions and full-size motifs for the fruit mats are on pages 182 and 183.

## 20

### Colourful Machine Appliqué for a Cheerful Easter Table

On festive occasions, the home should be decorated accordingly. Even if you spend a quiet holiday with the immediate family, without guests to entertain, an appropriately bedecked room reflects the tender loving care put into it and contributes to a warm and cosy atmosphere.

Our Easter tablecloth is just such a thoughtful touch. It's a speedy sewing project that's bound to be a favourite with the children. Special makes like this one are what childhood memories are made of. In future years, the children may fondly recall happy holiday images of the family sitting round a table clad in this gaily embellished cloth.

Our Easter hens are likely to be so popular with the young ones that you'll have a difficult time reserving the cloth for holiday use only. They'll want to use it all year round.

The tablecloth is quite simple to make. Our instructions tell you how to make it from scratch, but you may prefer to decorate a purchased table covering. The big white hen, above, serves as your trace-off pattern. Have your children assist you in cutting out the Easter eggs from fabric scraps. All the cut-outs are first fused on to the cloth with adhesive web, then each shape is outlined with machine overcasting.

Instructions for the Easter tablecloth are on page 183.

# 16

## Flowers and Birds to Embroider

**Stitches:** Satin stitch, stem stitch, French knots.

**Materials:** Red stranded embroidery cotton (floss); 2 skeins for large motifs, 1 skein for smaller motifs. Crewel needle.

**Preparation:** Full-size embroidery patterns are given, at right. Select the motifs of your choice, then copy them on to tracing paper to determine their positions on the finished item. By using tracings, you can combine individual motifs to make larger designs or you can work out repeating border patterns. To do this, make multiple tracings of one or more motifs, then juggle them around until you find a pleasing arrangement. Transfer the completed embroidery design on to the fabric.

**Embroidery:** Use three strands of thread to embroider on closely woven fabric; on other fabrics use four strands of thread throughout. Work lines in stem stitch, solid areas in satin stitch and dots in French knots. The flower petals and leaves can either be filled in with satin stitch or left as outlines, according to your wishes.

# 17
## Romantic Pillowcases

**Size:** Approx. 30 × 40 cm (12 × 16 in), without frill or border.

**Stitches:** Stem stitch, padded satin stitch, broderie anglaise (cutwork eyelets).

**Materials:** *Embroidery thread:* Anchor Stranded Cotton (Anchor Bates/u.s.), in white no. 2: five skeins for pillowcase 1, six skeins for pillowcase 2 and eight skeins for pillowcase 3. Crewel needle. Round embroidery frame (hoop). Sharp embroidery scissors. *You also need:* 1 m (1⅛ yd) of 90 cm (36 in)-wide shirting linen or firmly woven cotton for frilled pillowcases 1 and 3; 0.6 m (⅝ yd) for pillowcase 2. For each: 1.4 m (1¼ yd) of contrasting pastel-coloured cord. Matching sewing thread.

**Instructions:** Cut out a 40 × 50 cm (16 × 20 in) fabric rectangle for each pillowcase front. Transfer the embroidery design on to it, in a centred position. Before you embroider, outline all the petals and circles in running stitch. Work each pillowcase as follows, using two strands of thread throughout:
*Pillowcase 1:* embroider all lines in stem stitch, all petals and the circles in broderie anglaise.
*Pillowcase 2:* embroider all lines in stem stitch, all petals in padded satin stitch and all the circles in broderie anglaise.
*Pillowcase 3:* embroider all lines in stem stitch, all petals and all circles in padded satin stitch.

**Broderie anglaise** (cutwork eyelets): Outline the eyelet hole in running stitch, then snip it across and lengthwise using sharp embroidery scissors. Turn under the four corners and overcast around the edge (the less fabric caught up, the better the shape of the hole). On the wrong side, trim off excess fabric close to stitching.

**Padded satin stitch:** Outline the shape in running stitch

*Continued on page 180*

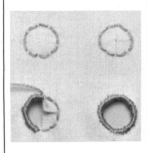

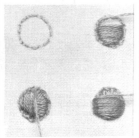

and fill in the central area (within the outline) with satin stitch. Two more satin stitch layers are worked over this. Stitch each successive layer in the opposite direction, with stitches closer together than in the previous layer. On the final layer, embroider over the running stitches, covering them completely.

**Finishing:** Make up each pillowcase with a back opening, so that it can be laundered. The instructions for sewing project 27 (pages 68–9) may be helpful as a reference. To make frills for oval pillowcases 1 and 3: join 10 cm (4 in)-wide strips of fabric together to form a ring. Fold ring in half lengthwise and gather along raw edges. Stitch frill on to pillowcase front, distributing the gathers. Rectangular pillow 2 has a flanged border. Trim each pillowcase with cord, as shown.

# 18
## Embroidered Terry Towels

**Sizes:** *Bath towel:*
80 × 140 cm (32 × 55 in)
*Hand towel:* 50 × 100 cm
(20 × 40 in)
*Guest towel:* 30 × 50 cm
(12 × 20 in)
*Flannel (face cloth) (not shown):* 30 × 30 cm
(12 × 12 in)

**Stitches:** Satin stitch.

### MATERIALS

**Embroidery:** *Embroidery thread:* Anchor Stranded Cotton (Anchor Bates/U.S.), in the following colours and quantities: *Set 1 (chain link motif):* olive no. 281, *Set 2 (rose motif):* dark red no. 44, *Set 3 (Oriental knot motif):* dark cobalt blue no. 132. For each small motif one skein, for each larger motif two–three skeins and for a continuous border three–four skeins. Crewel needle. White organdie (for design transfer). Small round adjustable embroidery frame (hoop). Pair of tweezers.

**Towels:** *To make one set of towels, you need:* 2.4 m (2⅝ yd) of 90 cm (36 in)-wide reversible terry towelling (terry cloth) in the appropriate colour (olive green, pink or blue). 11 m (12⅛ yd) of 24 mm (1 in)-wide cotton bias binding in a colour to match the corresponding embroidery thread. Matching sewing thread. NOTE: embroidery is worked on the finished towels to prevent fraying. For this reason, sewing instructions are given first.

**Cutting out:** For each set of towels, cut out all the pieces from terry towelling in the dimensions specified above, without seam allowance. Make templates out of card as guides for cutting the rounded corners (on all the towels) and the wavy top and bottom edges on Set 2 (rose motif towels). Draw fairly shallow curves to simplify application of bias binding.

**Sewing:** Fold binding in half lengthwise and press so that one long edge extends 2 mm (⅛ in) beyond

*Continued on page 182*

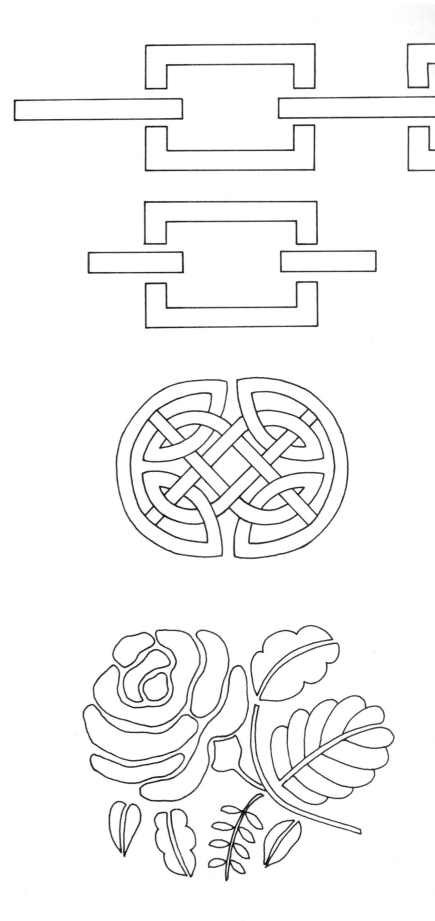

the other. *Bind each towel:* insert the fabric into the binding so that its raw edge is flush with the centre binding fold. Lay the beginning of the folded binding flat on the fabric. Work the binding all round each towel, easing it round the corners and/or curves and basting it in place through all layers. Turn the remaining binding end under 1 cm (⅜ in) and lap it over the beginning. Carefully stitch the bias binding in place, making one seamline through all fabric layers. The narrower binding width belongs on the right side of the towel.

**Embroidery:** Full size trace-off motifs are given on pages 180–1. The organdie method (see Embroidery Course, page 235) is used to transfer embroidery designs on to the textured towelling. Trace each desired motif on to the organdie. When you cut it out, leave enough organdie all round to fit comfortably into the frame. Baste the organdie patterns on to each towel in the correct position. Position the appropriately sized motifs as follows:

*Set 1 (chain link motif):* flannel: 5 cm (2 in) above lower edge, guest towel: 7 cm (2¾ in) above, hand towel: 8 cm (3 in) above and bath towel: 12 cm

(4¾ in) above. For the flannel and guest towel, embroider a single motif centred between both sides, as shown. For the hand towel and bath towel, work a repeating border along the entire width. Embroider the chain motifs using straight satin stitch and four strands of thread throughout.

*Set 2 (rose motif):* flannel: 2 cm (¾ in) above deepest point of curve, guest towel: 5 cm (2 in) above, hand towel: 10 cm (4 in) above and bath towel 14 cm (5½ in) above. Centre the motif between both sides in all cases. Embroider the roses using straight satin stitch and four strands of thread throughout.

*Set 3 (Oriental knot motif):* flannel: 4 cm (1½ in) above lower edge, guest towel: 5 cm (2 in) above, hand towel: 9 cm (3½ in) above and bath towel: 13 cm (5 in) above. Centre the motif between both sides in all cases. Embroider using diagonal satin stitch, following the motif outlines to create the illusion of under- and overlapping cords, as shown. Use four strands of thread throughout. Finishing: trim off the organdie, leaving 2 cm (¾ in) all round each motif. Withdraw the threads one at a time, using the pair of tweezers.

# 19

## Fruit Motif Place Mats

**Size:** 34 × 44 cm (13¼ × 17¼ in)

**Stitches:** Encroaching satin stitch, satin stitch, backstitch, stem stitch and French knots.

### Materials
*Embroidery thread:* for each place mat, you need Anchor Stranded Cotton (Anchor Bates/U.S.) in the following colours and quantities:
*Apples:* six skeins of orange no. 925, five skeins of dark red no. 19 and one skein of green no. 279.
*Strawberries:* four skeins of dark red no. 19, three skeins of green no. 279 and one skein each of red no. 35 and cinnamon brown no. 370.
*Pears:* six skeins of yellow no. 291, five skeins of orange no. 925, four skeins of golden tan no. 363 and one skein of green no. 279.
*Cherries:* four skeins of red no. 29; two skeins each of cinnamon brown no. 370, dark red no. 19 and green no. 279.
*You also need:* crewel needle. 1 m (1⅛ yd) of 90 cm (36 in)-wide semi-fine linen (enough for four mats). Matching sewing thread.

### Cutting out/preparation:
For each place mat, cut out a 40 × 50 cm (15¾ × 19¾ in) piece of linen along the grain. Full-size trace-off embroidery patterns are given below. Transfer the motifs on to each piece of fabric, forming a border design. (Use the photo on pages 172–3 as a guide for motif placement.) Position the fruit motifs 5 cm (2 in) from the raw edges and spaced equidistantly apart. Position a motif diagonally in each corner, as shown. It is best to work out the spacing of the motifs on tracing paper first.

### Embroidery:
Use the photo on pages 172–3 and the motif outlines, right, as stitch and colour placement guides. Embroider each place mat as follows, using all six strands of thread throughout:
*Apple mat:* embroider single-coloured apples in orange using encroaching satin

stitch, two-coloured apples in orange and dark red using satin stitch. Outline all apples with dark red backstitching. Work leaf and bud (at bottom) in green satin stitch.
*Strawberry mat:* work the strawberries in dark red using encroaching satin stitch and the stems in brown stem stitch. Embroider the leaves in green satin stitch. On selected strawberries, work French knots in the lighter red.
*Pear mat:* work single-coloured pears in yellow or golden tan using encroaching satin stitch. Embroider two-coloured pears in yellow and orange using satin stitch. Outline all pears with orange backstitch. Work each leaf in green satin stitch, then add a green satin stitch bud

at the bottom of each pear (see photo on pages 172–3).
*Cherry mat:* embroider single-coloured cherries in red using encroaching satin stitch and two-coloured cherries in red and dark red using satin stitch. Work the stems in brown satin stitch and the leaves in green satin stitch.

**Finishing:** the place mat hem lies on the right side of the fabric. Turn edges under 3 cm (1¼ in) all round; mitre the corners, leaving the last 5 mm (¼ in) unstitched. Press corner seams open. Turn the hem on to the right side of the place mat; baste it down, turning under the 5 mm (¼ in) allowance. Sew the hem using decorative overcasting stitches worked in the dominant colour of the place mat.

# 20

## Easter Tablecloth in Machine Appliqué

**Size:** 132 × 132 cm (52 × 52 in)

**Materials:** 3 m (3⅜ yd) of 90 cm (36 in)-wide green cotton fabric. 0.65 m (¾ yd) of 90 cm (36 in)-wide white cotton fabric (for hens). Assorted printed cotton fabric scraps. 5 m (5½ yd) of red soutache braid. Four 1 m packs of 20 cm-wide iron-on adhesive web (1⅛ yd of 36 in-wide adhesive web). Matching and contrasting sewing thread. Red fabric dye or textile paint. Black permanent-ink marker.

**Making up:** *Tablecloth:* two widths of fabric are joined to make up the tablecloth dimensions. Cut the green fabric into two equal pieces. Stitch the centre seam. Trim to a 148 cm (58 in) square. The tablecloth hem lies on the right side of the fabric. Turn edges under 8 cm (3 in) all round; mitre the corners, leaving the last 1 cm (⅜ in) unstitched. Press corner seams open. Turn the hem on to the right side of the fabric, baste it down, turning under the 1 cm (⅜ in) allowance. Stitch the soutache braid on over the hemline on the right side of the fabric, catching in all layers. *Appliqué:* use the full-size photo of the hen as a trace-off pattern. Cut out twenty-four hens from both white fabric and adhesive web. Colour in the red areas of each hen's head with fabric dye or textile paint, as shown. Draw in the eye with a permanent-ink marker. From the printed cotton scraps, cut out lots of egg shapes, each measuring about 4 × 6 cm (1½ × 2¼ in). For each egg shape, cut out an identical piece of adhesive web. Position the hens and eggs around the cloth, forming a border above the hem, as shown. The spacing doesn't have to be absolutely precise, but there should be five or six hens on each side of the tablecloth. Pin on each appliqué with a matching piece of adhesive web underneath. Iron-on each appliqué, one by one, using a dry iron and a damp press cloth. Machine-overcast all round the edges of each cut-out using closely spaced zigzag stitching. Machine-embroider the remaining details of each hen (wing, claws, parts of the head) as shown, also using closely spaced zigzag stitching. You can, of course, make the tablecloth up in any size you wish.

## Roses for a Gracious Hostess

The coffee-warmer, place mats and serviettes (napkins) are all decorated with matching designs worked in satin stitch. Even those with less needlework experience will soon master the technique. All the items are trimmed with rose-coloured bias binding, to emphasize the dominant colour of the stitchery.

Instructions and full-size embroidery patterns for the coffee ensemble are on pages 194 and 195.

# 22

## No Maintenance House Plants: Preserved in Counted Cross-stitch

No green fingers (or green thumb) necessary for tending these delightful flowering pot plants; nimble fingers are an asset, however, because they're worked in the popular technique of counted cross-stitch.

Cross-stitch is the oldest known embroidery stitch and it's enjoying renewed interest today, with good reason. It's a simple skill which produces beautiful and versatile results. In grandmother's day it was used for making delicate embroidered miniatures as well as for decorating the usual household and apparel items. Our splendid cross-stitched house plant designs will probably suggest their own applications to you. Here, you see them as cushions and as framed 'portraits'.

The striking, stylized designs, in rich jewel-like tones, are worked thickly to give a lush, highly textured appearance. Make them up as a gift for your favourite indoor gardener.

Instructions and pattern diagrams for the house plant designs are on pages 195, 196 and 197.

## Hemstitching Adds an Extra-special Touch to Fine Linen

The table- and bed linen from our grandparents' day is now highly treasured, not just because of its age but because it was embroidered with loving care. Hemstitching was one of the most popular decorative techniques used. Perhaps you were introduced to this skill in school needlework lessons. As a schoolgirl, you might have found this kind of drawn thread embroidery pretty useless, just something you put up with to get good results at the end of term. Now, however, you probably appreciate its beauty and wish you'd paid more attention. Our instructions will pleasantly refresh your memory. There's also a page on hemstitching in the Embroidery Course, with helpful step-by-step photos.

Hemstitching is really extremely easy and it's an ideal way of trying your hand at needlework. Linen is the most suitable

**23**

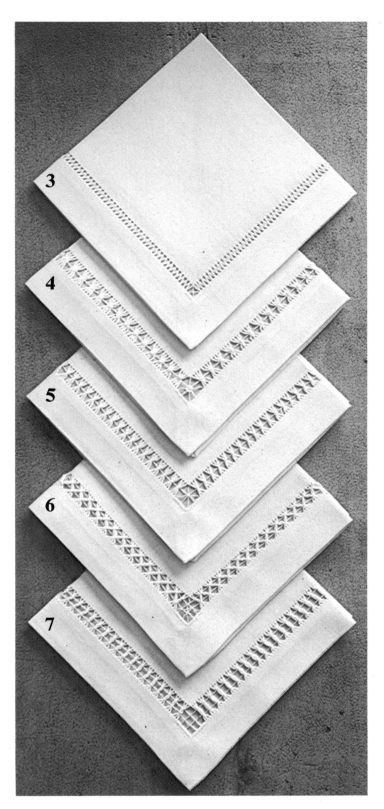

fabric choice because its construction lends itself to the withdrawal of threads. Hardly any other decorative stitch is as versatile as this one. We have selected small projects for you to start with. After you've practised hemstitching on these place mats and serviettes, you can progress to bigger items, like tablecloths, top sheets and cushion covers.

Instructions for the hemstitched table linen are on page 198.

# 24

## Mexican Patterns in Satin Stitch for a Highly Individual Rug

Any small rug or carpet will add a touch of comfort and beauty to a room. Whether you put your carpet down on polished parquet flooring or on top of wall-to-wall floor covering, your room will immediately become cosier and more inviting. Of course, the colour scheme of your decor should harmonize with that of the rug.

This magnificent rug, inspired by traditional Mexican folk art designs, will become the focal point of any room. It is worked in satin stitch on rug canvas using thick, hard-wearing woollen rug yarn. You won't finish this project overnight, but as you can see for yourself, it's well worth the

effort. Although this is a large-scale project, it's interesting to work because of the constantly changing colour and pattern areas. Once you've finished, you have a beautiful conversation piece which is also durable enough to withstand the wear and tear of everyday life. You needn't fear treading on this 'work of art'. It's a good idea to place a non-slip rubber mat beneath the rug, particularly if it is in a central location or on a waxed floor. The mat can be purchased at any department or carpet store.

If this rug is placed in a well-trafficked area, the lighter colours will eventually become grubby. When the carpet needs a clean, shampoo it with a rug shampooer (this can be rented) and a dry shampoo. This

light foam cleanser will not damage the rug, and it successfully gets rid of dirt and grime, so that the colours will be as bright and fresh as new. Should you still find stubborn stains, just put the rug in the bath and wash it using warm water, a special detergent for woollens and a brush.

The many rich colours of the rug are not overpowering because the colour combination is balanced. The rug, therefore, comes across as a single unit. In a simply decorated room, it looks particularly effective. You might wish to display it as a wall hanging, to add warmth to a brick or masonry wall.

Instructions and pattern grid for the rug are on pages 198 and 199.

## Knitted or Crocheted – the Embroidery adds Flair

You can transform knitted and crocheted garments into works of art with simple stitchery. See for yourself on these two pages. It doesn't need

to be something new. You're bound to have lots of sweaters and blouses tucked away in your wardrobe which could be brightened up with needle and thread and a bit of imagination.

The colourful bolero on the left-hand page is knitted

up quickly in garter stitch using thick wool. We then embellished it by weaving through the knitted loops with silver Lurex thread and yarn remnants. Instructions with photos show you how to work these folkloristic patterns.

The sweet and

summery crocheted top, above, is decorated with a delightful counted cross-stitch flower arrangement. You work the embroidery before making up the blouse. The top has jersey front and back sections which are joined to filet crochet side panels

and a short peplum. Elastic cinches in the waistline and picot edging complete this very delicate and feminine look.

Making up and embroidery instructions for the knitted bolero and crocheted top are on pages 199 to 201.

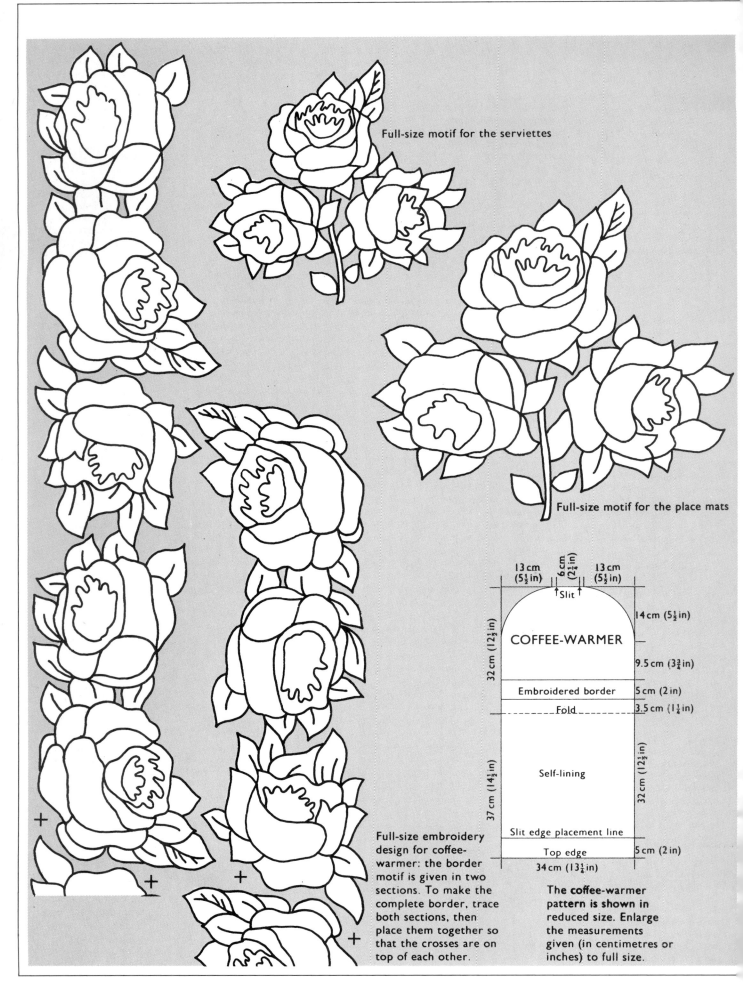

Full-size motif for the serviettes

Full-size motif for the place mats

13 cm (5½ in)  6 cm (2¼ in)  13 cm (5½ in)
↑Slit

14 cm (5½ in)

**COFFEE-WARMER**

9.5 cm (3¾ in)

Embroidered border — 5 cm (2 in)

Fold — 3.5 cm (1¼ in)

32 cm (12½ in)

Self-lining

32 cm (12½ in)

37 cm (14½ in)

Slit edge placement line

Top edge — 5 cm (2 in)

34 cm (13½ in)

Full-size embroidery design for coffee-warmer: the border motif is given in two sections. To make the complete border, trace both sections, then place them together so that the crosses are on top of each other.

**The coffee-warmer pattern is shown in reduced size.** Enlarge the measurements given (in centimetres or inches) to full size.

# 21

## Rose Motif Coffee-warmer, Place Mats and Serviettes

**Stitches:** Satin stitch, stem stitch.

### Coffee-warmer

**Size:** 34 × 37 cm (13¼ × 14½ in)

**Materials:** *Embroidery thread:* Anchor Stranded Cotton (Anchor Bates/U.S.) in the following colours and quantities: three skeins each of pink no. 36, heather no. 39, light green no. 261 and grass green no. 244; two skeins of deep pink no. 38. Crewel needle. *For coffee-warmer you need:* 0.8 m (⅞ yd) of 90 cm (36 in)-wide semi-fine cotton or linen fabric. 1.4 m (1⅝ yd) of 24 mm (1 in)-wide rose-coloured bias binding. Two 40 × 40 cm (16 × 16 in) pieces of 1 cm (⅜ in)-thick foam rubber (or use heavy-weight synthetic wadding [batting]). Matching sewing thread.

**Cutting out/preparation:** Enlarge the coffee-warmer pattern, then cut it out roughly twice. The full-size trace-off border pattern is given on the opposite page. Mark the limits of the embroidery and then transfer the border motif on to each piece of fabric. Cut out two pieces of foam rubber or wadding, without seam allowance, to the same size as the outer section of the coffee-warmer, but 12 mm (½ in) shorter.

**Embroidery:** Use the photo on page 185 as a guide for colour placement. Embroider with three strands of thread throughout. Work the roses and leaves in satin stitch. Use stem stitch to embroider the veins of the leaves.

**Sewing:** After completing the embroidery, trim the seam allowances to 1 cm (⅜ in), apart from the short sides, which are without seam allowance. With right sides together, stitch the *sides as far as the top slit opening*. Clean-finish the raw edges of the side seams. Topstitch all round the top slit opening. Clip 5 mm (¼ in) into the seam allowances on the slit edge placement line, then turn under and stitch down the short lengths of seam allowance between the placement line and the straight open edges. Apply bias binding all round the straight open edges. Turn coffee-warmer right side out. Now, fold the self-lining inside along the fold line and bind the folded edge. Overcast the side edges of the two foam rubber (or wadding) pieces together by hand, leaving top slit and bottom edges open. Slip the padding into the top portion of the coffee-warmer, then turn under the self-lining and draw its bound edges through the slit. Fan out the edges.

### Place Mat

**Size:** 30 × 40 cm (12 × 16 in)

**Materials:** *To make one place mat, you need:* embroidery thread: Anchor Stranded Cotton (Anchor Bates/U.S.) in the following colours and quantities: one skein each of pink no. 36, deep pink no. 38, heather no. 39, grey no. 398, light green no. 261 and grass green no. 244. Crewel needle. *You also need:* 30 × 40 cm (12 × 16 in) piece of semi-fine cotton or linen. 1.5 m (1¾ yd) of 24 mm (1 in)-wide rose-coloured bias binding. Matching sewing thread.

**Cutting out/preparation:** Cut the place mat out roughly, then trace the full-size embroidery motif (given opposite) on to the lower right-hand corner.

**Embroidery:** Use the photo on page 185 as a guide for colour placement. Note that the rose motif on the place mat contains a grey accent not present on the coffee-warmer border. Embroider with three strands of thread throughout. Work the roses and leaves in satin stitch. Use stem stitch to embroider the veins of the leaves.

**Sewing:** After completing the embroidery, trim the place mat to the exact size (specified above). Bind the raw edges of the mat, mitring the corners.

### Serviette (napkin)

**Size:** 30 × 30 cm (12 × 12 in)

**Materials:** *To make one serviette, you need:* embroidery thread: same colours and quantities as for place mat. *You also need:* crewel needle. 30 × 30 cm (12 × 12 in) piece of semi-fine cotton or linen. 1.3 m (1⅜ yd) of 24 mm (1 in)-wide rose-coloured bias binding. Matching sewing thread.

**Instructions:** Embroider and sew same as for place mat.

# 22

## Four House Plants in Counted Cross-stitch

**Size:** Each motif measures approx. 13 × 18.5 cm (5 × 7½ in)

**Stitches:** Cross-stitch.

**Materials:** *Embroidery thread:* Anchor Stranded Cotton (Anchor Bates/U.S.), in the colours and quantities specified overleaf. Tapestry needle. *For four cushion fronts or pictures you need:* 0.8 m (⅞ yd) of 115 cm (44–45 in)-wide Hardanger fabric (thread count: 9 double threads per cm [22 per in]). Coloured basting thread.

**Stitch gauge:** 45 cross-stitches = 10 cm (4 in).

**Cutting out/preparation:** Cut out four fabric squares, each measuring 40 × 40 cm (16 × 16 in), including a 5 cm (2 in) seam allowance all round. Each piece makes a cushion front with a finished size of 30 × 30 cm (12 × 12 in). Clean-finish the edges of each piece to prevent fraying. Mark the vertical and horizontal centres of each piece of fabric with lines of coloured basting stitches. If you are making pictures, trim the fabric to the required size after the embroidery is completed, leaving extra fabric all round for mounting.

**Stitch diagrams:** Pattern grids for each of the four house plant motifs are given overleaf. Thread colour numbers and quantities are specified in the colour key which appears in the column next to each pattern grid. Each motif measures 57 squares across and 82 squares down. Each coloured square represents one cross-stitch in the appropriate colour worked over two double fabric threads both vertically and horizontally. Each empty square represents two double fabric threads (both directions) of the background fabric.

**Embroidery:** Cross-stitch over two double fabric threads both vertically and horizontally. Use four strands of thread throughout. The arrows on each diagram should coincide with the basting stitches on each piece of fabric.

*Patterns overleaf*

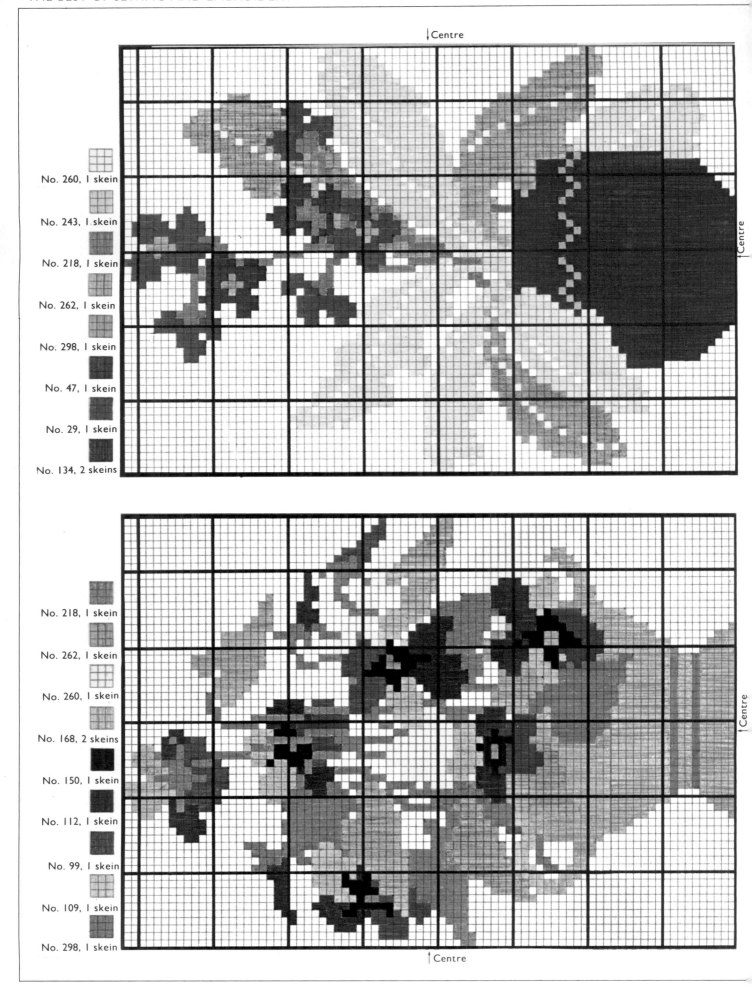

No. 260, 1 skein

No. 243, 1 skein

No. 218, 1 skein

No. 262, 1 skein

No. 298, 1 skein

No. 47, 1 skein

No. 29, 1 skein

No. 134, 2 skeins

No. 218, 1 skein

No. 262, 1 skein

No. 260, 1 skein

No. 168, 2 skeins

No. 150, 1 skein

No. 112, 1 skein

No. 99, 1 skein

No. 109, 1 skein

No. 298, 1 skein

Centre

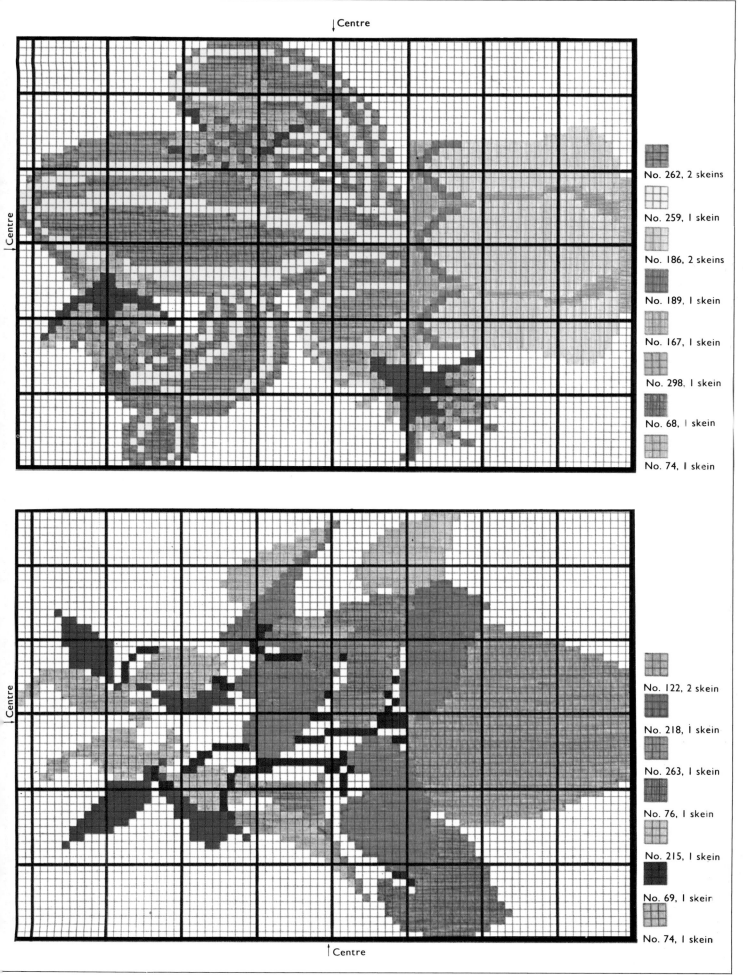

Centre

No. 262, 2 skeins

No. 259, 1 skein

No. 186, 2 skeins

No. 189, 1 skein

No. 167, 1 skein

No. 298, 1 skein

No. 68, 1 skein

No. 74, 1 skein

Centre

No. 122, 2 skein

No. 218, 1 skein

No. 263, 1 skein

No. 76, 1 skein

No. 215, 1 skein

No. 69, 1 skein

No. 74, 1 skein

Centre

# 23

## Hemstitching Fine Linen

**Sizes:** *Place mat:* 30 × 40 cm (12 × 16 in)
*Serviette (napkin):* 30 × 30 cm (12 × 12 in)

**Stitches:** Ladder hemstitch, zigzag hemstitch, various knotted hemstitches.

**Materials:** *Semi-fine pure linen:* 1.6 m (1¾ yd) of 90 cm (36 in)-wide fabric makes four place mats and four serviettes. *Embroidery thread:* white non-stranded embroidery thread in same thread weight as linen. Crewel needle. Basting thread.

**Cutting out:** Cut along the grain of the fabric. For each place mat, cut linen 40 × 50 cm (16 × 20 in); for each serviette, cut a 40 × 40 cm (16 × 16 in) piece. This gives a finished hem width of 2.5 cm (1 in), made up of two 2.5 cm (1 in) turnings. The last fold can be cut a little narrower, but then the edge of the shorter turning may form a visible ridge.

**Withdrawing the threads/ preparation:** On the wrong side, mark the length and width of the hem strip using pins or a fine pencil. For patterns 1–3, the hemstitching is 5 mm (¼ in) wide; for patterns 4–7, it is 1 cm (⅜ in) wide. On the place mat, the hem strips intersect and run to the edge of the fabric, so the threads are withdrawn from edge to edge. To do so, pull out the outer threads of each hem strip, then pull out the ones in between. To withdraw threads for interior designs (place mat 1, serviette 2) and hem strips with corners (all serviettes), cut through the middle of the outer threads, then pull them out towards the corners. Do the same for the threads in between. Trim off the threads close to each corner, then turn under and sew down the thread ends. *For place mat and all serviettes:* before you begin the embroidery, turn under and baste down, then hem (two 2.5 cm [1 in] turnings), mitring the corners.

**Embroidery:** When hemstitching, the hem is caught up along the outer edges as you work. The top and bottom of each hem strip are secured using simple hemstitching: on design 1 the stitches are aligned to make ladder hemstitch, on design 3 the stitches are staggered to make zigzag hemstitch. For designs 2 and 3, there are four threads in each bundle; the other designs have three threads in each bundle. These bundles are grouped together for the decorative stitches: for designs 5 and 7, group three bundles together; for designs 4 and 6, group four bundles together. Below is a stitch key which identifies the various stitches used for each design. Detailed instructions for these stitches are given on pages 226–7 of the Embroidery Course. *Interior design areas:* on the place mat (1) and serviette 2, work the interior drawn thread areas first, then work the hem strip. *Place Mat:* since the hemstitching goes right to the edge, there is a triple thickness of fabric within the hem allowance. When working the hemstitching, treat the triple thickness as a single layer by aligning the threads on top of one another. *To fill corner gaps:* on the narrow hem strips (designs 1–3) stitch criss-crosses diagonally, as shown. Fill wider gaps (designs 4–7) with more elaborate stitches (for example, needleweaving) to match the stitch used. Do not make the tension on these stitches too tight. *Finishing:* wash the linen and iron it carefully on the wrong side.

**Stitch key**
Design no.
1 Ladder hemstitch
2 Ladder hemstitch with wrapped thread bundles
3 Zigzag hemstitch
4 Simple knotted hemstitch with embroidered bundles
5 Simple knotted hemstitch
6 Zigzag-knotted hemstitch
7 Double-knotted hemstitch

# 24

## Mexican Rug

**Size:** 110 × 210 cm (43½ × 83 in)

**Stitches:** Satin stitch on canvas.

**Materials:** 2.2 m (2½ yd) of 158 cm (63 in)-wide Zweigart 'Sudan' rug canvas (article no. 1106/ 132), with 3 holes per 2.5 cm (1 in). Rug needle or size 13 tapestry needle. 7 m (7⅝ yd) of 40 mm (1½ in)-wide rug binding. Strong carpet or buttonhole thread.
*Rug yarn:* a good-quality continuous-length rug wool in the following colours and quantities: 200 g (7 oz) of yellow; 400 g (14 oz) each of blue, dark green, gold, light pink and light green; 500 g (17½ oz) of dusty rose; 600 g (21 oz) of white/cream; 700 g (24½ oz) each of black and burgundy.

**Stitch diagram:** The background lines on the diagram represent the double threads of the rug canvas. Each coloured line represents *two* satin stitches worked over the indicated number of canvas threads, in the indicated colour. The colour key to the right of the diagram identifies the colours of all the yarns. To make the pattern diagram easier to follow, those areas meant to be worked in white are shown in

turquoise. One pattern repeat is given in both the lengthwise and widthwise directions. The lengthwise pattern is repeated twice along the length of the rug. The widthwise pattern repeat is worked five and a half times.

**Embroidery:** The rug is worked in satin stitch using one strand of rug yarn throughout. Satin stitch on canvas is explained on pages 224–5 of the Embroidery Course. Trim the canvas down to 220 × 115 cm (87 × 45½ in). Leave 5 cm (2 in) unworked along the top and bottom edges, 2.5 cm (1 in) along the sides. All the stitches are worked in the lengthwise direction. Take each satin stitch over the indicated number of canvas holes lengthwise, with two stitches worked between each pair of double canvas threads in the widthwise direction. Work the widthwise pattern repeat a total of five and a half times. One half of the lengthwise pattern is given. When you reach the lengthwise centre of the rug, repeat the colour and pattern sequence in the reverse order.

**Finishing:** Stretch (block) the rug if necessary. To do this, place the rug face down on an ironing board or a flat surface and press using a steam iron and a press cloth. Trim the

canvas down to 2.5 cm (1 in) all round; clip diagonally across corners. With rug right side up and with width of rug binding extending on to rug surface, sew binding all round rug by hand, using strong thread. The ends of the binding should overlap by 5 cm (2 in). Sew along the outer edge of the binding, keeping stitches as close as possible to the first row of embroidery. Next, turn binding under on to wrong side of rug. Stitch binding down, mitring the corners.

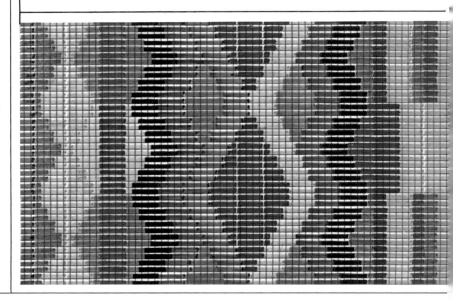

# 25

## Embroidered Quick-Knit Bolero

**Size:** Small (8–10 [6–8 U.S.])

**Embroidery stitches:**
Blanket stitch, backstitch, lazy daisy stitch, overcasting and various needle-weaving techniques.

**Materials:** Five 50 g balls of Phildar Kadisha. One pair of 5½ mm (u.s. no. 9) knitting needles.
*Embroidery thread:* silver Lurex thread, assorted colourful remnants of yarn and soft embroidery cotton (matte embroidery cotton). Tapestry needle.
*Tension (gauge):* 13 stitches and 26 rows to 10 cm (4 in) measured over garter stitch.
*To knit the bolero:*
The bolero is knitted in one piece beginning at left side seam edge.
Cast on 100 stitches loosely and work in garter stitch as follows: *1st row:* K to end. Repeat last row for 18 cm (7 in).
*Shape neck and left front as follows:*
*Next row:* cast off (blind off) 54 sts, K 46. Work straight for 20 rows.
*Shape neck and right front as follows:*
*Next row:* K 46, make 54 sts. Work straight until same no. of rows are completed as for left front. Cast off (bind off) loosely.

**Embroidery:** Use Lurex and remnants of yarn and embroidery thread, doubling the thinner strands. First, embroider all edges of the bolero in blanket stitch. In the vertical direction, work over the cast on/cast off row + 1 ridge in depth and embroider into every knitted stitch. Horizontally, space the stitches two ridges apart, working over two knitted stitches in height. Then, using Lurex, overcast along the second row above the blanket stitching, sewing into each knitted stitch/ridge. Next, embroider the vertical border along the full length of the bolero back and front. Start at the left side seam and overcast the first free ridge with yarn, then overcast the second ridge with Lurex.
*First border:* Skip two ridges and work the repeat pattern over the following three ridges. Catch up opposite loops on the first and third ridges, then turn and stitch through the adjacent loop on the third ridge, then through the loop directly opposite on the first ridge (see photo 1). Turn and stitch through the adjacent loop on the first ridge, then the loop opposite. Continue in this way, forming a wavy pattern. In a contrasting colour, work a lazy daisy stitch two ridges long through each loop.
*Second border:* The next two

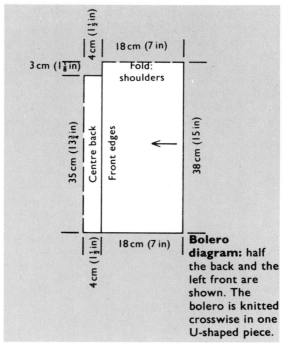

ridges are embroidered with a V-shaped chain. To start, * bring the needle out between two ridges, then stitch through the nearest 'bottom' loop and the

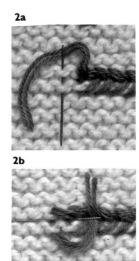

**2a**

**2b**

18 cm (7 in)

3 cm (1⅛ in) | 4 cm (1½ in)

Fold: shoulders

35 cm (13¾ in) | Centre back | Front edges

38 cm (15 in)

4 cm (1½ in) | 18 cm (7 in)

**Bolero diagram: half the back and the left front are shown. The bolero is knitted crosswise in one U-shaped piece.**

bottom loop on the ridge directly opposite (see photo 2a). Insert the needle where it first emerged and bring it out between the two ridges, inside the loop you have just made (photo 2b). Repeat the sequence from *, as necessary to complete the row. To finish the border, work one row of backstitch down the centre in Lurex, encircling each 'V'-shape.
*Third border:* The zigzag pattern repeats over three ridges. Sew through a

bottom loop of the first ridge, then through the next-but-one bottom loop of the second ridge, then through the next-but-one bottom loop of the third ridge. Turn, then catch up the next loop of the third ridge, then the next-but-one loop of the second ridge, then the next-but-one loop of the first ridge. Turn, and repeat the sequence to complete the row (see photo 3). Work

*Continued overleaf*

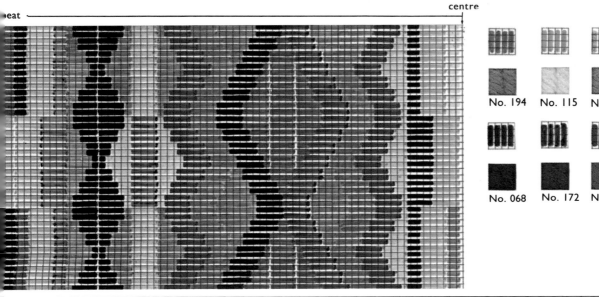

eat

centre

| No. 194 | No. 115 | No. 229 | No. 040 | No. 216 |
| No. 068 | No. 172 | No. 024 | No. 225 | No. 226 |

3

4

the next line of stitching in a contrasting colour, one row higher, in exactly the same way. Finally, in a third colour, work a lazy daisy stitch at each inner point on the second row of zigzag stitching.
*Fourth border:* To start, embroider the next *two ridges* in the wavy pattern used for the first border (see photo 1). At the end of the row, reverse direction and finish off the stitching through the same loops. To finish the border, work one row of backstitch down the centre in a contrasting colour, encircling each vertical thread (see photo 4).
*To finish embroidery:* for the back, repeat the second border, then work the first border down the centre back. From centre back, work the remaining half in reverse order. Finally, using the Lurex, stitch a ridge of overcasting to either side of the borders, as shown.

**Finishing:** Using the same yarn as was used for the blanket stitch edging, join the lower 18 cm (7 in) of the side seams together with overcasting stitch.

# 26

## Top With Cross-Stitch Plus Crochet

**Size:** Medium (10–12 [8–10 U.S.])

**Materials:** *For blouse front and back sections:* 0.4 m (½ yd) of 115 cm (44–45 in)-wide cotton jersey fabric. Waist measurement + 3 cm (1⅛ in) of 5 mm (¼ in)-wide elastic. Matching sewing thread.
*For embroidery:* Anchor Stranded Cotton (Anchor Bates/U.S.) in the colours and quantities indicated in the colour key next to the pattern diagram, at right. Crewel needle. Piece of cotton single-thread canvas with twelve holes per 2.5 cm (1 in), measuring 25 × 25 cm (10 × 10 in). Pair of tweezers. Coloured basting thread.
*For crochet:* 2 balls of Twilleys Lyscordet. crochet hook no. 3.00 mm (No. 2/U.S.).

**Embroidery stitches:** Cross-stitch.

**Cross-stitch diagram:** The canvas transfer method, described on page 235 of the Embroidery Course, is used to work the cross-stitch design on the knitted fabric. Each coloured square on the grid represents one cross-stitch in the appropriate colour worked over one intersection of the canvas grid. Each empty square represents an unembroidered canvas thread intersection. The design measures 101 cross-stitches across and 90 cross-stitches down.

**Cutting out/Preparation:** Enlarge the pattern pieces and cut out one front and one back section from the jersey, adding 1 cm (⅜ in) seam allowance all round. Clean-finish the edges to prevent ravelling.

**Embroidery:** The design is embroidered 2.5 cm (1 in) above the cut bottom edge of the blouse front section. Baste the canvas on to the blouse front and mark the vertical and horizontal centres with lines of coloured basting stitches. Cross-stitch over one canvas intersection, using

four strands of thread throughout. The arrows on the diagram should coincide with the basting stitches on the blouse front. It is easiest to work the design if you start the embroidery from the bottom edge. When embroidery is completed, trim canvas close to stitching and remove canvas threads one at a time, using a pair of tweezers.

*Crochet blouse*
*Tension* (gauge): 25 stitches and 9 rows to 10 cm (4 in).
*Side panels:* make 2. A seam allowance of 1 cm (⅜ in) has been allowed on each side of panels. Commence with 28 ch loosely to measure 11 cm (4½ in).
*Foundation row:* 1 tr (dc) into 6th ch from hook (1 ch, miss (skip) next ch, 1 tr [1 dc] into next ch) 11 times, turn
*1st row:* 4 ch, miss (skip) first tr (dc), * 1 tr (1 dc) into next tr (dc), 1 ch; repeat from * ending with 1 tr (1 dc) into 3rd of 4 ch, turn.
Repeat 1st row until work measures 22 cm (8⅝ in) from beginning. Fasten off.
*Peplum:* working in continuous rounds, commence with 180 ch to measure 76 cm (30 in). 1 ss (sl st) into first ch to form a ring.
*Foundation round:* 1 dc into same place as ss (sl st), 1 dc (1 sc) into next ch, 1 ss (sl st) into first dc (sc); 180 dc (180 sc).
*1st rnd:* 4 ch, * miss (skip) next dc (sc), 1 tr (1 dc) into next dc (sc), 1 ch; repeat from * to within last dc (sc), end with 1 ss (sl st) into 3rd of 4 ch.
*2nd rnd:* 4 ch, miss (skip) first tr (dc), * 1 tr (1 dc) into next tr (dc), 1 ch; repeat from * ending with 1 ss (sl st) into 3rd of 4 ch. Repeat 2nd round six times more.
*9th rnd:* 1 dc (sc) into first tr (dc), * 1 dc (1 sc) into next 1 ch sp, 1 dc (1 sc) into next tr (dc); repeat from * ending with 1 dc (1 sc) into last 1 ch sp, 1 ss (sl st) into first dc (sc).
*10th rnd:* * 5 ch, 1 ss (sl st) into 5th ch from hook, miss (skip) next dc (sc), 1 dc (1 sc) into next dc (sc); repeat from * ending with 1 ss (sl st) into first ch. Fasten off.
*Neck edging:* working in

continuous rounds commence with 135 ch to measure 56 cm (22 in), 1 ss (sl st) into first ch to form a ring.
Repeat foundation round of peplum once.
*Last rnd:* * 5 ch, 1 ss (sl st) into 5th ch from hook, miss (skip) next 2 dc (2 sc), 1 dc (1 sc) into next dc (sc); repeat from * ending with 1 ss (sl st) into first ch. Fasten off.
*Armhole edging:* make 2. Working in continuous rounds, commence with 102 ch to measure 43 cm (17 in), 1 ss (sl st) into first ch to form a ring.
Repeat foundation round of peplum once. Repeat last round of neck edging once. Fasten off.

**Finishing:** With right sides together, stitch blouse front to back at shoulder seams. Turn under and press seam allowances along front and back side seams and insert crocheted side panels in between, using small hand stitches. Turn under and press all remaining seam allowances. Pin on peplum, neckline and armhole trims with right sides together and straight edges even; sew on to blouse by hand using small overcasting stitches. Join elastic to form a ring; sew on to waistline on wrong side of blouse, using herringbone stitch (catchstitch).

No. 6, 2 skein

No. 35, 1 skein

No. 212, 1 skein

No. 210, 2 skeins

No. 97, 1 skein

No. 25, 1 skein

No. 102, 1 skein

No. 298, 1 skein

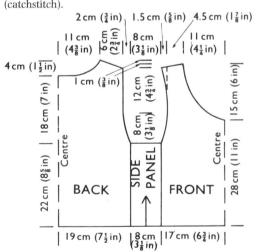

Blouse pattern is shown in reduced size: half back, side panel and half front. Enlarge the measurements given (in centimetres or inches) to full size. The front and back panels are cut from knit fabric. The side panels are crocheted.

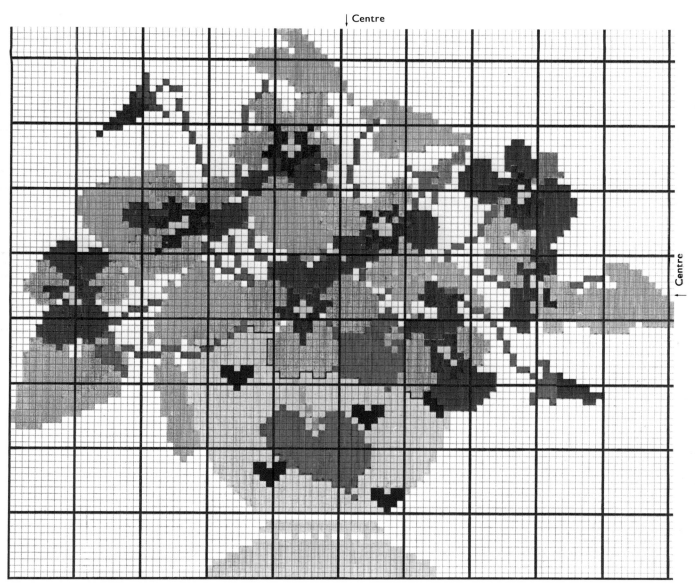

| Centre

Centre

**Embroidery pattern:** Each square represents one cross-stitch worked in the appropriate colour. Empty squares represent unembroidered background fabric. The canvas transfer method is used. Work each stitch over one mesh intersection.

# 27

**Cuddly Lambs to Guarantee Sweet Dreams**

We embroidered these whimsical motifs on pastel-striped bed linen using satin stitch. Your child will certainly sleep peacefully in such delightful surroundings. He or she will probably clamber into bed without too much persuasion. On the right-hand page, you can see the lambs full size. They are so irresistible you'll be tempted to use them on adult bedding.

These designs can be worked equally well on nightdresses, pyjamas or dressing-gowns. Embroider these fleecy friends on both sheets and nightwear and your little ones will eagerly await bedtime. Since children's things undergo frequent laundering, make sure that you purchase colourfast embroidery thread.

The big lamb, at the top, is embroidered with the initials of its owner. You will find all the letters of the alphabet in full size in the instructions section.

Instructions and full-size embroidery patterns for the lambs are on pages 212 and 213.

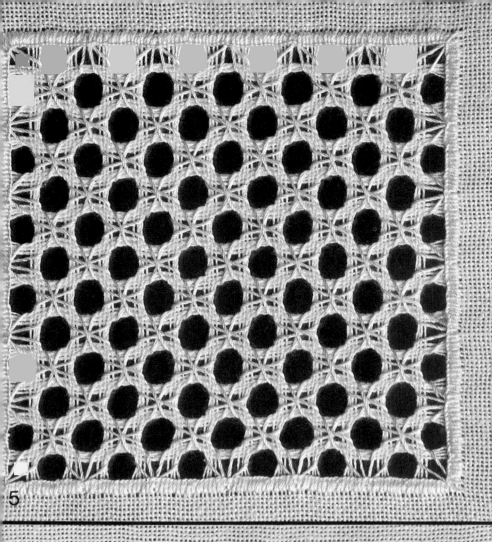

5

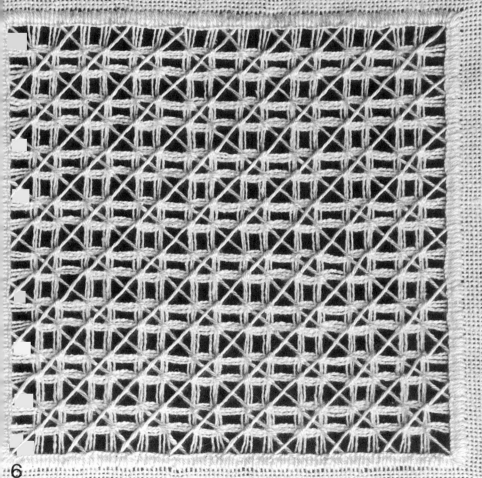

6

## 28
## Openwork Embroidery: Six Multi-Purpose Designs

Openwork embroidery falls into the category of 'whitework', as it is most often stitched with white thread on a white base fabric. Traditionally, it has been used to decorate table and bed linens, but there is no reason why you can't – or shouldn't – break these conventions. Openwork can be worked quite effectively using either contrasting-coloured thread or fabric. Why not use it to enhance curtains, cushions or items of clothing? That way, you can lovingly revive and update an almost lost art.

The lace-like appearance of these designs is created by withdrawing fabric threads and then grouping the remaining threads to form patterns. The six designs at left are described in detail with explanatory photos in the instructions section. There are four border patterns and two square insets.

Instructions for these openwork designs are on pages 213, 214 and 215.

# 29
## Naive-style Farmyard Scene in Embroidered Appliqué

This homely and attractive picture is bound to receive lots of admiring comments. It was created from colourful scraps of cotton fabric and embellished with decorative stitchery details worked in leftover bits of embroidery thread.

The farmyard scene is assembled using iron-on adhesive web. This speeds up the appliquéing process because it makes it unnecessary to turn under seam allowances round each and every shape. All you have to do is fuse on the cut-outs in the correct order. Accuracy is required, but a smaller dose of patience is called for than in the past. The results will enhance any living room.

Once you've mastered the simple technique, you can use it to make appliquéd pictures based on children's drawings or book illustrations.

Instructions and a full-size pattern for the farmyard scene are on pages 216, 217 and 222.

# 30
**Alpine Village: Picture Stitched with Needle and Thread**

This winter landscape is truly a masterpiece. It wasn't made using brush and paint though; it was worked in needlepoint tapestry to create this naive, romantic effect.

Long winter evenings when you wish to pass a few pleasant hours are ideal for a project like this. During this time you can relax and recover from the trials of the day. The picture is embroidered in tent stitch which is explained on page 234 of the Embroidery Course. You need a certain amount of patience for this, but the results are well worth the effort. You should always work a larger piece like this in an embroidery frame to prevent distortion. We tell you how to mount the canvas correctly in the frame on page 233 of the Embroidery Course section.

Instructions and the pattern grid for the winter landscape are on pages 218 and 219, and 222.

# 31

**Six Scenes of Idyllic Country Life Embroidered with Loving Care**

Cheerful, vivid colours and attractive naive-style motifs are the secret of the success of these embroidered pictures. Compare the large picture with the six smaller ones and you will soon discover that it is comprised of these six scenes.

You need lots of perseverance to complete the large picture because it is made up of almost 60,000 stitches. If that sounds a bit overwhelming, start with one of the small pictures. If you enjoy that, you can progress to the next one. In this way you will be able to make the large picture more quickly than you imagined.

If you don't manage to complete it, it doesn't really matter because each vignette looks quite attractive when framed on its own. They are worked in cross-stitch, using stranded embroidery cotton. The Embroidery Course shows you how to cross-stitch on canvas on pages 223–4.

If you do manage to finish the large picture, you will be a cross-stitcher par excellence. The next logical step will be to create your own original, more complicated designs, a suggestion which we have repeatedly made in the book in regard to cross-stitch. Anyone who successfully meets the challenge of this picture is so truly experienced that more difficult projects will present no problem.

Instructions and a pattern grid for the country life scenes are on pages 220–221, and page 222.

# 27

## Cuddly Lamb Nursery Linen

**Stitches:** Satin stitch.

**Materials:** Anchor Stranded Cotton (Anchor Bates/U.S.) in soft pink no. 968, deep pink no. 972, light blue no. 144, deep blue no. 148 and white no. 2. For the large motif, you need one skein of light blue, one half skein of each of the other colours; you need the same quantities for the long border. Crewel needle.

**Preparation:** We embroidered on store-bought bed linens. Transfer the motifs on to the fabric, positioning them as shown (see page 235). Centre the appropriate initials in the middle of the big lamb's body, with the point (period) after each letter under- or overlapping as shown. If you are embroidering the border on to a top sheet, make sure that the border is placed correctly on the right side of the turn-back, with bottom of the border parallel to the edge of the sheet.

**Embroidery:** Work the embroidery in satin stitch, using two strands of thread throughout. Use the photo on page 203 as a guide for stitch direction. Work the lambs in light blue, stitching the curly fleece in scalloped rows as shown. Embroider white hooves, soft pink ears and face and light blue eyelashes and nose. Embroider the ground soft pink, the flower petals alternately soft pink and deep pink, the stem and sepals blue, and each leaf half light blue and half deep blue. Work the initials in deep pink with white outlines.

# 28
## Openwork Designs

**Stitches:** Basic hemstitching, buttonhole stitch, loop knots, needleweaving.

**General instructions**
If you are unfamiliar with the technique of drawn thread work, it might be a good idea to perfect your skill by working project 23 (Hemstitching fine linen) before attempting this more advanced one. It is also advisable to read the Embroidery Course sections on hemstitching (pages 226–7) and Hardanger embroidery (page 229).

Openwork embroidery should be worked on an evenweave cotton or linen base fabric from which the threads can easily be withdrawn. Work the embroidery with a tapestry needle, using non-stranded embroidery thread in the same weight as the fabric threads. To withdraw threads, cut through the middle of each thread to be removed and pull it out towards the edges. Trim off the thread ends close to the end of each side of the openwork area, then turn under and sew down the thread ends with backstitch. These ends will later be secured with hemstitching or buttonhole stitching. On border patterns 1–4, the hemstitching along the top and bottom edges is worked two fabric threads from the edge, with each stitch encircling two fabric threads. Start the embroidery without making a knot; just secure the thread with a few running stitches in the fabric. After completing the embroidery, clean-finish the remaining edges using buttonhole stitch; then trim off the thread ends.

*Pattern overleaf*

Within each openwork area, the fabric threads are grouped together in bundles. Each bundle is fastened with a loop knot. To work a loop knot, lay the working thread as a loop over the threads to be bundled together, then insert the needle at the top right, encircling the appropriate number of threads. Then pull the needle out, bringing it through the loop (see left-hand needle, photo 4). Pull the thread firmly.

**Pattern 1** (Border with criss-crossing thread bars): all the threads are withdrawn in the lengthwise direction: pull out four threads and leave one, a total of three times; then pull out twelve threads and leave one. Then pull out four threads and leave one twice more. To finish, pull out four threads. Stitch the loop knot rows as follows, working inwards towards the centre of the border: on the two outer rows, bundle four threads together; on the second row to either side, bundle four threads together, but staggered; on the two middle rows, bundle twelve threads together (see left-hand needle in photo 1). Work the needlewoven thread bars between the middle loop knot rows in two criss-crossing zigzag rows: to form a thread support for the needlewoven bars, secure the working thread in the fabric, level with the top row of loop knots. Working on a downwards slant, loop the working thread behind the right four-thread bar of the first thread bundle on the lower row of loop knots, then bring the needle back to the point where it first emerged. Work a needlewoven thread bar round the two strands of the thread loop, working from top to bottom (see Embroidery Course, page 227). When the first bar is completed, push the needle through in the bottom row, in front of the four-thread bar on the left of the first thread bundle. Working on an upwards slant, loop the working thread round the top right-hand four-thread bar of the second bundle, then insert the needle at

the point where it emerged. Work needleweaving round this thread loop, too. Complete the row, then work the second row of zigzag needleweaving in exactly the same way, but with zigzags going in the opposite direction, as shown. The needlewoven thread bars will overlap. Hemstitch the long edges of the border; work buttonhole stitch on the short sides.

**Pattern 2** (Greek key border): all the threads are withdrawn in the lengthwise direction: pull out four threads and leave one a total of eight times; then pull out four threads. Work a total of eight loop knot rows, bundling the fabric threads together in groups of four, as shown (see left-hand needle, photo 2). Embroider the Greek key pattern in needleweaving, using the photo on page 204 as your stitch placement guide. Always work the needleweaving in the lengthwise direction: to make the design lines which run parallel to the long sides, weave in and out along the full length of each line (see centre needle, photo 2). Work design lines which are parallel to the short sides in units of two squares at a time, as necessary to complete the pattern (see lower right-hand needle, photo 2). To start a new thread, fasten it down on the underside, but do not make a knot. To finish, hemstitch the long edges of the border; work buttonhole stitching on the short sides.

**Pattern 3** (Border with diamond-shaped thread bars): all the threads are withdrawn in the lengthwise direction: pull out four threads and leave one, a total of three times; then pull out nine threads, leave one and pull out nine more threads. To finish, leave one thread and pull out four, a total of three times. Work the loop knot rows as follows: on the two outer rows, bundle the fabric threads together in groups of four; on the two following inward rows on either side, bundle the threads together in staggered groups of four. In

**PATTERN 1**

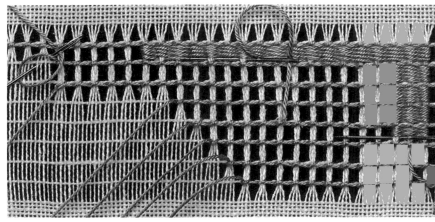

**PATTERN 2**

**PATTERN 3**

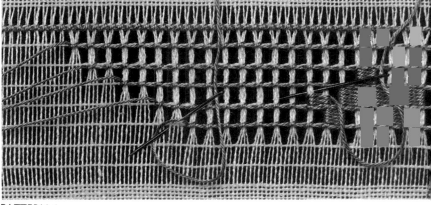

**PATTERN 4**

the centre three rows, bundle groups of eight fabric threads together, splitting up every second bundle of the previous row, to either side of each bundle. Work the needlewoven thread bars between the three middle loop knot rows, in a manner similar to pattern 1. Work the thread support loops as shown, anchoring each around the four-thread bar in each bundle, as the double-thread bars are too weak for this purpose. The thread support loop should pass through the loop knot on the middle row. For added support, stitch through the centre thread bundle when working each needlewoven bar. First work the needlewoven bars in a zigzag pattern, then work the remaining diagonal bars in the opposite direction; each of these bars must be needlewoven in two halves (see centre top needle, photo 3). To finish, hemstitch the long edges of the border; work buttonhole stitch along the short sides.

**Pattern 4** (Zigzag 'filet' border): withdraw threads as for pattern 2. Work loop knot rows as follows: bundle the two outer rows together in thread pairs; on all other rows, bundle the threads together in groups of four. Start the zigzag pattern in the centre of the border, between the fourth and fifth row of loop knots. Beginning at the right-hand side, needleweave pairs of thread bundles together (see right-hand needle, photo 4). After you have finished the centre row in this way, work the necessary needleweaving blocks to the left in the row above and to the right in the row below, to complete the zigzag pattern (see photo, page 204). To finish, work hemstitching along the lengthwise edges of the border and buttonhole stitching along the sides.

**Pattern 5** (Square inset with mesh pattern): for this pattern, the number of fabric threads must be divisible by 8 + 4. Pull out four fabric threads alternately vertically and horizontally and then leave four. Finally, pull out four threads each way. Fasten

the embroidery thread in the upper right-hand corner of the openwork square and wind the thread round each square fabric thread intersection as shown, working diagonally towards the bottom left-hand corner. Insert the needle at the bottom left-hand corner and then work diagonally back towards the upper right-hand corner, winding the embroidery thread round each square fabric thread intersection, as before (see right-hand needle in photo 5). When you reach the upper right-hand corner, slide the needle down through the folded fabric edge and bring it out in the middle of the *second* square fabric thread intersection to the right or left. Stitch this and all following rows in the same way as the previous row, working outwards to either side of the centre diagonal. Then work the remaining diagonal rows in the same manner, but in the reverse direction: diagonally from top left to bottom right (see left-hand needle in photo 5). Do not pull the embroidery thread too tight. If you should run out of thread while working either pattern 5 or pattern 6, always begin a new working thread from the edge of the openwork square. Fasten each new working thread, but not too firmly, as it will be secured by the buttonhole stitching, just like the ends of the drawn threads. To finish, work buttonhole stitching all round the edges of the openwork square; trim the thread ends.

**Pattern 6** (Square inset with criss-crossing threads): for this pattern, the number of fabric threads both horizontally and vertically must be divisible by 12 + 4. *Pull out four fabric threads alternately vertically and horizontally, leave three, pull two, leave three, repeat from *. Finally, pull out four threads each way. Start the embroidery in the upper left-hand corner, and stitch diagonally towards the bottom right-hand corner, working one loop knot round each square fabric thread intersection. Work the following rows of loop knots in the same

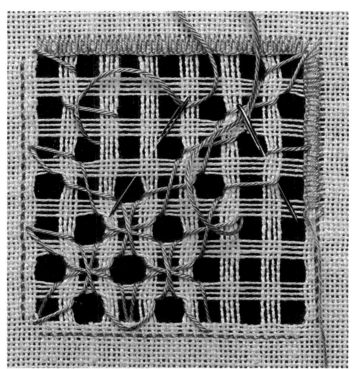

**PATTERN 5**

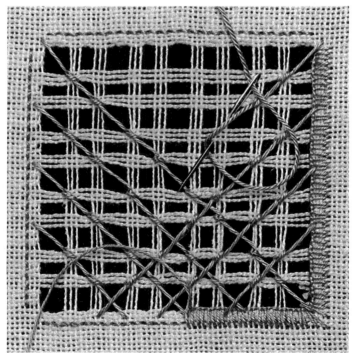

**PATTERN 6**

way, to either side of the diagonal, always beginning in the corner of a large empty square and skipping the small empty squares. Then work the diagonal rows from right to left, in the same manner (see right-hand needle, photo 6). If you run out of embroidery thread, start a new working thread from the edge of the openwork

area. To finish, work buttonhole stitch all round the edges of the openwork square, catching in the drawn thread ends and embroidery thread ends; trim all thread ends.

# 29

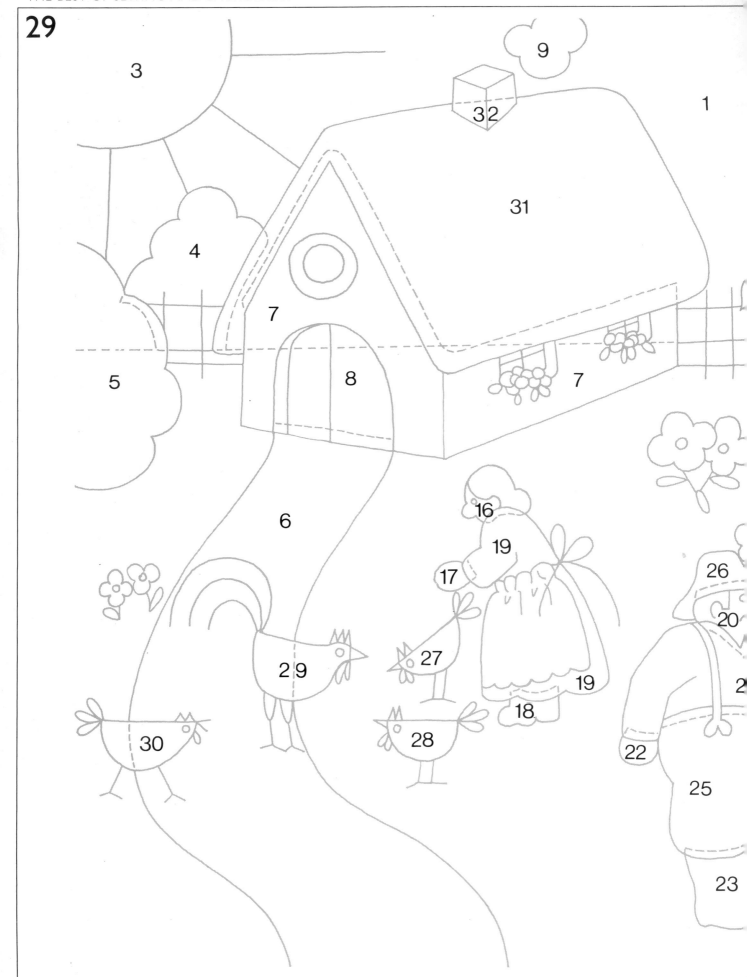

**Alpine village:** The needlepoint design is given in grid form below. Each square represents one tent stitch in the appropriate colour. The picture is worked on single thread canvas using soft embroidery cotton (matte embroidery cotton). See page 222 for thread requirements and full instructions.

| | |
|---|---|
| No. 2 | 5 skeins |
| No. 288 | 3 skeins |
| No. 298 | 7 skeins |
| No. 316 | 4 skeins |
| No. 46 | 3 skeins |
| No. 20 | 2 skeins |
| No. 24 | 2 skeins |
| No. 8 | 2 skeins |
| No. 68 | 4 skeins |
| No. 100 | 3 skeins |
| No. 112 | 2 skeins |
| No. 133 | 2 skeins |
| No. 150 | 1 skein |
| No. 145 | 7 skeins |
| No. 169 | 6 skeins |
| No. 186 | 3 skeins |
| No. 255 | 17 skeins |
| No. 225 | 8 skeins |
| No. 258 | 3 skeins |
| No. 245 | 9 skeins |
| No. 218 | 4 skeins |
| No. 281 | 5 skeins |
| No. 372 | 3 skeins |
| No. 374 | 1 skein |
| No. 340 | 3 skeins |
| No. 370 | 3 skeins |
| No. 371 | 2 skeins |
| No. 397 | 3 skeins |
| No. 398 | 2 skeins |
| No. 403 | 2 skeins |

# 29

## Farmyard Scene to Appliqué and Embroider

**Size:** 25 × 38 cm (approx. 10 × 15 in)

**Materials:** Assorted printed and plain scraps of cotton fabric. *For base:* 35 × 48 cm (14 × 19 in) piece of cotton fabric. *You also need:* Two 1 m packs of 20 cm-wide iron-on adhesive web (¾ yd of 36 in-wide iron-on adhesive web). Leftover bits of stranded embroidery cotton (floss) and yarn. Crewel needle. Scrap of lace (for apron). Contrasting sewing thread.

**Appliqué diagram:** A full-size pattern for the farmyard picture is given on pages 216–7. Each shape on the pattern is numbered to indicate the order in which the fabric cut-outs are ironed on to the base fabric. The broken lines are guidelines for the positioning of the underlapping parts of the cut-out motifs. The motifs on top overlap them by approx. 5 mm (¼ in).

**Instructions:** Use the photo on pages 206–7 as a reference for colour and stitch placement. First, make a tracing of the whole picture and then make individual tracing paper patterns for each appliqué shape. Cut out each shape once from an appropriate fabric and once from adhesive web. Position each cut-out on the base fabric, with the corresponding piece of adhesive web underneath. Centre the picture on the base fabric (there's a 5 cm [2 in] allowance all round). The large tracing serves as a placement guide. Pin the top edge of the tracing on to the piece of base fabric, within the seam allowance. Lift the tracing up and down to check that the shapes are correctly positioned. The edges of each motif should coincide with the appropriate outline on the tracing. Iron each appliqué shape on to the base fabric in the order shown, using a dry iron and a damp press cloth.

**Embroidery:** After all the pieces have been ironed in place, embroider round each motif with contrasting sewing thread, using small overhand stitches. To make the woman's apron, gather the top of a small scrap of lace, then sew it in place. For the apron ties, sew on a yarn bow. Add details to the picture using the following embroidery stitches: work apples, birds, hair on the farmer and his wife, farmer's pipe, chickens' combs, many of the flower petals and the leaves on the sunflowers in satin stitch. Embroider the fence, rays of sunshine and the details on the cottage in stem stitch. The ladder and the farmer's braces (suspenders) are embroidered in chain stitch. Work sunflower petals in lazy daisy stitch. Use backstitch for the chickens' legs and some of the flower stems. The basket is worked in basic couching (see Embroidery Course, page 228).

# 30

## Alpine Village Needlepoint Picture

**Size:** 27 × 42 cm (10½ × 16½ in)

**Stitches:** Tent stitch.

**Materials:** 0.5 m (⅝ yd) of 90 cm (36 in)-wide single thread canvas with 12 holes per 2.5 cm (1 in). Size 20 tapestry needle. Straight-sided embroidery frame.
*Embroidery thread:* Anchor Soft Embroidery cotton (matte embroidery cotton, Anchor Bates/U.S.), in the following colours and quantities: one skein each dark cornflower blue no. 148, canary yellow no. 298, dark forest green no. 218, medium grass green no. 244, pink no. 6, dark cardinal red no. 20, deep orange no. 332 and black no. 403; two skeins of geranium red no. 13; three skeins each of cobalt blue no. 128 and grey no. 397; four skeins each of chocolate brown no. 936, light delphinium blue no. 121 and light brown no. 310; six skeins of tangerine orange no. 316; ten skeins of kingfisher blue no. 161 and twelve skeins of white no. 1.

**Diagram:** Each square on the pattern grid represents one tent stitch in the appropriate colour. You can find the pattern grid on pages 218–9.

**Embroidery:** Trim canvas down to 50 × 60 cm (22½ × 24½ in). Mount the canvas in the embroidery frame as described on page 233 of the Embroidery Course. Work the design in tent stitch, following the pattern grid. Start with the houses in the middle of the picture. Leave 9 cm (3¾ in) unworked along the short sides of the picture, 11.5 cm (6 in) along the long sides.

**Finishing:** Stretch (block) canvas if necessary. Mount in picture frame.

# 31

## Country Life Pictures

**Size:** *Large picture:* approx. 53 × 80 cm (21 × 31½ in)
*Each small picture:* approx. 26.5 × 26.5 cm (10½ × 10½ in)

**Stitches:** Cross-stitch on canvas.

**Materials:** Zweigart double mesh canvas (article no. 500/38) with 9/10 holes per 2.5 cm (1 in), 60 cm (24 in) wide: for the large picture 0.95 m (1⅛ yd); for each small picture 0.35 m (⅜ yd). Size 22 tapestry needle. Straight-sided embroidery frame.
*Embroidery thread:* Anchor Stranded Cotton (Anchor Bates/U.S.). Colours and quantities for the large picture are listed in the colour key next to the pattern grid on page 221. Following are the colours and quantities for the small pictures:
*Picture 1* (Hiking): one skein each colour no. 288, 298, 316, 46, 20, 24, 8, 100, 112, 169, 258, 245, 218, 281, 372, 374, 340, 371, 397, 398, 403 and 2. Two skeins each colour no. 145 and 225. Three skeins colour no. 255.
*Picture 2* (Fishing): one skein each colour no. 288, 316, 46, 20, 8, 68, 100, 112, 169, 258, 245, 218, 372, 374, 340, 370, 371, 397, 398, 403 and 2. Two skeins each colour no. 298, 145 and 225. Three skeins colour no. 255.
*Picture 3* (Shepherd): one skein each colour no. 288, 298, 316, 46, 20, 24, 8, 68, 100, 112, 133, 169, 186, 258, 245, 218, 281, 372, 374, 340, 370, 371, 398, 403 and 2. Two skeins each colour no. 145 and 225. Three skeins colour no. 255.
*Picture 4* (Wedding): one skein each colour no. 288, 298, 316, 46, 20, 24, 8, 68, 100, 112, 133, 169, 186, 225, 258, 218, 281, 372, 340, 370, 371, 397, 398, 403 and 2. Two skeins colour no. 245. Three skeins colour no. 255.
*Picture 5* (Dancing): one skein each colour no. 288, 316, 46, 20, 24, 8, 68, 100, 112, 133, 150, 145, 169, 186, 258, 218, 281, 372, 370, 371, 397, 398, 403 and 2. Two skeins each colour no. 298 and 245. Three skeins colour no. 255.
*Picture 6* (Milking): one skein each colour no. 288, 298, 316, 46, 20, 24, 8, 68, 100, 112, 145, 169, 186, 225, 218, 281, 372, 374, 370, 371, 397, 398, 403 and 2. Two skeins each colour no. 255 and 245.

**Diagram:** Each square on the pattern grid represents one cross-stitch in the appropriate colour worked over two canvas threads (one mesh intersection) both horizontally and vertically. The large picture is 200 stitches high by 300 stitches wide. Each small picture is 100 stitches high by 100 stitches wide. The heavy black lines on the grid divide the large picture into the six smaller scenes. You can find the pattern grid on pages 220–221.

**Embroidery:** Mount the canvas in the frame as described on page 233 of the Embroidery Course. Cross-stitch over two canvas threads (one mesh intersection) both horizontally and vertically using all six stranded threads throughout. Leave 7.5 cm (4 in) unembroidered along the short sides of the large picture, 3.8 cm (1½ in) along the long sides. On each small picture leave 4.3 cm (1½ in) unembroidered all round. Draw the thread through the canvas holes carefully to prevent the strands from separating. Make sure that the top stitch on all the crosses lies in the same direction.

# EMBROIDERY COURSE

*A Basic Guide to Embroidery Techniques*

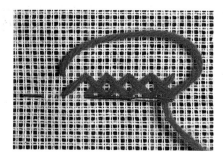

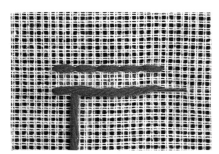

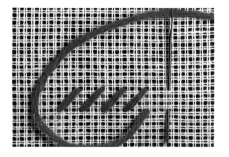

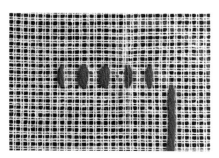

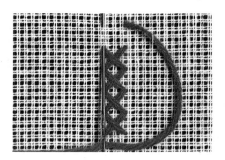

## Cross-stitch on canvas, working horizontally from the right

1) This is the basic stitch, in which you embroider each cross individually. For the first cross only, bring the needle up at the lower left-hand corner of the cross. At the top, insert the needle the width of the entire cross.

2) Insert the needle at the lower right-hand corner and bring it out twice the width of the cross to the left.

3) Check: on the underside there are two parallel horizontal rows. On the bottom row, the yarn is double.

## Cross-stitch on canvas, working horizontally from the left

1) First embroider a row of slanting understitches from left to right, inserting needle as shown.

2) Work the top layer of stitches on the return row, in the opposite direction.

3) Check: on the back there are vertical double stitches.

## Cross-stitch on canvas, working vertically from the bottom

1) Embroider each cross individually. For the first cross-stitch only, bring the needle out at the upper right-hand corner. Insert the needle on the lower left-hand corner and bring it out the height of one stitch above the last.

2) On the right-hand side, insert the needle and bring it out the height of two stitches above the last.

3) Check: on the underside there are two parallel vertical rows. On the left-hand side, the yarn is double.

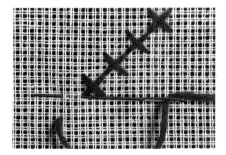

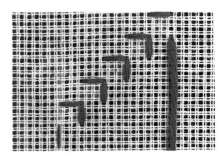

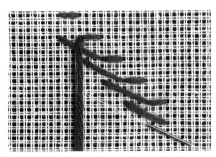

## Cross-stitch on canvas, working diagonally from top left

1) Embroider each stitch individually. For the first cross only, bring the needle up at the lower left-hand corner. At the top, insert the needle the width of one cross-stitch from right to left.

2) To start the next cross-stitch, insert the needle at the lower right-hand corner, then bring it out the height of one cross-stitch below.

3) Check: on the underside there is a diagonal line of horizontal and vertical stitches at right angles to each other.

## Cross-stitch on canvas, working diagonally from top right

1) Embroider each stitch individually. For the first stitch only, bring the needle out at the lower left-hand corner. At the top right-hand corner, insert the needle the width of the cross; bring it out at the top left-hand corner.

2) Take the needle diagonally downwards, inserting it at the lower right-hand corner, then bringing it out at the lower left-hand corner of the next stitch.

3) Check: on the underside there are short horizontal stitches and slanting stitches which are twice as long.

## Satin stitch on canvas

1) Satin stitch is a flat filling stitch. Embroidered horizontally: insert the needle and stitch over the specified number of squares. Bring the needle through at the start of the row of squares directly above.

2) Embroidered vertically: insert the needle and stitch over the specified number of squares, from bottom to top. Bring the needle through at the bottom of the adjacent row. The stitches are diagonal on the underside.

3) For all further stitches, regardless of whether they are horizontal or vertical: always work the row of squares adjacent to the previously embroidered row.

4) Embroidered at an angle: work in the indicated direction, over the number of squares specified in height and width. To start an area next to a completed one, insert the needle in the appropriate adjacent square.

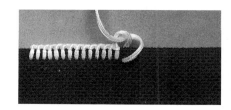

## Buttonhole stitch (blanket stitch)

1a) Buttonhole stitch and blanket stitch are usually used for edging. They are made in the same way, except that buttonhole stitches are spaced closely together and blanket stitches are spaced apart. There are two methods, both worked from left to right. Make a stitch of the appropriate length. Wrap the thread round the needle and pull the needle through.

1b) The other method: insert the needle as in 1a and pull it through. Instead of wrapping thread round the needle, draw the needle through the top loop, from back to front. Pull the thread through.

2) This is how it looks before the thread has been tightened. The position of the threads is identical in both methods.

3) Tighten the thread, keeping the tension uniform for each stitch. This produces an even ridge of knots. If the fabric you are edging frays easily, fold the edge under. If not, work the stitches over the raw edge.

## Interlinked buttonhole- or blanket stitch

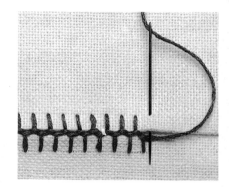
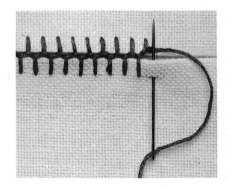

1) This stitch is used to join fabric edge-to-edge. First, push needle through upper piece of fabric, about 5 mm (¼ in) above folded edge, with needle facing downwards. Thread is under the point of the needle. Pull the needle through.

2) Insert the needle into the lower piece of fabric, 5 mm (¼ in) below the folded edge and to the right of the top stitch. Thread is under the point. Pull the needle through and repeat from the first step, working top and bottom edges alternately.

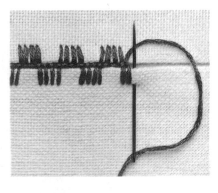

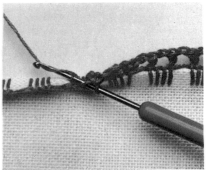

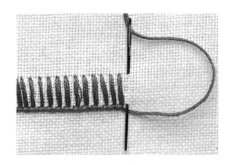

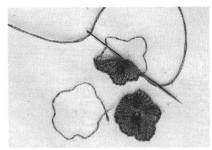

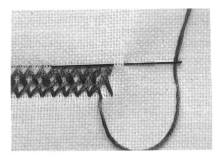

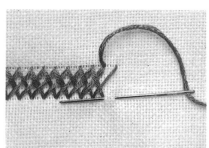

## Groups of interlinked buttonhole stitch

1) For a larger pattern, work alternate groups of four closely spaced stitches. This gives a box-like effect.

2) To add a crocheted border, work trebles (doubles) on the underside of the embroidery inserting hook around every first and fourth interlinked stitch.

## Buttonhole stitch (interior)

Buttonhole stitch can be used to fill in or outline interior design areas; it is not exclusively an edging stitch. Work it in the usual way, from left to right, with the thread under the point of the needle. When using it to fill in flower shapes or circles, outline the design in running stitch first. A hole will form in the centre, at the point where the needle is brought up.

## Herringbone stitch

Herringbone stitch is a type of cross-stitch, often used for borders. Work it from left to right, taking backstitches which zigzag alternately between upper and lower imaginary parallel guidelines. The threads may weave over and under each other several times, depending upon the length of the stitch. On the underside, two parallel rows of backstitch are visible.

## Drawn thread work: hemstitch

1) Zigzag hemstitch: withdraw the necessary number of fabric threads. Embroider from left to right on the wrong side of the fabric. Encircle a fixed, even number of vertical threads from right to left; pull them into a bundle.

2) Take a short vertical stitch from behind and to the right of each bundle; come out one to three fabric threads below the drawn threads. To work the second row, turn the fabric upside down so that the upper edge becomes the lower edge.

3) To make the zigzag effect, divide each original bundle in half. On the second row, each new bundle consists of half the threads from one bundle and half the threads from the adjacent bundle. This row begins and end with half a group.

4) Here, ladder hemstitch is shown. To work it, stitch the second row the same way as the first. Edge the corners with closely spaced buttonhole stitch. To fill a corner gap, make a thread criss-cross, then work buttonhole stitch.

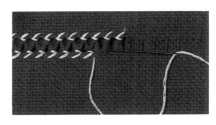

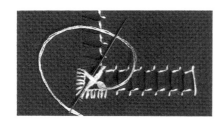

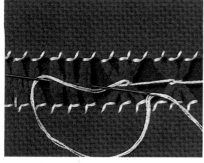

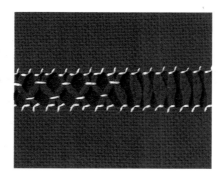

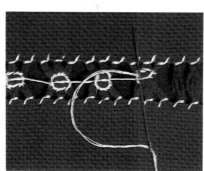

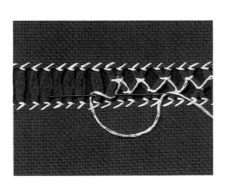

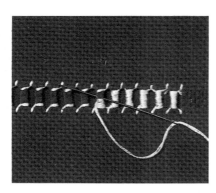

## Hemstitching: decorative stitches

1) Simple knotted effect: work ladder hemstitch first. The number of knotted bundles must be a multiple of the number of bundles in the second row. Anchor the working thread at the centre of the right-hand side of the drawn thread border. On the right or wrong side of the fabric, make a loop with the working thread. Pass the needle under the desired number of bundles (here, three) and through the loop. Pull the thread tight and repeat for the following bundles. Space the bundles evenly apart.

2) Double knotted effect: embroider two parallel rows of loop knots in the same way. Work from right to left on the right or wrong side of the fabric, equal distances apart.

3) Zigzag knotted effect: work ladder hemstitch first. Here, the bundles are secured with loop knots, in staggered groupings. Since the working thread runs visibly from one knot to the next, you must embroider on the underside. Knot together two bundles at the bottom, about one third of the way up the drawn thread border.

4) The next loop is worked about two-thirds of the way up the drawn thread border: take the thread upwards and encircle the last bundle of the lower knot together with the following thread bundle. Secure the knot.

5) This is the way this particular decorative stitch looks on the right side of the fabric.

6) Here, a simple knotted effect is embellished. A small circle embroidered in backstitch is worked on to each group of knotted bundles.

7) In this pattern, embroidery thread is wrapped tightly round the individual thread bundles.

8) To make an openwork grid, work closely spaced overcasting over the outer edges. Then wrap embroidery thread tightly round the remaining fabric bars, both horizontally and vertically.

## Couching

1) Couching can be used to outline or fill in an area. In this technique the couching yarn is stitched over the laid yarn to hold it in place. The laid yarn and the couching yarn are often of contrasting colours. Here, we demonstrate how to couch using a single yarn for both the laying and the couching. Basic couching: lay the yarn in a straight line from the bottom to the top of the area you wish to cover. Insert the needle at the top and bring it out at the second square down on the row to the right. Take a horizontal couching stitch over the laid yarn and insert the needle in the second square on the row to the left. Take the next couching stitch four squares down from the previous one.

2) Couch the entire length of the laid yarn with these horizontal stitches. At the end of the row, bring the needle out in the second square to the left of the first laid yarn. Lay the new yarn parallel to the first, inserting the needle at the top in the second square to the left of the first laid yarn.

3) In the second row, the horizontal couching stitches are worked midway between the couching stitches in the first row. To do this, bring the needle out in the square to the left, level with the top of the new laid yarn. Space the rest of the couching stitches four squares apart. Stagger the couching stitches this way in all following rows.

4) To make slanting couching stitches, bring the needle out one square to the right of the point where the laid yarn emerges. Bring the yarn diagonally across and insert the needle four squares down and one square to the left of the laid yarn. Space all following couching stitches five squares apart.

5) For all further rows, bring the needle out for the laid yarn in the second square to the left of the previous laid yarn. Work the couching stitches next to each other, as described in step 4.

6) Here each second row of diagonal couching stitches is worked in reverse to the previous row. Work the first row as described in step 4. In the second row, bring the needle out one square to the left of the laid yarn and make the couching by inserting the needle in the same square that was used for the previous row (this forms a V-shape). Repeat the first and second rows.

7) In Bokhara couching, the slanting couching stitches align to form diagonals across the filling area. Work the first row as described in step 4. For the next row, bring the needle out to the right of the laid yarn, in the second square above the one where the needle was inserted in the previous row. Space the following couching stitches five squares apart. Position the staggered couching stitches two squares further down with each new row.

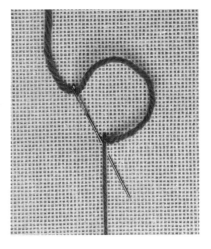
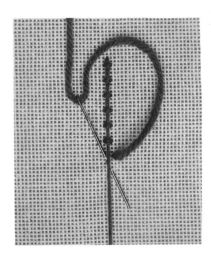

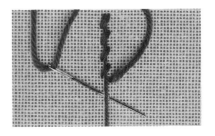

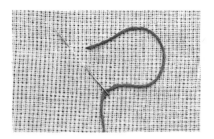

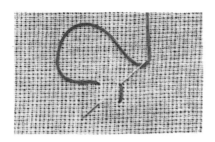

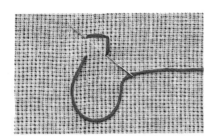

## Four-sided stitch, worked diagonally

First, make one whole square (see four-sided stitch). When you take the last stitch, bring the needle out two stitch-widths to the right. Complete the square as instructed above; work all following stitches this way.

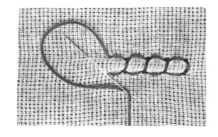

## Hardanger embroidery

Hardanger embroidery is a type of counted thread, openwork embroidery which originated in Norway. It features rectangular blocks of satin stitch, called kloster blocks, which usually consist of five stitches worked over five fabric threads. Kloster block formations outline each Hardanger motif. Selected threads are then cut or withdrawn from the interior of the motif. The remaining threads are embroidered with woven bars or overcasting.

1) First, outline the shape of the motif in backstitch. Embroider the kloster blocks working clockwise from block to block. The last stitch of each block forms the first stitch of the next. Wherever the threads are to be cut, there must be kloster blocks on opposite sides of the motif. Work the outer ring of blocks, then the inner ring. When the design is complete, cut the selected threads close to the satin stitching, forming the openwork grid.
2) Now embroider the openwork grid. Weave under and over each bar to cover it. To do so, bring up the needle in the middle of the four-thread bar, then weave over and under each thread pair. Do not pull the working thread too tightly. Begin with the top horizontal bar and work diagonally towards the bottom left. Then reverse direction and proceed upwards and to the right. Cover all the bars in the openwork area in this way.

## Pulled thread work: four-sided stitch

1) Pulled thread work is a type of counted thread embroidery; work it with a tapestry needle on evenweave fabric. Use embroidery thread which is similar in weight and texture to the base fabric. To work four-sided stitch: bring the thread up and insert the needle vertically, taking a stitch of the desired length. Bring the needle diagonally across to the upper left-hand corner of the square. The distance between the upper left-hand corner and the point where the needle first emerged is the same as for the first stitch.

2) Re-insert the needle at the point where it first emerged. Bring the needle diagonally across to the lower left-hand corner. The stitch length is the same as for the previous stitches.

3) Insert the needle at the lower right-hand corner, then bring it diagonally across to the upper left-hand corner. To work a horizontal row of stitches, repeat from step 1 for all following stitches. The last side of each square is then the first side of each adjacent square. To simply complete one individual square, insert the needle in the lower left-hand corner.

## Four-sided stitch (thread pulled)

This is how this type of embroidery actually looks after the thread has been pulled tight. The tightly bound thread pulls back the fabric at the points where the needle was inserted, forming an openwork pattern.

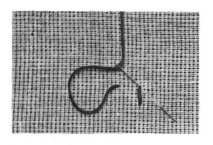

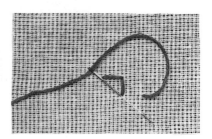

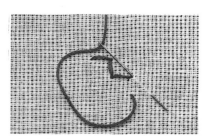

## Single faggot stitch, diagonal

1) Work the beginning the same as for the four-sided stitch. Then insert the needle diagonally, bringing it out one stitch width to the bottom right.

2) Re-insert the needle at the point where it was inserted for the very first stitch, then bring it up one stitch-width below the point where it last emerged.

3) To work all following stitches, repeat this process from step 1.

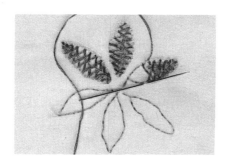

## Shadow work

This is done using sheer fabric. Outline the design in running stitch. On the wrong side, fill in these areas with closely spaced herringbone stitch. This produces a muted matt effect on the right side. The outline stitches emphasize the shaded areas.

## Narrow satin stitch

This stitch is narrower than basic satin stitch. It is useful for broderie anglaise (cutwork: eyelet lace): outline the shape using running stitches. Cut into the fabric, fold the raw edges under and embroider round the edge in narrow satin stitch/ overcasting to stop fraying. Trim off the excess fabric.

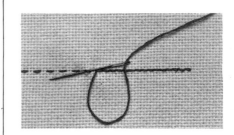

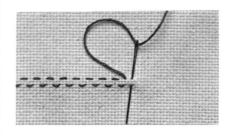

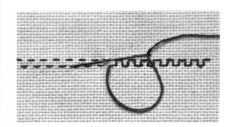

## Holbein stitch

1) Work a straight line with two journeys of evenly spaced running stitch. On the return journey, insert the needle in the same holes as the first. When working the Holbein stitch diagonally, space the running stitches over an equal number of thread intersections.

2) *Crenellation stitch:* on the first journey work two parallel rows of staggered stitches, using a single length of thread. Insert the needle vertically, as shown. Pick up the same number of threads for each stitch and leave the same amount of space between the stitches and also between the two rows.

3) On the return journey, work vertical stitches, inserting the needle horizontally behind the stitches of the first journey. Insert the needle in the same holes as before. This stitch looks the same on both sides of the fabric.

## Chain stitch

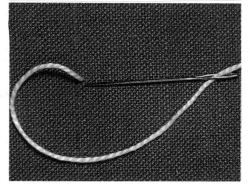

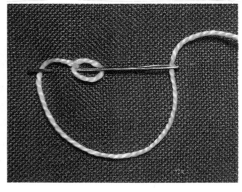

1) Chain stitch is a versatile stitch, particularly suitable for working curves. Bring the needle up, then re-insert it into the same hole, forming a loop.

2) Bring the needle out the desired stitch length away, at the far end of the loop. The thread must be under the point of the needle. Pull the needle through, but do not draw the thread too tight.

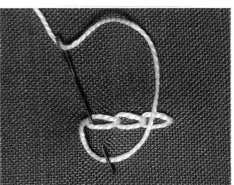

3) Re-insert the needle at the point where it emerged at the far end of the completed loop, then bring it out to form a stitch of the same size.

4) To turn a corner: bring the needle out at the desired location below the previous stitch; then complete the stitch in the usual way.

## Stem stitch

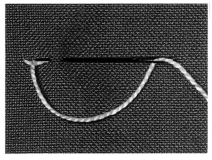

1) To make the first stitch, bring the needle up, insert it again and then bring the needle out half way along the length of the stitch.

2) To make following stitches, bring the needle out slightly above the point where it was inserted for the previous stitch.

3) Work stem stitch from left to right and always keep the thread below the needle.

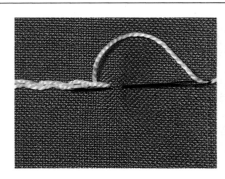

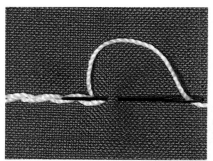

## Staggered stem stitch

1) To do this, work the first stitch with the thread placed below the needle.

2) On the second stitch, place the thread above the needle. Work these two stitches alternately.

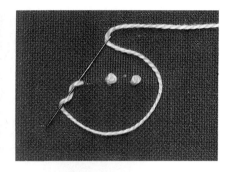

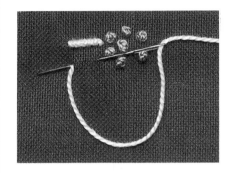

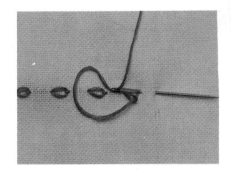

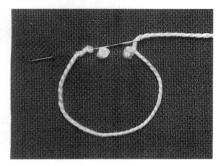

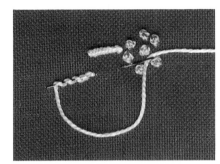

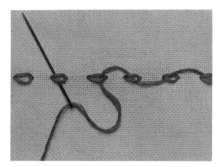

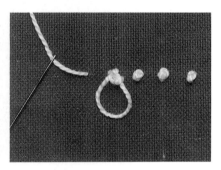

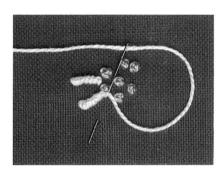

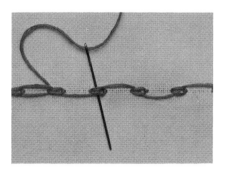

## French knot

1) Mount the fabric in a round embroidery frame (hoop); this leaves both hands free to work the stitch. Bring the needle up, then twist the thread round the needle twice, as shown, holding the thread firmly.

2) Slide the thread twists down the needle and on to the fabric surface. Insert the needle close to the point where it emerged, still holding the thread firmly.

3) Carefully pull the needle through, forming the knot. To make a bigger French knot, increase the number of twists round the needle.

## Bullion knot stitch

1) For best results, use a thick needle and a short piece of thread. First, bring the needle up and take one backstitch of the desired length.

2) Twist the thread around the needle as many times as necessary, depending on the length of the stitch (5–7 twists are average). Hold the thread firmly round the needle and gently pull the needle and thread through the twists.

3) Carefully pull the thread to tighten the twists, then reverse the direction of the coil and re-insert the needle at the point where it was inserted before. As you do so, bring the needle up for the next stitch.

## Threaded chain stitch

1) To start, work a row of detached chain stitches, spaced equidistantly apart. (To make a detached chain stitch, bring the needle up, then re-insert it into the same hole, forming a loop. Bring the needle out at the end of the loop, with the thread under the point. Take a small stitch over the loop to secure it.)

2) Next, weave the embroidery thread through the chain stitches, forming a wavy line. Weave under both threads of each chain stitch and draw the working thread through evenly.

3) Work the return row the same way, in the opposite direction. Do not pull too tightly. This stitch is particularly attractive when a contrasting colour is used for the weaving.

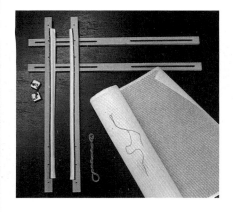
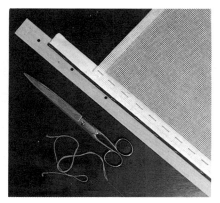

## Needlepoint tapestry

1) Basic equipment for needlepoint tapestry: an adjustable embroidery frame, needlepoint canvas, yarn and a blunt-ended needle.

2) To mount canvas in frame: cut canvas to size along the grain. Sew top and bottom edges of the canvas on to the tapes attached to the top and bottom rollers. Wind canvas on to rollers.

3) Lace the side edges of the canvas on to the side struts of the frame using strong thread.

4) The finished frame. Make sure that the canvas is always taut and evenly stretched.

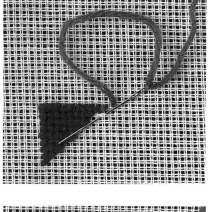

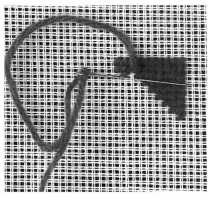
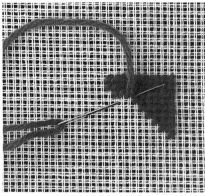

## Working corners on needlepoint tapestry

1) Diagonally to the left: bring the needle out one square below and to the left.

2) Next change of row: return to the point where the needle last emerged.

3) Diagonally to the right: take the needle one square further to the right.

4) Then insert the needle one square below and to the left.

## Tent stitch

1) Working from right to left, insert needle one square above the point where it first emerged.

2) Bring needle out two squares to the left, next to the point where the needle last emerged. Once again, insert the needle one square above the point where it last emerged. Repeat this sequence across the row.

3) To change rows: bring the needle back to the point where it was brought up for the stitch before the last.

4) The return row, from left to right: insert the needle one square below and to the left, then bring it out two squares to the right, above. Insert the needle one square below and to the left, then bring it out two squares to the right, above. Continue across the row in this way.

5) Changing rows, again: bring needle up one square below the last insertion point.

6) Insert needle one square above and to the right, as for step 1. Repeat the entire stitch sequence as necessary.

Tent stitch is the principal needlepoint stitch. It is always worked over one mesh intersection. Here, it is being worked on double-thread canvas.

In a double-thread canvas, the vertical and horizontal threads are arranged in pairs. The other main type of needlepoint canvas is single-thread canvas, in which only one vertical and one horizontal thread cross at each mesh intersection. There is also an interlock type of single-thread canvas, in which two vertical threads are intertwined around each horizontal thread. This produces a canvas of greater stability. When working satin stitch on canvas, either interlock or double-thread canvas should be used to prevent yarn slippage.

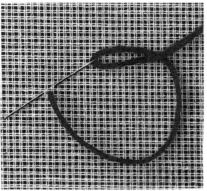
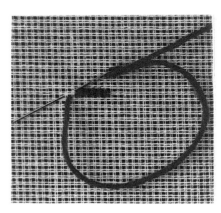

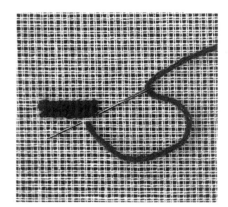

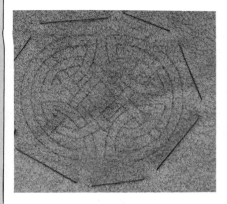
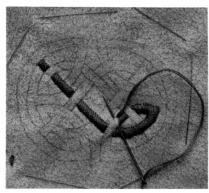

## Design transfer: organdie method

1) Use this technique to transfer an embroidery design on to a difficult surface. Trace the motif outline on to the organdie. Make sure that the piece of base fabric is large enough to fit into the embroidery frame (hoop). Baste the organdie in place.

2) Depending upon the type of design, work the stitches in straight or slanting satin stitch with stranded embroidery cotton (floss).

3) When the design is finished, trim the organdie off all round and possibly even clip into the design area, then withdraw the threads one by one with a pair of tweezers.

## How to transfer designs:

**Basting**
This technique is suitable for simple, linear designs. Trace the design on to tissue paper, then pin it on to the fabric you wish to embroider. Baste along the design lines, through both tissue paper and fabric. Gently tear the tissue paper away, then embroider the design. When the design is completed, remove the basting thread from the wrong side of the fabric. This method is particularly good for knitted fabrics or velvet.

**Organdie and canvas methods**
The organdie method is shown in detail on page 000 of this course. It is especially useful for transferring designs on to highly textured surfaces. Needlepoint canvas can be used in a similar way, to enable you to embroider counted thread designs (for example, cross-stitch) on to a dark ground, on to a non-evenweave fabric or on to a knitted fabric when the stitches themselves are not being used as a grid. Use only flexible single-thread canvas (without interlocking meshes) for this purpose. Baste the canvas on to the fabric; work the design. Trim the canvas close to the stitching, then withdraw the threads one by one, using a pair of tweezers. Knitted items have a tendency to shift beneath the canvas, so take extra care to avoid a lopsided design.

**Tracing with a pencil or dressmaker's carbon paper**
Pencil markings do eventually wash out, so it is advisable to use pencil to transfer designs on to light-coloured fabrics whenever possible. Copy the design on to tracing paper, then turn the tracing over on to the wrong side and pencil over the outlines. Pin the tracing on to the fabric, right side up. Go over the design lines with a pencil, pressing firmly to transfer the design clearly. Dressmaker's carbon paper is available in dark or light colours, to contrast with the fabric ground as necessary. The marks it leaves are permanent, so be sure to cover the design outlines completely with embroidery. Sandwich the dressmaker's carbon, carbon side down, between the fabric and the design (right side up). Position the design carefully. Pin all three layers together. Trace the design with a pencil or stylus, pressing very firmly.

**Direct transfer: with and without the aid of a light source**
These methods are suitable for light-coloured fabrics and can be used to copy designs from existing pictures as well as tracings. A design can be copied directly on to fine (sheer) fabric. Simply tape the design on to a firm surface, tape the fabric over it and trace along the design lines with a pencil. If the fabric is semi-transparent or opaque, tape the design on to a window, then tape the fabric over it: sunlight will illuminate the design, making it visible for tracing. A more effective version of this technique is a home-made light box. Rest a plate of glass between two chairs and shine a bright bulb underneath it. Trace the design as before.

**Pricking and pounce method**
This technique is preferred by experienced needlewomen. Copy the design on to firm tracing paper. Place the tracing on a padded surface, then use a pin or awl to prick closely spaced holes along the design lines. (An unthreaded sewing machine can do this job quickly; just stitch along the design lines.) Pin the design, right side up, on to the embroidery fabric. Spread pounce (inking powder) over the pricked outlines, then rub it in using a brush or a small pad of felt. Remove the pins, then lift the paper carefully to avoid smudging. Blow off any excess powder. An artist's fixative can be used to set the powder spots or you can go over the design lines with a dressmaker's pencil. Pounce is available at good specialist needlework shops.

# USEFUL INFORMATION

## Common Measurements: Approximate Equivalents

| METRIC | U.S. STANDARD/ IMPERIAL | PURCHASABLE FABRIC AMOUNTS |
|---|---|---|
| 2 mm | $\frac{1}{16}$ in | — |
| 3 mm | $\frac{1}{8}$ in | — |
| 5 mm | $\frac{1}{4}$ in | — |
| 1.0 cm = 10 mm | $\frac{3}{8}$ in | — |
| 12 mm | $\frac{1}{2}$ in | — |
| 1.5 cm = 15 mm | $\frac{5}{8}$ in | — |
| 2.5 cm = 24 mm | 1 in | — |
| 0.1 m = 10 cm | 4 in | $\frac{1}{8}$ yd |
| 0.2 m = 20 cm | 8 in | $\frac{1}{4}$ yd |
| 0.3 m = 30 cm | 12 in | $\frac{3}{8}$ yd |
| 0.4 m = 40 cm | 16 in | $\frac{1}{2}$ yd |
| 0.5 m = 50 cm | 20 in | $\frac{5}{8}$ yd |
| 0.6 m = 60 cm | 24 in | $\frac{3}{4}$ yd |
| 0.7 m = 70 cm | $27\frac{1}{2}$ in | $\frac{7}{8}$ yd |
| 0.8 m = 80 cm | $31\frac{1}{2}$ in | $\frac{7}{8}$ yd |
| 0.9 m = 90 cm | 36 in = 1 yd | 1 yd |
| 1.0 m = 100 cm | 39.5 in = $1\frac{1}{8}$ yd | $1\frac{1}{8}$ yd |

## Purchasable Fabric Amounts (Higher metrages/yardages)

| METRIC | U.S. STANDARD/ IMPERIAL |
|---|---|
| 1.0 m | $1\frac{1}{8}$ yd |
| 1.5 m | $1\frac{3}{4}$ yd |
| 2.0 m | $2\frac{1}{4}$ yd |
| 3.0 m | $2\frac{3}{4}$ yd |
| 3.5 m | $3\frac{7}{8}$ yd |
| 4.0 m | $4\frac{3}{8}$ yd |
| 4.5 m | $4\frac{7}{8}$ yd |
| 5.0 m | $5\frac{1}{2}$ yd |

## Equivalent Fabric Widths:

| METRIC | U.S. STANDARD/ IMPERIAL |
|---|---|
| 90 cm | 36 in |
| 115 cm | 44/45 in |
| 120 cm | 48 in |
| 140 cm | 54 in |
| 152 cm | 60 in |
| 180 cm | 72 in |

## Crochet Hook Conversion Table

**Regular range** (for medium to heavy yarns)

| METRIC | AMERICAN SIZES B–K |
|---|---|
| 2.00 mm | B |
| 2.50 mm | C |
| 3.00 mm | D |
| 3.50 mm | E |
| 4.00 mm | F |
| 4.50 mm | G |
| 5.00 mm | H |
| 5.50 mm | I |
| 6.00 mm | J |
| 7.00 mm | K |

**Steel crochet hooks** (for fine yarns)

| METRIC | AMERICAN |
|---|---|
| 0.60 mm | 14 |
| | 13 |
| 0.75 mm | 12 |
| | 11 |
| 1.00 mm | 10 |
| | 9 |
| 1.25 mm | 8 |
| 1.50 mm | 7 |
| | 6 |
| | 5 |
| 1.75 mm | 4 |
| | 3 |
| | 2 |
| 2.00 mm | 1 |
| 2.50 mm | 0 |
| 3.00 mm | 00 |

## Equivalent Dress Sizes

| BRITISH | 8 | 10 | 12 | 14 | 16 | 18 | 20 |
|---|---|---|---|---|---|---|---|
| AMERICAN | 6 | 8 | 10 | 12 | 14 | 16 | 18 |

## Equivalent Zip (Zipper) Lengths

| cm | 10 | 12 | 15 | 18 | 20 | 23 | 25 | 28 | 30 | 35 | 40 | 45 | 50 | 55 | 60 |
|---|---|---|---|---|---|---|---|---|---|---|---|---|---|---|---|
| in | 4 | 5 | 6 | 7 | 8 | 9 | 10 | 11 | 12 | 14 | 16 | 18 | 20 | 22 | 24 |

## Abbreviations used in Crochet and Knitting Instructions

dc — double crochet; K — knit; 1p(s) — loop(s); rnd — round; sc — single crochet(U.S.); sp — space; ss — slip stitch; tr — treble crochet.
* Asterisk. Repeat instructions following the asterisk as many times as specified in addition to the original.
( ) Brackets. Repeat instructions in brackets as many times as specified.

# British/American Glossary

This glossary is meant to serve as a handy, at-a-glance reference for our American readers. The word list below relates to sewing, needlework, crafts and apparel terms used within this book; it is not meant to be a comprehensive vocabulary. The British term is given along with its closest American equivalent.

Throughout this book, the American term, when it differs from the British, is given in parentheses following the British word. The U.S. Standard/Imperial equivalent measurement is given in parentheses after the metric figure.

| BRITISH | AMERICAN |
|---|---|
| adhesive web | fusible web |
| bias, crossgrain | bias |
| blindstitch, catchstitch | blindstitch |
| braces | suspenders |
| broderie anglaise | cutwork, eyelet lace |
| calico (unbleached) | unbleached muslin |
| card | cardboard |
| chunky yarn | bulky yarn |
| clean-finish, neaten | finish |
| crutch | crotch |
| (curtain) rail | (curtain) rod |
| cushion | pillow |
| cushion pad | pillow form |
| double crochet | single crochet |
| drawing-pin | thumbtack |
| fancy dress | costume |
| filling | stuffing |
| flannel, face flannel | face cloth |
| frill, ruffle | ruffle, frill |
| furnishing fabric | upholstery fabric |
| haberdashery | notions |
| herringbone stitch (embroidery) | herringbone stitch (embroidery) |
| herringbone stitch (sewing) | catchstitch (sewing, especially for hems) |
| made-to-measure | custom-made |
| millinery petersham | grosgrain ribbon |
| miss (knitting, crochet) | skip |
| needlepoint tapestry | needlepoint |
| net curtains | sheer curtains |
| oversew, overcast | overcast |
| pelmet (wooden board placed across top of window to conceal curtain rod) | cornice |
| pelmet, valance (short curtain across window top) | valance |
| plain (fabric) | solid-colored (fabric) |

| BRITISH | AMERICAN |
|---|---|
| press-stud, snap fastener | snap fastener, snap |
| round embroidery frame, tambour frame | embroidery hoop |
| rubber solution | rubber cement |
| rucksack | knapsack |
| serviette, napkin | napkin |
| sewing cotton, sewing thread | sewing thread |
| set square | right angle, right triangle |
| single crochet, slip stitch | slip stitch |
| slate frame, straight-sided embroidery frame | scroll frame, straight-sided embroidery frame |
| sleeve head | sleeve cap |
| soft embroidery cotton | matte embroidery cotton |
| soft furnishings | upholstery fabrics |
| soft toy | stuffed toy |
| sticky tape | cellophane tape |
| stitch unpicker, seam ripper | seam ripper |
| stranded cotton | stranded embroidery floss |
| tack, baste | baste |
| tea-towel | dish towel |
| tension (knitting, crochet) | stitch gauge |
| terry towelling, towelling | terry cloth |
| tights | pantyhose |
| treble crochet | double crochet |
| trousers | slacks, pants |
| unboxed cushion | knife-edged pillow |
| waistcoat | vest |
| windcheater | windbreaker |
| zip | zipper |

## Supplies and Suppliers

**To our British readers:**

The materials needed to make the projects in this book should be readily available in fabric and needlework departments and in specialist shops.

*The following merchants provide a mail order service:*

Needlework supplies, including Paterna Persian Yarn:
Royal School of Needlework, 25 Princes Gate, London SW7 1QE.
Telephone: (01) 589 0077

Needlework supplies, including Zweigart embroidery fabrics:
The Danish House, Arts and Crafts, P.O. Box 502, Maidstone, Kent ME17 3UZ.
Telephone: (0622) 46744

Needlework, art and craft supplies, including rug yarn:
Dryad, P.O. Box 38, Northgates, Leicester LE1 9BU.
Telephone: (0533) 50405

**To our American readers:**

Anchor embroidery threads, which are specified for many of the embroidery projects, are available in the United States under the Anchor Bates brand name. The color numbers are the same, but the range of available colors may not be as great as in the United Kingdom. For this reason, it is advisable to select all the necessary embroidery threads before beginning a project. If you are unable to obtain the specified colors, choose the nearest shade. For information regarding the closest retail store write to Susan Bates, Inc., 212 Middlesex Ave., Chester, CT 06412.

All the other materials needed to make the projects in this book should be readily available in fabric and needlework and craft departments, and in specialty shops.

# PROJECT INDEX